SIGNIFICANT BENEFITS

HIGH/SCOPE
EDUCATIONAL RESEARCH FOUNDATION
Ypsilanti, Michigan

Monographs of the
High/Scope Educational Research Foundation
Number Ten

SIGNIFICANT BENEFITS

The High/Scope Perry Preschool Study Through Age 27

Lawrence J. Schweinhart
Helen V. Barnes
David P. Weikart

with

W. Steven Barnett
Ann S. Epstein

commentaries by

Edward Zigler and Victoria Seitz
Yale University

Sadie A. Grimmett
Indiana University

THE HIGH/SCOPE PRESS

Published by
High/Scope® Press

A division of the
High/Scope Educational Research Foundation
600 North River Street
Ypsilanti, Michigan 48198-2898
(313)485-2000, FAX (313)485-0704

Marge Senninger, High/Scope Press Editor

Linda Eckel, Cover and Text Design

Library of Congress Cataloging-in-Publication Data

Schweinhart, L. J. (Lawrence J.), 1947-
   Significant benefits : the High–Scope Perry preschool study
through age 27 / Lawrence J. Schweinhart, Helen V. Barnes, David P. Weikart; with W. Steven Barnett, Ann S. Epstein; commentaries by Edward Zigler and Victoria Seitz, Sadie A. Grimmett.
   p. cm. — (Monographs of the High/Scope Educational Research Foundation; no. 10)
   Includes bibliographical references.
   ISBN 0-929816-57-9: $25.00
   1. Perry Preschool Project (Ypsilanti, Mich.)—Longitudinal studies.   2. Socially handicapped children—Education—Michigan—Ypsilanti—Longitudinal studies.   3. Education, Preschool—Michigan—Ypsilanti—Longitudinal Studies.   4. School children—Michigan—Ypsilanti—Social conditions—Longitudinal studies. 5. Educational surveys—United States.   I. Barnes, Helen V., 1939-.   II. Weikart, David P.   III. Title.   IV. Series.
LC4092.M42S37   1993   c.2
371.96'7'0977435—dc20
                                                                93-30791
                                                                CIP

Printed in the United States of America

Contents

Tables and Figures

Tables

Figures

Preface

Building on the hopeful findings of the age-19 phase of the High/Scope Perry Preschool Project, the hypothesis of the age-27 phase of the study was that positive effects of a good preschool program would continue into program participants' adult lives. Now, combined with data already collected on study participants from ages 3 through 19, the new data collected at age 27 provides an unprecedented opportunity to learn whether and how a preschool program's positive effects have stayed with program participants into their adults years.

This report, which summarizes the High/Scope Perry Preschool Project while focusing on the age-27 phase, joins and draws upon a large collection of previous reports and summaries of the longitudinal study through age 19. The initial findings of each phase of the study were published in a preliminary report (Weikart, 1967); a postprogram report (Weikart, Deloria, Lawser, & Wiegerink, 1970); a report through age 10 (Weikart, Bond, & McNeil, 1978); a first economic analysis (Weber, Foster, & Weikart, 1978); a report through age 15 (Schweinhart & Weikart, 1980); a report through age 19 (Berrueta-Clement, Schweinhart, Barnett, Epstein, & Weikart, 1984); and an economic analysis through age 19 (Barnett, 1985b). Professional education journals have published summaries of the study (Barnett, 1985a; Farnworth, Schweinhart, & Berrueta-Clement, 1985; Schweinhart, Berrueta-Clement, Barnett, Epstein, & Weikart, 1985a, 1985b; Schweinhart & Weikart, 1981a, 1988a; Weikart, 1967). Several books edited by distinguished social scientists have included chapters summarizing the study (Berrueta-Clement, Schweinhart, & Weikart, 1983; Schweinhart & Weikart, 1981b, 1983, 1987, 1989, 1992; Schweinhart, 1988b, 1992; Schweinhart, 1987). In the work leading to publication of two such chapters, the Consortium for Longitudinal Studies and the American Psychological Association Task Force on Prevention provided unusual scrutiny of the study. Helen Barnes's master's thesis (1989) and dissertation (1991) were based on data from the study through age 19.

During three decades of operation, the High/Scope Perry Preschool Project, in its many phases, has involved a large number of people and institutions in various roles. We owe them all our gratitude. We thank in particular the Ford Foundation and the Administration on Children, Youth, and Families in the U.S. Department of Health and Human Services for funding this age-27 phase of the study. Previous phases of the study have been funded by the U.S. Department of Education's Office of Special Education Programs; the National Institute of Mental Health; the Rosenberg Foundation; the Levi-Strauss Foundation; the Administration on Children, Youth, and Families; Carnegie Corporation of New York; the Spencer Foundation; and, in the 1960s, the U.S. Office of Education. The opinions expressed in this report do not necessarily reflect the positions or policies of any of these funding sources.

Individuals to whom we are grateful include the more than 100 researchers who have worked on the study in the years since David Weikart began planning it in 1960. For the age-27 study, Steven Barnett conducted the cost–benefit analysis (Chapter 7) and Ann Epstein wrote the case studies (Chapter 9). The principal data collector, for the age-27 study was Van Loggins. His extraordinary ability and persistence in finding study participants, and the resultant lack of missing data and attrition, have set a new standard for longitudinal studies. Others who made possible this latest report are these: Kay Long, Kay Elder, Nell Duke, Karen Parsell, Lyn Griffin, and Nancy Burandt prepared coding manuals and coded, entered, and verified data. Molly (Zhongxin) Gong, Jodie Roth, Mei-yu Yu, John Weiss, and Zhenkui Ma all assisted in carrying out the computerized data analysis. Mark Feldkamp, David Tholen, and David Mackoff-Borisy collected information from crime records. Marge Senninger carefully edited the final draft, with Diana Knepp providing both editorial and secretarial assistance. Steve McHugh also provided secretarial and editorial assistance throughout the age-27 phase of the study, including meticulous completion of the tables and the reference list.

Members of the age-27 study's advisory panel were Andrew Billingsley of the University of Maryland, Harriette Pipes McAdoo of Michigan State University, Lyle Jones of the University of North Carolina at Chapel Hill, and Donald Campbell of Lehigh University. They brought to the study sensitivity to the African-American population and expertise in experimental design and statistical analysis. Statisticians Marcia Feingold and Kenneth Guire also provided valuable consultation, particularly on the problem of how best to analyze nonparametric variables.

Various agencies provided us with valuable access to the records of study participants who had given us permission to look at their records: We received information from general, special, and adult education records of the Michigan public school districts of Ypsilanti, Ann Arbor, Willow Run, Lincoln, Milan, Belleville, and Van Buren. We also obtained information from the Highland Park (Michigan) Community High School, Osborn High School in Detroit, the Washtenaw Intermediate School District, and the Michigan Department of Education. Postsecondary transcripts were provided to us by several institutions in Washtenaw County, Michigan—Eastern Michigan University, the University of Michigan, Concordia College, Washtenaw Community College, and Cleary College. We also received transcripts from Michigan State University, Sumpter Area Technical College in South Carolina, San Jose City College in California, and Central Texas College.

Access to crime records was provided by the Washtenaw County Juvenile and Circuit courts, the Michigan District Courts 14-A, the Washtenaw County Sheriff's Department, the Monroe County (Michigan) Circuit Courts, and the Recorder's and Federal courts in Detroit. Records searches were facilitated by the Michigan State Police; the Michigan Department of Corrections; the California Department of Justice; and the state police of California, Massachusetts, Nebraska, Pennsylvania, and Texas. Access to social services records and searches of those records were made possible by the Michigan Department of Social Services and the Social Services Division of the Washtenaw County Human Services Department.

Special thanks go to the study participants themselves, who participated in extensive interviews and gave us permission to examine their lives, and to the parents of the study participants, who originally agreed to participate in the study and then consented to being interviewed several times. We also thank those parents, as well as other family members and friends, for helping us locate the study participants for the various phases of the project.

The High/Scope Perry Preschool Project could not have been completed without the cooperation of funding agencies, study participants, their parents, many public and private agencies and institutions, and High/Scope research and support staff. Because of their combined efforts, the study has made a contribution to what is known about changing and benefiting the lives of children born into poverty. We hope that this knowledge will be used to improve the opportunities available to all such children.

EXECUTIVE SUMMARY

The High/Scope Perry Preschool Study Through Age 27

The High/Scope Perry Preschool Project is a study assessing whether high-quality, active learning preschool programs can provide both short- and long-term benefits to children living in poverty and at high risk of failing in school. For almost three decades, the study has followed the lives of 123 such children from African-American families who lived in the neighborhood of the Perry Elementary School in Ypsilanti, Michigan, in the 1960s. At the study's outset, the youngsters were randomly divided into a *program group,* who received a high-quality, active learning preschool program, and a *no-program group,* who received no preschool program. Researchers then assessed the status of the two groups annually from ages 3 to 11, at ages 14–15, at age 19, and most recently, at age 27, on variables representing certain characteristics, abilities, attitudes, and types of performance. The median percentage of missing cases for these various assessments was only 4.9%, and only 4.9% of cases were missing for the age-27 interviews. The study's design characteristics give it a high degree of internal validity, providing scientific confidence that postprogram group-differences in performance and attitudes are actually effects of the preschool program.

As shown in Figure 1, study findings at age 27 indicate that in comparison with the no-program group, the program group had

- Significantly[1] higher monthly earnings at age 27 (with 29% vs. 7% earning $2,000 or more per month)

- Significantly higher percentages of home ownership (36% vs. 13%) and second-car ownership (30% vs. 13%)

- A significantly higher level of schooling completed (with 71% vs. 54% completing 12th grade or higher)

- A significantly lower percentage receiving social services at some time in the previous 10 years (59% vs. 80%)

- Significantly fewer arrests by age 27 (with 7% vs. 35% having 5 or more arrests), including significantly fewer arrests for crimes of drug making or dealing (7% vs. 25%)

As shown in Figure 2, over the years the program group had significantly higher scores than the no-program group in

---

[1]This report describes a group difference as **significant** if it has a two-tailed probability of less than .05.

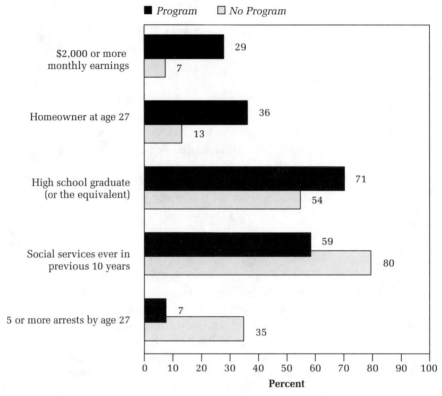

Figure 1

HIGH/SCOPE PERRY PRESCHOOL PROJECT —
MAJOR FINDINGS AT AGE 27

■ *Program*　□ *No Program*

$2,000 or more monthly earnings: 29 / 7

Homeowner at age 27: 36 / 13

High school graduate (or the equivalent): 71 / 54

Social services ever in previous 10 years: 59 / 80

5 or more arrests by age 27: 7 / 35

Percent (0–100)

Note. All findings are significant at $p < .05$, two-tailed.
See Tables 9, 18, 22, 25, and 26 for details.

- General literacy at age 19 (on the Adult Performance Level Survey; American College Testing Program, 1976)

- School achievement at age 14 (on the California Achievement Tests; Tiegs & Clark, 1971)

- Intellectual performance (IQ) from the end of the first year of the preschool program to the end of first grade at age 7 (on the Stanford-Binet Intelligence Scale, Terman & Merrill, 1960)

Moreover, as compared with the no-program group, the program group

- Spent significantly fewer years in programs for educable mental impairment (with 15% vs. 34% spending a year or more in EMI programs)

- Had a significantly higher percentage reporting at age 15 that their school work required preparation at home (68% vs. 40%)

As a group, the program females reported significantly higher monthly earnings at age 27 than the no-program females did (with 48% vs. 18% earning over $1,000) because more of the program females (80%

Figure 2

HIGH/SCOPE PERRY PRESCHOOL PROJECT —
MAJOR EDUCATIONAL PERFORMANCE FINDINGS

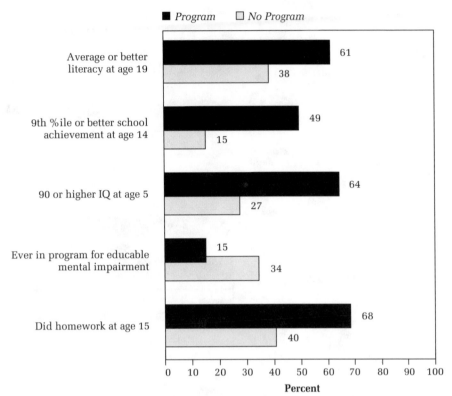

Note. All findings are significant at $p < .05$, two-tailed.
See Tables 10, 12, 13, 14, and 15 for details.

vs. 55%) had found jobs. The program males, as a group, had significantly higher monthly earnings at age 27 than the no-program males (with 42% vs. 6% earning over $2,000) because the program males had better paying jobs. Of employed males in the two groups, 53% vs. 8%, respectively, were earning over $2,000, which is a significant difference.

As shown in Figure 3, unlike the significant differences in monthly earnings, which were found for *both* females and males, the following significant differences between the program group and the no-program group at age 27 were found to hold for males only or for females only. As compared with no-program females,

- Significantly more program females were married at age 27 (40% vs. 8%), and significantly fewer of the births to program females were out of wedlock (57% vs. 83% of births).

- Significantly more program females completed 12th grade or higher (84% vs. 35%).

- Significantly fewer program females spent time in programs for educable mental impairment (8% vs. 37%).

Figure 3

HIGH/SCOPE PERRY PRESCHOOL PROJECT —
MAJOR FINDINGS THROUGH AGE 27, BY GENDER

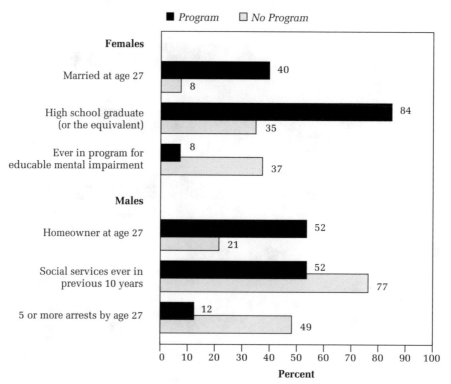

Note. All findings are significant at $p < .05$, two-tailed.
See Tables 11, 19, 25, and 28 for details.

As compared with no-program males,

- Significantly more program males owned their homes at age 27 (52% vs. 21%).

- Significantly fewer program males received social services at some time between ages 18 and 27 (52% vs. 77%).

- Significantly fewer program males had 5 or more lifetime arrests (12% vs. 49%).

The findings listed here have economic values that are benefits to society. Compared with the preschool program's cost, these benefits make the program a worthwhile investment for taxpayers as well as for society in general. **Over the lifetimes of the participants, the preschool program returns to the public an estimated $7.16 for every dollar invested.**

These findings are remarkable. Their positive implications for improved quality of life for participants, their families, and the community at large are of tremendous importance. No evidence available when this study was initiated even suggested that a preschool program for children 3 and 4 years old could set in motion a chain of events leading to such lifetime effects on the children. Yet the internal validity of the study constitutes a powerful argument that all the outcomes stated here are in fact due to the program that the young children experienced at the outset of the High/Scope Perry Preschool Project.

When the preschool studies of the 1960s were begun, people spoke of "breaking the cycle of poverty" and "inoculating" children against failure. However, life and poverty are much more complicated than this all-or-nothing rhetoric suggests. This study nevertheless shows that amidst this complexity, a good program can make **significant** differences. The rhetoric of the 1990s should reflect this more sophisticated understanding of the complexity of poverty. *People don't break the cycle of poverty: Some people ease out of it a little. The preschool "inoculation" is not universally successful, like polio or smallpox vaccinations. But like many other medicines, it brings about significant differences.*

The High/Scope Perry Preschool Project findings present us with the challenge to develop and maintain widespread preschool programs similar to the program developed for this study. Such a program, like other preschool programs that have demonstrated lasting success, would

- Provide for all 3- and 4-year-olds living in poverty a classroom program operating at least 12$\frac{1}{2}$ hours each week

- Use developmentally appropriate practices that encourage child-initiated learning activities

- Have a high level of outreach to parents as partners

- Maintain a child-staff ratio of no more than 10 children per adult

- Employ staff who are well trained in early childhood education

- Provide consistent staff supervision and staff training in the developmentally appropriate curriculum approach used

It is essential that we invest fully in high-quality, active learning preschool programs for all children living in poverty. Since the national Head Start program and state-funded preschool programs now serve fewer than half of these most vulnerable of our children, the nation is ignoring tremendous human and financial potential.

- We must spend what it takes. This means full funding for the national Head Start program and similar programs—enough to not only *serve all eligible children but also adequately serve each child,* so programs can help all children reach their potential.

- We must ensure that the policies and procedures in place for all early childhood programs are of the quality necessary to permit staff to do their jobs well.

- Early childhood program staff must do their jobs well, bringing to them a firm sense of purpose, a deep love of children, and solid competence in early childhood education.

Doing all this is sure to bring significant benefits to the lives of the next generation.

SIGNIFICANT BENEFITS

I Preschool Program Effects

Among studies on the effects of early childhood programs, High/Scope's Perry Preschool Project stands out both for the boldness of its design and for its longevity. This chapter begins by examining why the High/Scope Perry Preschool Project was initiated, why the study focused on young African-American children living in poverty, and why it has followed study participants through age 27. Next comes a review of the various problems people living in poverty face—problems having to do with schooling, unemployment, single parenting, welfare dependence, and crime. The chapter concludes with an examination of whether and how preschool programs address the problems of poverty. Several related studies and groups of studies, together with the High/Scope Perry Preschool study, provide mounting evidence that preschool programs can have far-reaching effects.

Why This Study, With This Sample?

When the High/Scope Perry Preschool Project and other studies like it began in the 1960s, an answer to poverty seemed far beyond the scope of any of the studies—indeed, beyond the scope of feasible research. Nevertheless, at the time, leading educators and social scientists *hoped* that preschool programs would help children escape the cycle of poverty—that such early programs would break the chain of causes and effects linking family poverty to children's school failure and to their subsequent poverty as adults. And despite some early findings that appeared to contradict this hypothesis (Westinghouse Learning Corporation, 1969), research evidence *has* accumulated over the past three decades to indicate that good preschool programs can have such an impact (relevant studies, other than the Perry study, are reviewed in the latter part of this chapter).

The principal hypothesis of the High/Scope Perry Preschool study through age 27 was that good preschool programs can help children in poverty make a better start in their transition from home to community and thereby set more of them on paths to becoming economically self-sufficient, socially responsible adults. This pattern of effects was hypothesized to counteract to some extent, at each step, the cycle in which family poverty and related problems lead children to school failure and continuing poverty as adults. In this cycle, children's school failure often begins with poor intellectual performance that leads to a negative disposition towards learning, then to special education placement and low school-achievement, and finally, for many, to dropping out of high school. This sequence of events constituting school failure appears to be partly responsible for, or at least predictive of, such undesirable social and economic outcomes as crime, welfare dependence, unemployment, and adult poverty (Schweinhart, 1985). The entire poverty cycle is a series of causes and effects in the relative, scientific sense: A certain degree of change in one variable causes a certain degree of change in a related variable, and so on. The preschool program is seen as interrupting this cycle at an important developmental stage—early enough to improve children's intellectual performance and disposition towards learning as they start elementary school and thus early enough to induce improvements in the subsequent chain of variables.

Perry Project staff chose for the study a group composed entirely of black children living in poverty. Children of other races would have been included as well, had the National Institute of Mental Health chosen to fund the study proposal as it was originally conceived in 1960. However, subsequently limiting the study to participants of one race simplified the design by eliminating racial differences. With this simplified design, the study qualified, after it began in 1962, for funding as a Cooperative Research Project of the U.S. Office of Education. Blacks in particular were selected as study participants because, in the 1960s, they were experiencing high rates of poverty and related school problems. That this situation has largely continued for blacks in America is borne out by the statistics of the 1970s and 1980s.

The Intractable Problems of Poverty

During the decades in which the children in the Perry sample were growing up, the poverty-rate decline seen in the late 1960s ended (Danziger, Haveman, & Plotnick, 1986). From 1969 to 1978 the poverty rate remained steady, and then in 1978 it began once again to rise. Poverty, especially persistent poverty lasting several years, was endemic among black children (Duncan & Rodgers, 1988). More than 6 out of 7 black children lived in families with incomes below the federal poverty level at some time during the 15 years from 1968 to 1982, and at least 1 out of 4 black children was poor for 10 or more of those years. According to a 1989 report of the National Research Council's Committee on the Status of Black Americans (Jaynes & Williams, 1989), despite substantial improvements in the past few decades, blacks are still not as well-off as other Americans.

The history of the Perry study participants who did not attend the preschool program—the no-program group—vividly portrays the ways in which poverty is related to many of America's social problems. At study entry, fewer than 1 in 5 of the parents of the children in the no-program group had completed high school; 49% of the children lived in families headed by single parents; 45% of the families were on welfare. The mean IQ of the no-program group, 79 at study entry, never rose above 87 over the decade of assessment. The group's mean achievement-test score at age 14 was only at the 6th percentile. The average child from the no-program group spent 2.8 years in programs for educable mental impairment; 46% of no-program children were considered handicapped at some time while they were in school; and only 54% of them graduated from regular or adult high school or received a certificate of General Educational Development (GED). This last statistic compared with 78% of black 22-year-olds and 83% of all 22-year-olds in the U.S. (Frase, 1989). The average 27-year-old in the no-program group had been arrested 4.6 times; 69% had been arrested at least once; 35% had been arrested 5 or more times; 32% had served time in a state prison or county jail. Only 59% of the no-program group were employed when interviewed at age 27. In the group at age 27, 54% of males and 82% of females earned less than $1,000 a month; of no-program group members who were married, 57% reported household earnings below $2,000 a month. Eighty percent of the no-program group had received social services at some time in the 10 years before the age-27 interview, and they had spent an average of 26.3 months receiving public assistance during that time.

The no-program group's outcomes illustrate the cycle: Childhood poverty often leads to school failure, which is highly correlated with adult poverty (Schweinhart, 1985). The problems of adult poverty include male unemployment, female single parenthood, and welfare dependence. People living in poverty also experience, either as victims or perpetrators, more than their share of violent and drug-related crime. The High/Scope Perry Preschool Project, in developing a high-quality, active learning preschool program, sought to counteract these short- and long-term effects of poverty. But these are problems that have proved resistant to many other forms of treatment (Levin, 1977; Murray, 1984). To fully understand the challenge undertaken by the High/Scope Perry Project, it is important to have some understanding of the extent and seriousness of poverty's various effects over the past three decades.

School Failure

A specific goal of the High/Scope Perry Preschool study, when it began in the 1960s, was to discover whether a good preschool program could assist young children who were at high risk of school failure to successfully develop the intellectual abilities needed to succeed in school and thus graduate from high school. In those days, over 50% of the students in the Perry Elementary School had been retained in grade at least once by the age of 10; fewer than half could be expected to graduate from high school.

In the decades since the 1960s, American society has continued to struggle with the problems of low school-achievement and high school-dropout, especially among black and Hispanic youths (Natriello, McDill, & Pallas, 1990; Wilson, 1987). In the mid-1980s 22% of black males dropped out of the nation's high schools (Frase, 1989), and dropout rates were considerably higher than this in major cities (Ellwood, 1988; Lomotey, 1990). Factors influencing black males to drop out of school have included their alienation from the system, negative peer-influence, lack of appropriate male role models, involvement in crime and drug abuse, and a growing perception that high school graduation does not assure employment or escape from poverty (Auletta, 1982; Ogbu, 1986; U.S. Department of Justice, 1988; Wilson, 1987). Indeed, in the mid-1980s, unemployment rates of young black urban males were above 50% (Ellwood & Summers, 1986). Moreover, the percentage of black male high school graduates aged 25–34 earning wages below the federal poverty line rose from 20% in 1969 to 50% in 1986 (Danziger, 1989).

Black females have fared only slightly better academically. In the mid-1980s 17% of black females dropped out of high school; studies in Harlem and Philadelphia found the factors influencing them to drop out to be (a) early childbearing, (b) other family problems, and (c) grade retention (Fine & Zane, 1989).

The patterns of school failure described here are what the Perry Project staff hoped to change.

Male Unemployment, Female-Headed Families, and Welfare Dependence

Another specific goal of the High/Scope Perry Preschool Project was to link preparation for school to success in school and, through the latter, to success in the real world of jobs, families, and community. Almost all the parents of the study participants were, at study entry, either unemployed or employed in low-skill jobs. It seemed that their children would need major assistance to avoid the same fate.

Many of the families of children in the High/Scope Perry study were characterized by male unemployment, a female head-of-household, and consequent welfare dependence. The hope of those who designed and ran the Perry Preschool Project—it was too bold at the time to be called a hypothesis—was that the program would help participants to do better in school, so they might grow up to have jobs with decent pay that would help them to avoid this characteristic pattern.

The pattern we speak of, which has been a long time in developing, continues to prevail. In the past several decades the employment rate for black males has plunged from 80% in 1930 to 56% in 1983 (Wilson & Neckerman, 1986). Ellwood (1988) reported that the unemployment rate for minority men aged 20–24, which did not include those who became discouraged and stopped looking for work, dropped to almost 30% by 1983. This pervasive male unemployment has been at least one of the factors involved in blacks foregoing marriage and having children out of wedlock (Wilson, 1987).

Minority households headed by women are particularly likely to experience poverty, welfare dependence, and other concomitant problems. In 1985 almost two thirds of black or Hispanic children living in female-headed households were poor (Smolensky, Danziger, & Gottschalk, 1988). The 1960s and 1970s saw the percentage of female-headed black families increase dramatically—from 21% of all black families in 1960 to 44% in 1985 (Ricketts, 1989). The proportion of out-of-wedlock births to black women aged 15 to 24 grew from 41% in 1955 to 68% in 1980 (Wilson & Neckerman, 1986). These percentages have been even higher in urban areas; for instance, Wilson (1987) reported that nearly three fourths of all black births in Chicago in 1983 were to unmarried women. Out-of-wedlock births and resultant female-headed households are highly related to long-term poverty and dependence on AFDC (Aid to Families with Dependent Children; Duncan, Hill, & Hoffman, 1988; Smolensky et al., 1988).

Single parenthood brings with it hazards related to or in addition to poverty. For example, single parenthood and poverty are stressors that place mothers at greater risk of depression, which may negatively affect their parenting (Belle, 1982). In particular, poverty has been found to be associated with high rates of child abuse (Steinberg, Catalano, & Dooley, 1981). Also, in comparison with two-parent families, single-parent families tend to provide their children with less supervision and control; the children, especially sons, are more prone to delinquency (Dornbusch et al., 1985). Daughters of single mothers are more likely to have children while they themselves are teenagers and unmarried (Garfinkel & McLanahan, 1986). And infants born to black teen mothers living in poverty are at high risk of having low birth weight, which may lead to developmental and educational disabilities (Kopp & Kaler, 1989b; National Commission to Prevent Infant Mortality, 1988; National Center for Clinical Infant Programs, 1986).

Dependence on welfare assistance and other social services often accompanies poverty. Among black males, welfare dependence goes hand in hand with high unemployment. Among poor black women, welfare dependence is most strongly associated with being a teen mother or a single parent.

Research findings are mixed about the relationship between welfare dependence as a child and as an adult (Duncan et al., 1988). One study (McLanahan & Bumpass, 1988) found that black women from single-parent homes, most of them raised in poverty, were more likely to give birth early in their lives, when they were unmarried, and they were more likely at some time to have their marriages break up. Thus, these women were more likely than other women to become female heads of families, poor, and welfare-dependent.

Most mothers who have been on AFDC for 8 years or more—about 30% of those receiving AFDC—are of minority ethnicity, have never married, and have dropped out of high school (Wilson, 1987; Duncan et al., 1988). One study reported that over 40% of the never-married mothers of young children who began receiving AFDC before age 25 had received it for 9 or more years (Duncan et al., 1988).

The preschool staff who taught Perry Project participants sincerely hoped that the young children they served would be able to achieve a better pattern of life than the one just described.

Delinquency and Crime

Another hope for the High/Scope Perry Preschool Project—again, too bold at the time to be framed as a hypothesis—was that program participants would do better in subsequent schooling and therefore engage in less delinquency and crime. The increasing concentration of unemployment and poverty in black urban communities has been associated with escalating substance abuse, delinquency, and crime (Brunswick, 1988; National Institute of Justice, 1989; U.S. Department of Justice, 1988). Blacks, while 12% of the U.S. population in 1985, accounted for 27% of all arrests and 47% of all arrests for violent crimes (U.S. Department of Justice, 1988). In 1978, nearly 10% of blacks were arrested, as compared with only 3.5% of whites; and from 1974 to 1985, 47% of all prison inmates were black (Jaynes & Williams, 1989). Moreover, these statistics indicate the risks of arrest and incarceration for blacks in general; and the Perry study participants, because they were blacks who were young, poor, and urban, were at even greater risk of engaging in crime or being incarcerated.

Crimes by blacks most strongly affect the residents of black communities (the findings mentioned in this paragraph can all be found in Jaynes & Williams, 1989). Black property-crime and violent-crime offenders have been found to most often victimize fellow blacks. Their criminal activities usually take place in areas near their homes, with the incidence of victimization highest for persons who have incomes of less than $10,000 per year. Compared with whites, blacks have been found to be about twice as likely to be victims of aggravated assault and between six and seven times as likely to be victims of homicide. Blacks are also about twice as likely as whites to be victims of robbery and vehicle theft. Besides having negative emotional, physical, and economic effects on individuals and families, high crime rates in black communities negatively influence economic and social development. Because robberies, burglaries, and violence are common, insurance rates are high, lenders are extremely cautious, and investors hesitate to put money and energy into business enterprises. Businesses as well as community and religious organizations relocate or fail to survive, and able individuals who might serve as leaders and role models move elsewhere.

Substance abuse, especially the "crack epidemic," has not only been associated with increases in property and violent crime in poor, black communities in recent years, as just described; it has also been related to impaired family-functioning. This is particularly evidenced in a dramatic rise in the numbers of children with prenatal exposure to illegal drugs and therefore with high risk of educational difficulties (Kopp & Kaler, 1989a). These same youngsters also face higher chance of abuse and neglect (Howard, Beckwith, Rodning, & Kropenske, 1989). In many cases, drug-dependent mothers become incapable of providing responsible child care, and the burden of raising their young children falls on grandmothers (Gross, 1989).

Though the High/Scope Perry Preschool Project preceded the widespread drug and crime problems of the 1980s, study participants were surrounded by such problems in their adolescence and early adulthood. And these were certainly the kinds of problems that the Perry Project's teaching staff hoped to help children avoid in their future lives.

The Project's Conceptual Framework

When the High/Scope Perry Preschool Project and other preschool studies began in the 1960s, they were based on the hypothesis that preschool programs could make a difference in the development of human intelligence—that during the early years, the ability to do well in school could be improved. Weikart et al. (1970) derived the Perry study hypothesis from animal studies on environmental enrichment (Krech, Rosenzweig, & Bennet, 1960; Scott, 1962); from Bloom's observation that "50 percent of [variance in intellectual] development takes place between conception and age 4" (1964, p. 88); and from the emerging work of Piaget on the development of the thinking process in young children (Hunt, 1961; Piaget & Inhelder, 1969). The Perry study's hypothesis was also favored by the social context of the late 1950s and early 1960s, including the social mandate to provide equal educational and employment opportunities to all Americans. Also, on a more pragmatic level, the Perry Project's developer and director, David Weikart, who was a public school administrator and school psychologist, decided to turn attention to preschool education partly out of frustration with the slow pace of innovation in the public schools.

As the Perry study has continued, researchers have extended the study's conceptual framework, taking into account the development of the study participants from young children to young adults and the growth of theory and methodology in the relevant disciplines. As participants entered the study in early childhood, then advanced to later childhood, adolescence, and adulthood, continued positive findings have supported the extension of data collection and group comparisons. The study has also responded to specific critiques (e.g., Gottfredson, 1990; Locurto, 1991; Spitz, 1986; Zigler, 1987) by refining the methods of data analysis. For example, emergent concern about an initial difference between program and no-program groups in percentages of single mothers employed led to a lengthy analysis of the effects of this variable.

In the years since 1962, theory on the development of the thinking process has advanced on many fronts. Most important has been the development of theory on the temporal unfolding of the relationship between a person's heredity and environment. No longer is the question simply whether a personal trait such as intelligence is inherited or the product of experience. Rather, a trait is best viewed as a dynamic relationship between genetic material and environmental opportunities (e.g., Sameroff & Chandler, 1975). Effects of genetic inheritance and effects of experience are inseparably intermixed and indistinguishable; all that can be observed and measured is a person's performance in a setting. Human development may be modeled as a series of interactions or transactions between performance and setting.

This formulation can be enriched by general concepts originally developed by Elliott and his associates to explain the causes of delinquency from a social-psychological perspective (Elliott, Ageton, & Canter, 1979). They speak of internal and external factors in the development of behavior. Internal factors, such as commitment to schooling or school motivation, come from within a person. External factors, such as the opinions of peers and teachers, affect a person from outside. On the basis of these internal and external factors, social bonds develop between persons and settings in the course of human development. Strong social bonds to conventional settings, such as school, are seen as making delinquency less likely, whereas weak social bonds make delinquency more likely. Schweinhart and Weikart (1980) proposed a transactional model of schooling with three factors—the internal factors of **school achievement** and **commitment to schooling** and the external factor of **student-role reinforcement,** especially as expressed in regular versus special education placement. This thinking may be extended as well to the adult world of work. People are successful in work if they perform well and are rewarded for performing well. They become more committed to doing their work well and less prone to crime, welfare assistance, or having children out of wedlock.

Each domain of life may be viewed as a series of interactions between performance and setting. A **setting** is one of the several environments—school, work, home, community—in which a person functions day to day. Children are usually placed in settings by others. Parents decide when and where children live, where they receive child care and schooling, and where they visit; educators decide when and if children should go on to the next grade and when and if they need special school services. In contrast, for the competent, independent adult, placement in a setting—for example, the choice to take a job, to continue schooling, to buy a house, or to get married—is usually the result of a mutual choice by the individual and someone else.

Individual **performance** is behavior within a setting. The setting defines the appropriateness or inappropriateness of the behavior. The school defines the appropriateness of performance by evaluating it according to its own criteria of what constitutes a good, inattentive, or misbehaving student. The workplace defines and rewards the appropriate performance of the good worker and censures the performance of the poor worker. If a person's behavior becomes more broadly socially unacceptable, the criminal justice system does what it can to stop it.

Evidence for Preschool Program Effects

Evidence for the effectiveness of high-quality preschool programs for children living in poverty comes from examinations of sets of studies as well as individual studies, both intensive and extensive. Sets of studies we examined include reviews (e.g., Haskins, 1989; Ramey, Bryant, & Suarez, 1985; Berrueta-Clement et al., 1984); meta-analyses (McKey et al., 1985); and even collaboratively conducted research (Lazar, Darlington, Murray, Royce, & Snipper, 1982).

Like the High/Scope Perry Preschool study, most of the relevant studies have been *intensive*—single-site, with under 500 study participants but relatively tight experimental designs and attention to individual study participants. A few studies have been *extensive*—multisite or multiyear, with over 500 study participants but relatively loose, quasi-experimental designs and less attention to individual study participants. While it is theoretically possible to combine the positive qualities of intensive and extensive studies in a single study, it has seldom if ever occurred, at least in educational research. Thus, intensive studies and extensive studies complement each other: Intensive studies are often strong on internal validity but weak on generalizability. Extensive studies are often weak on internal validity but strong on generalizability. Good public-policy development needs both types of studies—intensive to guard against ambiguous findings; extensive to guard against inaccurate generalizations.

Sets of Studies

The Head Start Synthesis Project meta-analysis of all available studies of Head Start's effects identified 50 studies that found evidence of immediate improvements in children's intellectual performance, socio-emotional performance, and health that lasted several years. It also found that these Head Start programs provided and linked families with health, social, and educational services and influenced various institutions to provide such services (McKey et al., 1985). Ramey, Bryant, and Suarez (1985) identified another 11 experimental studies in which the mean intelligence test scores of children who participated in preschool programs were as high as or higher than the mean intelligence test scores of children in the studies' control groups. Lazar et al. (1982) analyzed data from the constituent studies of a collaborative effort called the Consortium for Longitudinal Studies. Based on earlier findings of constituent studies and a common follow-up assessment in the late 1970s, they reported findings of positive program effects on intelligence test scores at school entry, on special education placement, and on grade retention.

Individual Studies

Table 1 lists seven intensive long-term studies (like the High/Scope Perry Preschool study) and four extensive long-term studies that have found evidence that good programs for young children living in poverty produce statistically significant (at $p < .05$, two-tailed) long-term benefits. The intensive studies we reviewed are the following:

- **Evaluation of the Carolina Early Intervention Project** (Ramey, Bryant, Campbell, Sparling, & Wasik, 1988), combining the Abecedarian Project and Project CARE, a developmental child day care program throughout early childhood, and a toy-lending library

- **Evaluation of the Early Training Project** (Gray, Ramsey, & Klaus, 1982), a program of part-time classes for children in the summer, and weekly home visits to the children and their parents during the school year

- **The Harlem study** (Palmer, 1983) of a program of twice-weekly, one-on-one sessions of teachers with young males

- **Evaluation of the Milwaukee Project** (Garber, 1988),[2] a program of full-time, year-round classes for children throughout early childhood, and job training for mothers with low intellectual performance

- **Evaluation of the Mother-Child Home Program** (Levenstein, O'Hara, & Madden, 1983), a program of twice-weekly home visits to mothers and their children

---

[2]Although doubts have been raised about the veracity of the original project director, Rick Heber (who was sentenced to prison for offenses unrelated to this project), Garber (1988) provides a credible presentation of the project's methodology and findings.

- **Evaluation of the Rome (Georgia) Head Start Program** (Monroe & McDonald, 1981), an ordinary Head Start program operated in the first year of the national Head Start project

- **The Syracuse University Family Development Research Program** (Lally, Mangione, & Honig, 1988), a program of high-quality child day care year-round and weekly home visits for family support

The extensive studies we reviewed are the following:

- **Evaluation of the Chicago Child-Parent Center Programs** (Fuerst & Fuerst, 1993), a program for children from ages 3 to 8 that featured self-contained centers at public elementary schools, smaller classes, Direct Instruction in many classrooms, and parent involvement

- **Evaluation of Project HOPE, Home-Oriented Preschool Education** (Gotts, 1989), a program of daily television lessons enhanced by weekly home visits on the same topics, and weekly classes for children in a mobile classroom

- **Evaluation of the Houston Parent-Child Development Center** (PCDC; Johnson, 1988), a program that began with a year of home visits to parents every other week, then provided a year of classes for children and classes for parents

- **Evaluation of the New York State Prekindergarten Program** (Irvine, 1982), a program of part-time classes for children, and parent involvement

All the programs examined in these longitudinal studies served young children living in poverty and at special risk of school failure. Children entered the programs at some time between birth and age 5 and remained in them, at least, for one school year and, at most, through nearly their entire early childhood, from birth to school entry. In some of these studies assessment has not yet progressed beyond early childhood, while in others follow-up has continued up to age 21; most of the studies include the possibility of future follow-up with study participants at later ages. All but two of the studies were able to follow up on at least 70% of the original study participants. The Project HOPE follow-up study located only 43% of original study participants, and the Houston PCDC follow-up study located only 17% of original study participants. However, in both follow-ups, analyses indicated that the follow-up study samples were representative of the original study samples.

Findings of the Reviewed Studies

As shown in Table 2, each of the studies that collected data on early childhood intellectual performance found its program group to have a significantly higher mean intellectual performance score than its no-program group ($p < .05$, two-tailed), at least during the program and shortly thereafter. Significant differences favoring the program group

Table 1

DESIGN OF SELECTED STUDIES OF PRESCHOOL PROGRAM EFFECTIVENESS

Study	Preschool Program		Cases in Original Sample	Last Follow-up	
	Age	Type		Age	% Located
Intensive studies					
Carolina Early Intervention (Ramey et al., 1988)	0–5	Developmental day care center; toy-lending library	146	4½	84%
Early Training (Gray et al., 1982)	3–6	Part-time classes for children in summer; weekly home visits during school year	90	21	80%
Harlem (Palmer, 1983)	2–4	Sessions with individual children twice a week	315	13	81%
Milwaukee (Garber, 1988)	0–6	Full-time year-round classes for children; job training for mothers	40	15	88%
Mother-Child Home (Levenstein et al., 1983)	2–5	Home visits twice weekly	250	9–13	74%
Rome Head Start (Monroe & McDonald, 1981)	5–6	Part-time classes for children; parent involvement	218	20	71%
Syracuse University Family Development (Lally et al., 1988)	0–5	Weekly home visits for family support; high-quality day care year-round	108	14	76%
Extensive studies					
Chicago Child-Parent Centers (Fuerst & Fuerst, 1993)	3–8	Self-contained centers at schools with specialist teachers, smaller classes, Direct Instruction, parent involvement	683	19	75%
HOPE[a] (Gotts, 1989)	3–5	Daily television lessons, weekly home visits, weekly classes in mobile classroom	703	17	43%
Houston PCDC (Johnson, 1988)	1–3	A year of home visits every 2 weeks, then a year of classes for children and classes for mothers	about 800	8–11	17%
New York Prekindergarten (Irvine, 1982)	4–5	Part-time classes for children; parent involvement	2,058	9	75%

Note. All studies listed studied persons living in poverty and at high risk of school failure, with programs that began between birth and age 5.

[a]Served the general population, but findings are due mainly to young persons living in poverty.

Table 2

FINDINGS OF SELECTED STUDIES OF PRESCHOOL PROGRAM EFFECTIVENESS

Study	Age of Higher Program-Group Intellectual Performance	Rate of Special Education Placement	Rate of Grade Retention	Rate of Graduation From High School
Intensive studies				
Carolina Early Intervention (Ramey et al., 1988)	$\frac{1}{2}$–$4\frac{1}{2}$	–	–	–
Early Training (Gray et al., 1982)	5–10	3% vs. 29%*	53% vs. 69%	78% vs. 57%
Harlem (Palmer, 1983)	3–5	–	24% vs. 45%*	–
Milwaukee (Garber, 1988)	2–10	47% vs. 89%*	29% vs. 56%	–
Mother-Child Home (Levenstein et al., 1983)	3–4	14% vs. 39%*	13% vs. 19%	–
Rome Head Start (Monroe & McDonald, 1981)	–	11% vs. 25%*	51% vs. 63%	50% vs. 33%*
Syracuse University Family Development (Lally et al., 1988)	3–4	–	–	–
Extensive studies				
Chicago Child-Parent Centers (Fuerst & Fuerst, 1993)	–	–	–	62% vs. 49%*
HOPE (Gotts, 1989)	–	–	10% vs. 23%*	88% vs. 74%*
Houston PCDC (Johnson, 1988)	3	–	–	–
New York Prekindergarten (Irvine, 1982)	–	2% vs. 5%*	16% vs. 21%*	–

Note. In each comparison, the percentage of the program group is given first, followed by the percentage of the no-program group.

*$p < .05$, two-tailed.

over the no-program group in intellectual performance were found through age 10 in the Early Training Project and through age 10 in the Milwaukee Project. However, in the Milwaukee Project there were no significant differences between groups in intellectual performance at ages 12 and 14.[3]

In four of the intensive studies and one of the extensive studies, significantly fewer program-group than no-program-group members were ever placed in special education classes. The magnitude of the special education percentages in each study was a function of the initial degree of risk of school failure for the participants in that study. The significant

[3]The Milwaukee Project found a similar diminution of difference on school achievement. Compared with the no-program group, the program group had significantly higher school-achievement test scores in the first 4 years of school. However, by the end of the fourth year of schooling the two groups' achievement test scores were no longer significantly different.

differences in the percentages ranged from 2% for the program group versus 5% for the no-program group in the evaluation of the New York Prekindergarten Program to 47% for the program group versus 89% for the no-program group in the Milwaukee Project. The Perry study had similar results, specifically with respect to percentages of program-group versus no-program group members placed in classes for educable mental impairment.

In one of the intensive studies and two of the extensive studies, significantly fewer program-group than no-program-group members were ever retained in grade. In the four other intensive studies with grade-retention information, fewer program-group than no-program-group members were ever retained in grade, although for various reasons the differences were not significant.

Placement in special education and retention in grade, regardless of their efficacy, identify and attempt to respond to children's educational problems (see Shepard & Smith, 1989, for a critical assessment of retention in grade). As outcome variables in studies of the effects of preschool programs, such placements serve the function of identifying students' educational problems. It is only when they are considered to be mediating variables to later outcomes (see Chapters 3 and 8 of this report) that their own effectiveness in addressing problems comes into the picture.

In one of the intensive studies and two of the extensive studies, the program group had a significantly higher rate of high school graduation than the no-program group. In the other intensive study with such data (the evaluation of the Early Training Project), *nearly* significantly more program-group than no-program-group members graduated from high school ($p = .079$). In two of these studies that examined these findings by gender, program-group females had significantly higher graduation rates than no-program-group females had, while program and no-program males did not differ significantly regarding graduation rate (Gray et al., 1982; Fuerst & Fuerst, 1993). The Perry study found a similar disparity between females (program and no-program differed significantly on high school graduation) and males (program and no-program did not differ significantly on high school graduation; Barnes, 1989).

In addition, several of these studies had other findings that should be noted here because of their similarity to certain High/Scope Perry Preschool study findings presented in later chapters.

The Syracuse University Family Development Research Program found, in a search of court and probation department records when study participants were ages 13–16, that only 6% of the program group, as compared with 22% of the no-program group, had been placed on probation ($p < .05$). Further, whereas most of the program group's offenses only involved family discipline problems, most of the no-program group's offenses involved acts of personal violence. Program-group offenders were 2 males and 2 females; no-program-group offenders were 3 females and 9 males; so the group difference was largely attributable to males. In addition, at grades 7 and 8 the program-group members had significantly better perceptions of themselves than did the no-program-group members.

The Houston PCDC was one of three such centers originally evaluated by Andrews et al. (1982). The evaluation of the Houston center is included here because it included a long-term follow-up study (Johnson, 1988). In addition to the findings already reported, the follow-up also had findings based on teacher ratings and school achievement tests. According to teachers in grades 2–5, program-group children as compared with no-program-group children were significantly less restless, impulsive, obstinate, and disruptive, and less often involved in fights; they also had significantly higher composite scores on the Iowa Test of Basic Skills; and they were referred for special services less often (these data are not reported in Table 2 because percentages were not specified in the report).

Several studies have differentiated between findings for program males versus no-program males and findings for program females versus no-program females. Gray et al. (1982) pioneered this approach, and their work is examined in Chapter 3, in comparison with the findings of the Perry study. The two other studies with such findings (Syracuse and Chicago) are reviewed here.

The Syracuse University Family Development Research Program found at grades 7 and 8 that as compared with no-program-group females, program-group females had significantly higher grades, fewer absences, more-positive attitudes towards themselves and other people, and, according to teachers, greater school achievement and impulse control.

Fuerst and Fuerst (1993) have argued that their findings on the Chicago Child-Parent Centers show that the programs helped girls but not boys.[4] In fact, their findings appear to indicate that while the programs helped *both* girls and boys, they helped girls a little more than boys. In their comparison of achievement test grade-equivalent scores at eighth grade ($n = 949$), the program males had an average advantage over the no-program males of 0.57 grade equivalents, while the program females had an average advantage over the no-program females of 0.62 grade equivalents. In this study, 49% of program males, as compared with 40% of no-program males, graduated from high school—which is an advantage of 9 percentage points; 74% of program females, as compared with 57% of no-program females, graduated from high school—which is an advantage of 17 percentage points.

Fade-out of Preschool Program Effects?

Although some have claimed that most effects of good preschool programs for children in poverty fade away (e.g., McKey et al., 1985), there is virtually no evidence of fade-out of the effect on children's special education placement, high school graduation, or delinquency; fade-out evidence is mixed for effects on children's socioemotional behavior and school achievement. Clear evidence of fade-out has been found only for gains in children's intelligence-test scores. In the 1960s, the hypothesis was that even though early educational programs were found to raise young children's test scores, subsequent educational programs would not affect

---

[4]A Newsweek article (Kantrowitz, 1991) interpreted the data from this study loosely to suggest that Head Start programs do not have long-term effects on either boys or girls.

them. Instead, it may be argued, a difference in intelligence-test scores reflects a difference in educational settings. When children who have attended preschool programs and children who have not attended preschool programs come together into the same, standard elementary school classrooms, their intelligence test scores also come together.

Early Childhood Program Quality: Indispensable to Effectiveness

Quality is essential to the effectiveness of preschool programs, whether they address the critical problems of children and families living in poverty or the important child care needs of a broader population (Ruopp, Travers, Glantz, & Coelen, 1979; Whitebook, Howes, & Phillips, 1989). Based on the longitudinal studies of a variety of early childhood programs serving all kinds of families, the following generalizations may be made about the characteristics of effective programs, staff, and administrators (Schweinhart, 1988a, 1988b; Schweinhart & Weikart, 1988b).

- Effective programs use explicitly stated, developmentally appropriate active-learning curricula that support children's self-initiated learning activities (Schweinhart, Weikart, & Larner, 1986; Rescorla, Hyson, & Hirsh-Pasek, 1991).

- Effective teaching staff have been trained in early childhood education and do not change jobs often (Ruopp et al., 1979; Whitebook et al., 1989).

- Effective administrators provide systematic inservice training on site and supervisory support for their staff's curriculum implementation (Epstein, 1993).

- Effective programs maintain classes of fewer than twenty 3- to 5-year-olds for every pair of teaching adults (Ruopp et al., 1979).

- In effective programs, staff treat parents as partners and engage in extensive outreach to parents, such as home visits at least monthly, to learn from parents and to help them understand the curriculum and their children's development (Gray et al., 1982; Weikart, Rogers, Adcock, & McClelland, 1971).

The accreditation criteria of the National Academy of Early Childhood Programs (National Association for the Education of Young Children [NAEYC], 1984) embrace these characteristics of program quality. But popular understanding of what is *developmentally appropriate* does not always measure up to the definition articulated by the NAEYC. The challenge is to systemize developmentally appropriate practices so that diverse teaching staff can readily comprehend and implement them. Clear formulation is the first step; widespread dissemination is the second. Developmentally appropriate practices must be widely understood, first of all, by teacher trainers, and to use a Piagetian term, this understanding must be *operative*—capable of being put into practice. And the teacher trainers must actually train large numbers of teachers. Popularizing such a phrase as developmentally appropriate practice is helpful, but only the first step, in meeting a real need—the widespread, effective training of teachers.

Causal Paths of Preschool Program Effects

The following is a hypothetical causal model derived from the findings of the High/Scope Perry Preschool study, and other studies, on the short-term and long-term effects of high-quality preschool programs for young children living in poverty.

Early childhood education seems to produce its long-term effects not by producing sustained improvements in intelligence or immediate improvements in school achievement, as was once hoped, but by engendering the dispositions in children that enable them to achieve greater success as they begin school. This early success breeds higher motivation, better performance, and higher regard from teachers and classmates. More-successful school careers increase students' chances of graduating from high school, holding jobs, forming families, and avoiding involvement in criminal activity (Schweinhart & Weikart, 1980).

A good preschool program comes at a time in the child's development that is opportune for preventing the deleterious effects of family poverty on school performance. A good preschool program—part-day or full-day—provides care for children while family caregivers are otherwise occupied. The function that all preschool programs have in common is helping children to develop in a variety of ways, including preparing them for successful school performance that creates a foundation for life success.

For a good preschool program to affect children in future years, it must have some immediate effect on the children and probably on their families. The best-documented immediate effect of good preschool programs is the improvement in children's intellectual performance, and this is an effect that usually lasts no more than a few years. Yet these years include the crucial beginning of school, and children who have attended good preschool programs exhibit better intellectual performance as they adapt to the demanding school setting. Hence, children's intellectual performance becomes the connecting link between the preschool program and its later effects. There is also appeal in the hypothesis that parents provide a connecting link by gaining, from their child's preschool program, improved parenting skills that support children during schooling.

By our hypothetical model, a good preschool program enables children to better carry out the first school tasks they encounter. This better performance is visible to everyone involved—the child, the teacher, the parents, and other children. Realizing they have the ability to achieve classroom success, children believe and act accordingly, thereby developing a stronger commitment to schooling. Teachers recognize better school performance and react to it with higher expectations and eventually with school placements that reflect these higher expectations. If children cannot carry out school tasks, then teachers, parents, and the children themselves develop lower expectations for future performance.

Sometimes "placements" are made within the classroom by seating or grouping children according to ability. Grade retention is a type of "placement" that is often used, despite the mounting evidence against it (Shepard & Smith, 1989). Other placements involve assignment outside the classroom—to special education or compensatory education programs. In the model described here, intellectual performance evokes, in the child, the response of commitment to schooling and, in teachers, the response of rewarding children's performance and commitment with improved school-placement. Commitment to schooling and school placement then work together to influence school achievement. School placement, by determining the setting, regulates exposure to content. Children's commitment or motivation determines how well the content is assimilated. School achievement then reflects performance in the setting and resultant mastery of content.

In the hypothetical model under consideration, reduced crime is another effect of commitment to schooling and school placement. To use Elliott's term, both commitment and placement represent *bonds* between the student and the school (Elliott et al., 1979). The strength of these bonds keeps young people engaged in the schooling process and disengaged from delinquency. Crime is a kind of negative performance in the community setting. Studies have found that antisocial behavior patterns and teacher perceptions of inappropriate behaviors in the early elementary years predict later outcomes (Comer, 1989; Flax, 1990; Loeber, 1985; Steinberg, 1987). In the High/Scope Perry study, ratings by early elementary teachers of children's school and personal misconduct were significant predictors of children's subsequent years retained in grade, high school graduation, unemployment, and arrests by age 19 (Barnes, 1991).

School motivation and commitment are seen as leading to the highest year of schooling completed. The highest year of schooling is based on a series of mutual choices by the student and educators. At least through high school graduation, these decisions grow out of consideration of the student's school potential and achievement and consideration of the underlying commitment that permits potential to be realized. Of course, in decisions about postsecondary schooling that involve private investment, the factor of financial resources comes strongly into play as well.

The final step in this model is from schooling completed to employment and earnings, which indicate socially responsible success in the community. One of the major purposes of education is to prepare young people for the world of work. Productive employment is one of the principal features of adult competence. Education does, by and large, prepare people for work and resultant earnings. In 1991 in the U.S., the median earnings for full-year, full-time employment were $17,631 for high school dropouts and $21,891 (24% higher) for high school graduates who did not attend college. However, blacks earned less than whites at all levels of schooling. Among blacks the median earnings from full-year, full-time employment were $15,796 for high school dropouts and $18,620 (18% higher) for high school graduates who did not attend college (U.S. Bureau of the Census, 1992).

Working from this view of the role of education in human development, the Perry preschool program—with its curriculum that is now known as the High/Scope Curriculum—was designed to increase the future school and life success of its participants. Employing real-world measures of school achievements, delinquency and crime, employment and earnings, welfare assistance, and the like, the High/Scope Perry study sought to identify the linkages between early childhood education and adult performance on variables that have a clear value to the community and a clear economic value.

The next several chapters describe the study's methodology and findings. Looked at in detail are the following: study participants' educational performance, involvement in crime, economic status, and family formation and health; the preschool program's economic costs and benefits; a causal model for the study's data; and selected case studies. The last chapter interprets the study's findings and draws conclusions and implications for public policy and practice.

II Experimental Design

According to the design of the High/Scope Perry Preschool study, project staff

- *Identified 123 young African-American children in Ypsilanti, Michigan, who were living in poverty and assessed to be at high risk of school failure*

- *Randomly assigned them to a program group and a no-program group*

- *Operated a high-quality, active learning program for the program group at ages 3 and 4*

- *Collected data on both groups annually from ages 3 through 11, at ages 14–15, at age 19, and at age 27*

- *After each phase of data collection, analyzed the data and wrote reports of the study*

This chapter elaborates on each element of this experimental design. It concludes with an assessment of the effects of several potential threats to the internal validity of the study.

The Study Participants

The High/Scope Perry study has for almost 30 years followed the lives of 123 persons who, as children, attended the Perry Elementary School, which drew its attendance from its surrounding, predominantly black neighborhood on the South Side of Ypsilanti, Michigan (see The African-American Experience in Ypsilanti on p. 24). The project was conducted in the Ypsilanti school district because David Weikart, the project director, was director of special education services for the Ypsilanti school district as well as a doctoral candidate at the University of Michigan in Ann Arbor at the time of the study's inception. The Perry School became the site of the study because of the high rates of poverty and school failure among its students and because Eugene Beatty, the school's principal, was willing to support the effort.

Selecting Children With the Odds Against Them

Staff of the Perry Preschool Project identified children for the longitudinal study from (a) a census of the families of students then attending Perry School, (b) referrals by neighborhood groups, and (c) door-to-door canvassing. They selected families of low socioeconomic status with children showing low intellectual performance (measured at study entry) but no evidence of organic handicap. **Self-selection had virtually no role in selection of study participants,** since only three families with

The African-American Experience in Ypsilanti

The municipality of Ypsilanti was founded in 1823 as a trading post community called Woodruff's Grove. As a neighbor of Detroit, Ypsilanti has been greatly affected by the automotive industry ever since the first Ford plant opened at the beginning of the century. In the 1960s and 1970s, while the Perry study participants were attending public school, Ypsilanti's growth was steady. Beginning in the early 1980s, however, massive layoffs and closings in automotive and related industries resulted in high unemployment rates in this city of 30,000 residents. Other local industries have not been able to fill the gap this created. Ypsilanti does continue, however, to have a thriving educational community. Its public schools serve approximately 7,400 students in nine elementary schools, two middle schools, and one high school, and the city has three institutions of higher learning: a 4-year university, a community college, and a private business college.

Ypsilanti's African-Americans

Today, African-Americans make up approximately 20% of Ypsilanti's population. Blacks first arrived in the early 1850s, when the city was a stop on the Underground Railroad, but their numbers did not really grow until the automobile industry arrived some 50 years later. Conversion of the nearby Willow Run auto plant to make bombers during World War II brought to Ypsilanti a further influx of whites as well as blacks, many of whom traveled straight north from Kentucky.

In the 1950s, the city's African-American middle class, made up primarily of factory workers, began to grow. Some blacks began to accumulate money through buying, renovating, and renting local rooming houses and apartments. The Ypsilanti Negro Business and Professional League was created in 1952 and remains active today. The 1960s and 1970s brought even greater prosperity for Ypsilanti's black population. While the Civil Rights Act of 1965 opened up jobs previously closed to them in business and industry, automotive manufacturing continued to provide their major source of employment. The economic downturn of the 1980s, however, has meant a serious setback for black prosperity in Ypsilanti.

Housing

At least through the 1960s, housing for African-Americans was concentrated on the city's South Side (where Perry School is located) and near the auto plants in Ypsilanti Township. Most of this housing was substandard. Denied FHA and bank loans, blacks found it necessary to pool their resources and build their homes over a long period of time. It wasn't until the Fair Housing Act of 1968 that federal loans became available at all to black home-buyers. Also in the late 1960s, under the city's black mayor, John H. Burton, construction of city-owned public housing began in earnest. Though the South Side today remains predominantly black, housing patterns became more integrated in the 1970s and 1980s. Whites, who had abandoned the South Side, began returning there to buy and renovate homes. Also, homes in other areas of the city were no longer off-limits to African-Americans. For poor black families, however, Ypsilanti's South Side and distinct neighborhoods in Willow Run remain the primary residential options.

Education

The Ypsilanti schools have never been formally segregated, but because of housing patterns, the schools on the South Side had few white children. The major effect of the 1954 U.S. Supreme Court decision (Brown v. the Board of Education) was to open up employment opportunities for African-American teachers beyond positions in the mostly black Perry School or in Special Education Services. The local 4-year university also began hiring African-American professors and, since 1965, has actively recruited blacks into its faculty, administration, and student body.

The 1950s also saw blacks becoming active on the local school board. First, a dentist, Dr. Perry (for whom Perry School is named), served two terms on the school board. Other blacks followed him on the school board, and still others were elected to the city council. Those active on the educational and political scene began to draw attention to the high numbers of high school dropouts, particularly within the black population. Eugene Beatty, who became the first black principal of Perry School in 1940, recalls that at the time, no more than two black students graduated from Ypsilanti High School each year. Under Beatty's leadership, the elementary school began dual function as a community center, parent involvement was encouraged, and the message that high school graduation was an important goal slowly took hold. Beatty is remembered for his innovative idea that the school, as well as the church, could be a focal point for African-American families. Although graduation rates have gradually improved over the years, when compared with the rest of the county and state, Ypsilanti still has a high dropout rate, particularly among minority students.

In sum, the childhood and young adulthood of the Perry study participants were characterized by growth and expanding opportunities, when the worlds of both education and business were opening their doors to blacks. Just as the Perry preschoolers embarked on adulthood, however, doors began to close. Most recently, the local economy has suffered a prolonged downturn. Drugs, with crime and violence, have spread outward from Detroit into Ypsilanti. The situation is such that strong beginnings and early hope might see a growing person through the hard times—or fractured plans and disappointed dreams could give way to discouragement and alienation.

---

*Sources are the U.S. Bureau of the Census; Howe (1953); Tobias, Baker, and Fairfield (1973); interviews with A.P. Marshall, a noted local African-American historian, and Eugene Beatty.

children identified for the study refused to participate in it (Weikart et al., 1970).

Project staff identified families of low **socioeconomic status** (using an operational definition developed by Deutsch, 1962) by their low scores for parents' years of schooling, parents' occupational levels, and rooms per person in their households. These scores were computed as (a) half the total of both parents' highest years of schooling or half the single mother's highest year of schooling; (b) the father's or single mother's occupational level (2 = unskilled or unemployed, 4 = semi-skilled, 6 = skilled, 8 = professional); and (c) twice the rooms per person in the household (Weikart et al., 1970).

Use of these selection criteria meant that families whose children participated in the study were in most ways considerably worse-off than the U.S. population and slightly worse-off than the black population at the time (Schweinhart & Weikart, 1980). As shown in Table 3, half of the mothers in the study had left school by the end of 9th grade, and half of the fathers had left school at 8th grade. These were educational levels just months below the median of U.S. blacks but several years below the median of the U.S. population. Only about one fifth of the mothers and one tenth of the fathers in the study had completed high school, compared with one third of black adults and a little over one half of all adults in the U.S. in 1970. Nearly half of the children participating in the study lived in single-parent families in the 1960s and 1970s, as compared with one third of black families and one seventh of all families in the U.S. in 1970.

Table 3 indicates that about half of the fathers in the study were employed; this is somewhat lower than the 60% rate for black men nationally and considerably below the 74% rate for all men nationally in 1970. Although at study entry only one fifth of the mothers were employed, when study participants were 15 years old, 45% of mothers reporting were employed; this was about the same as the percentage of black women employed nationally and a little higher than the percentage of all women employed nationally in 1970. About half of the study children's families received welfare assistance; this compared with fewer than one fifth of all black families and one twentieth of all families nationally. Although study participants' residences were of typical size for urban areas, Perry study families were over twice as large and their households were twice as crowded as those of either the U.S. black population or the U.S. total population. Also, the mothers of 79% of the study participants were born in the South, and 36% of the study participants lived in public housing projects at study entry.

Project staff used the Stanford-Binet Intelligence Test (Terman & Merrill, 1960) to assess the **intellectual performance** of the young children of families of low socioeconomic status. They selected for the study those children whose IQs at this initial testing were in the range of 70 to 85, defined then as "borderline educable mentally retarded" by the State of Michigan, following the American Association on Mental Deficiency (Weikart, 1967). Between 1959 and 1973, the association set the upper IQ limit for mental retardation at 85, although both before and after that time, the limit has been set at only 70 (Grossman, 1973). Zigler (1987) stated that the IQs of Perry children at study entry were lower

Table 3

DEMOGRAPHIC STATUS OF STUDY PARENTS AND U.S. FAMILIES

Variable	Perry Parents in 1962–65[a] (1973–77)	African-Americans in 1970	U.S. Population in 1970
Schooling of mothers/ women			
Median years of school	9.7	10.0	12.1
Completed high school	21%	33%	53%
Schooling of fathers/ men			
Median years of school	8.0	9.6	11.8
Completed high school	11%	32%	54%
Family composition			
Husband-wife families	53% (46%)	69%	86%
Single-head families	47% (54%)	33%	14%
Employment of parents/ adults			
Not employed or looking for work	40%[b]	25%	17%
Mothers employed	20%[c] (45%)	47%	38%
Fathers employed[d]	47%	60%	74%
Unskilled	81%	35%	16%
Semiskilled	14%	30%	20%
Skilled	5%	25%	39%
Professional	0%	9%	25%
Family on welfare	49%	18%	5%
Household density			
Median persons	6.7	3.1	2.7
Median rooms	4.8	4.7	4.8
Median persons per room	1.40	0.66	0.56

Note. Data source for Perry parents is the initial parent-interview; data source for the African-American population and the U.S. population (males and females 25 and over) is the 1970 U.S. Census as reported by Schweinhart and Weikart (1980).

[a] Statistics for 1962–65 report the status at study entry of the parents of the 100 families of the 123 Perry study participants; mothers were ages 18–48, fathers were ages 22–52.

[b] Combines Perry mothers and fathers.

[c] Perry mothers' employment levels were either unskilled or, in 10 cases, unreported.

[d] Percentages at each specific employment level refer to percents *of those employed.*

than those of most black children living in poverty; some poor black children were in fact screened out of the sample because their IQs were above the cutoff point. However, median IQs of the Perry study's no-program group ranged between 80 and 86 over the years of the study, which is essentially the range of the median IQ for black children in the 1960s (Kennedy, Van de Riet, & White, 1963).

Of the 128 children originally selected for the study, 4 children did not complete the preschool program because they moved away, and 1 child died shortly after the study began; so the longitudinal study had 123 participants. Children entered the study annually, in five waves, beginning with Wave Zero (of 4-year-olds) and Wave One (of 3-year-olds) in the fall of 1962 and adding a new wave of 3-year-olds each year through the fall of 1965.

Table 4 presents the numbers of longitudinal study participants at entry and the calendar years of their ages at times of data collection. In October of 1962, 28 Wave Zero children entered the study at age 4, and 17 Wave One children entered at age 3, followed by 26 Wave Two children in 1963, 27 Wave Three children in 1964, and 25 Wave Four children in 1965. Project staff randomly divided the children in each wave into those enrolled in the preschool program and those not enrolled in any preschool program. Program-group children, except for those in Wave Zero, attended the preschool program at ages 3 and 4; Wave Zero children attended only at age 4. To the findings from all the assessments through age 19, this report adds the study findings at age 27, an age reached by Wave Zero in 1986 and by Wave Four in 1990.

All study participants were African-American, as was almost everyone in the Perry School neighborhood. Though limiting the sample to black children removed racial variation from the design, it has raised a question about generalizing findings to children of other races, who have in fact constituted the majority of poor children in the United States (Zigler, 1987). Poor black children and poor children of other races may differ in many important ways. Nevertheless, because the program addressed intellectual and social abilities common to all races, it is reasonable to believe that it would have had the same effects on poor children of any race. Indeed, positive effects for black children may have been even harder to achieve, since in addition to the problems they shared with poor children of other backgrounds, black children also faced considerable racial prejudice and discrimination both early and later in life (e.g., in schooling, housing, and employment).

Most of the parents of study participants had come from the South: The mothers of 79% of the children[5] said they (the mothers) had been born in the South (33% in Alabama; 32% in Georgia, Mississippi, or Tennessee; only 11% in Michigan; and 9% in other states). The mothers of 47% of the children[6] said they (the mothers) had been educated in the South; a few had even graduated from high school, married, and given birth to some of their older children in the South. Proportions born and educated in the South were similar for the fathers of the study

---

[5]Based on information on 108 children.

[6]Based on information on 115 children.

Table 4

SAMPLE SIZES AND YEARS OF DATA COLLECTION, BY WAVE

Category	Sample Size					
	Wave Zero	Wave One	Wave Two	Wave Three	Wave Four	All Waves
Total	28	17	26	27	25	123
Program	13	8	12	13	12	58
No-program	15	9	14	14	13	65

	Calendar Year					
	Wave Zero	Wave One	Wave Two	Wave Three	Wave Four	All Waves
Age of data collection						
Birth	1958	1959	1960	1961	1962	1958–62
Age 3	1961	**1962**	**1963**	**1964**	**1965**	1961–65
Age 4	**1962**	**1963**	**1964**	**1965**	**1966**	1962–66
Age 5	**1963**	**1964**	**1965**	**1966**	**1967**	1963–67
Age 6	1964	1965	1966	1967	1968	1964–68
Age 7	1965	1966	1967	1968	1969	1965–69
Age 8	1966	1967	1968	1969	1970	1966–70
Age 9	1967	1968	1969	1970	1971	1967–71
Age 10	1968	1969	1970	1971	1972	1968–72
Age 11	1969	1970	1971	1972	1973	1969–73
Age 14	1972	1973	1974	1975	1976	1972–76
Age 15	1973	1974	1975	1976	1977	1973–77
Age 19	1977	1978	1979	1980	1981	1977–81
Age 27	1985	1986	1987	1988	1989	1985–89

Note. The years presented are when the study participants in a given wave reached each age (with 3 exceptions, born in the December prior to the calendar year shown). The years during which the program groups attended the preschool program are boldfaced.

participants. Having migrated to the Ypsilanti area in relatively recent times, when the best jobs were already taken, study parents tended to have the last choices of available jobs and were often the first to be laid off (Scanzoni, 1971).

Assignment to Groups

The scientific strength of this study, its ability to assess preschool program effects even many years later, is due primarily to the experimental design in which study participants were **randomly assigned** to one of two groups: a program group, enrolled in the preschool program, or a no-program group, not enrolled in any preschool program. Parents, teachers, psychologists who tested the children—-none of these had any influence over children's group assignments. Therefore there is no reason to suspect group differences in children's or parents' abilities or dispositions before the preschool program began.

The study design called for the use of randomizing techniques at several steps in the assignment of study participants to groups. After the fall survey in each year from 1962 to 1965, project staff assigned children in the wave entering the study to program and no-program groups as follows:

1. From pairs of study participants **matched on initial Stanford-Binet IQ** (Terman & Merrill, 1960), they randomly assigned each pair member to either of two undesignated groups.

2. They then exchanged several similarly ranked pair members, so the two groups would be **matched on mean socioeconomic status, mean intellectual performance,** and **percentages of boys and girls.**

3. By flipping a coin, they **randomly assigned** one group to the **program condition** and the other to the **no-program condition.**

4. They **assigned younger siblings to the same group as their older siblings,** to prevent the preschool program from indirectly affecting siblings in the no-program group. This procedure in effect made the sampling unit the family rather than the child. The 123 children in the sample came from 100 families: 47 families in the program group (39 with 1 child-participant, 6 with 2, 1 with 3, and 1 with 4) and 53 families in the no-program group (41 with 1 child-participant and 12 with 2).

Initially, 64 children were assigned to the program group, and 64 children were assigned to the no-program group. But then, fearing overall sample attrition, staff transferred from the program group to the no-program group 2 children (with single mothers employed away from home) who were unable to participate in any of the program's classes or home visits. (A thorough review of the study's comprehensive original data could identify only two such transfers; the transferred children's names were independently identified by the program's head teacher.[7]) After the 2 transfers, the program group had 62 children, and the no-program group had 66 children. Then 4 children in the program group moved out of the area before completing the 2-year classroom program, and 1 child in the no-program group died, leaving the program group with 58 members and the no-program group with 65 members. No other families withdrew children from the study. The final sample for the longitudinal study was composed of 33 program-group males, 25 program-group females, 39 no-program-group males, and 26 no-program-group females.

---

[7]Because this transfer has become a point of question (e.g., Gottfredson, 1990; Schweinhart, 1990), a special effort was made to verify its extent.

The Preschool Program

For the Perry Preschool Project, teachers conducted a program comprising a daily 2½-hour classroom session for children on weekday mornings and a weekly 1½-hour home visit to each mother and child on weekday afternoons. The 30-week school year began in mid-October and ended in May. Of the 58 children in the program group, the 13 in Wave Zero participated in the program for one school year at age 4, and the 45 in Waves One through Four participated in the program for two school years at ages 3 and 4. Each pair of successive waves—Zero and One, One and Two, Two and Three, and Three and Four—attended the program together one school year, one wave being age 4 and the other being age 3. In 1966–67, the final year of the program, 11 three-year-olds who were not included in the longitudinal sample attended the program with the 12 four-year-olds in Wave Four. Thus, the 4 teachers in the program served 20 to 25 children each school year, resulting in a child-teacher ratio of 5.00–6.25 children per teacher. This ratio was set to accommodate the demands not of the classroom sessions but of the weekly home visits.

The teachers visited the homes of each child in their classes (a) to involve the mother in the educational process and enable her to provide her child with educational support and (b) to implement the curriculum with each child in the child's home (Weikart et al., 1971). The teacher also helped the mother remain involved in the home visit by helping her deal with any problems that arose during the visit. Teachers took about a half hour to prepare for the home visit, planning how to extend what the child was doing in the classroom. Initially, both teachers and mothers, coming from different backgrounds, had to overcome a certain hesitation about participating in home visits. But after the first few visits, teachers and mothers usually were able to establish the rapport that was essential to the success of home visits. Project staff also convened group meetings of mothers and of fathers.

Between 1962 and 1967, 10 teachers certified to teach in elementary, early childhood, and special education served in the program's 4 teaching positions. Over the years, this included 7 white and 3 black women serving as teachers, and there was always at least 1 black teacher on the staff. One of the 10 teachers remained throughout the project, from 1962 to 1967; 3 remained 2 to 3 years; and 6 remained 1 to 2 years. In addition to project director David Weikart, 9 researchers (2 or 3 at a time) worked on the study while the program was in operation between 1962 and 1967.

The Perry preschool program cost $1,510 per child per school year in the dollars of the 1960s (Berrueta-Clement et al., 1984), which is the equivalent of $7,252 in 1992 dollars. This cost included *all* program costs, even school-district administration and building overhead costs. The high cost was principally due to having 4 public school teachers, paid 10% above the district's standard pay scale—1 teacher for every 5.7 children (overall project average). Since this program was experimental, the district did not strive for high economic efficiency. It is reasonable to assume that the quality of the program could have been maintained if the number of children per staff member had been increased to 10. The High/Scope Preschool Curriculum Comparison Study (Schweinhart et al., 1986) found that preschool programs could be highly effective with 8 children per staff member; and the National Day Care Study (Ruopp et al., 1979) provided evidence that program effectiveness does not decline substantially until the number of children per staff member exceeds 10. Increasing even to 8 children per staff member but making no other changes would have reduced the program cost to about $5,187 per child in 1992 dollars.

Developing the High/Scope Curriculum

The Perry Project's program staff developed a systematic approach to classroom and home-visit activities that was based on principles of active learning. Originally called the Cognitively Oriented Curriculum to distinguish it from approaches that did not include a systematic emphasis on cognitive development (Weikart et al., 1971), the approach was later named the High/Scope Curriculum (Hohmann, Banet, & Weikart, 1979; Hohmann & Weikart, in press; Weikart & Schweinhart, 1993). Beginning in 1962 and continuously throughout the program's duration, staff explicitly sought to develop an educational approach that supported the development of young children's cognitive and social skills through individualized teaching and learning. This approach was built on insights staff obtained from their classroom experience and their review of the studies of Jean Piaget and others (e.g., Brearly & Hitchfield, 1966; Flavell, 1965; Hunt, 1961; Piaget, 1960, 1968; Piaget & Inhelder, 1969; Piaget, Inhelder, & Szeminska, 1964; Smilansky, 1968).

During the five school years of the Perry Preschool Project, as staff developed their theoretical understanding of this curriculum based on active learning, they became increasingly systematic in its application. In the first year, they enthusiastically engaged in thoughtful experimentation; their lesson plans were not yet guided by an explicit developmental theory or set of objectives (Weikart et al., 1978). In the second year, six evening seminars on Piaget's theory inspired staff to articulate developmental goals and to make classroom teaching practices more individualized and developmentally appropriate. In the third year, staff began to apply Piaget's theory by developing a daily routine based on principles of active learning and by focusing on systematic assessment of the needs and interests of individual children in daily planning and evaluation. By the fourth year, the daily routine consistently included these elements: child-planning time, work time, cleanup time, recall time, snack time, small-group time, outdoor time, circle time, and dismissal. By the fifth year, staff had consolidated an essentially Piagetian theory-base and formulated a coherent approach to early childhood education (see Features of the High/Scope Curriculum on p. 34).

Throughout the curriculum development process, the focus was on evolving a conceptual framework with clearly stated principles to shape educational practices and permit objective evaluation of teacher-child activities. It is doubtful that the program's success with the first wave or two of children could have been sustained without this systemization of the educational approach.

Features of the High/Scope Curriculum

The High/Scope educational approach developed and used in the Perry Preschool Project's classroom and home visits was, and is today, an open framework of educational ideas and practices based on the natural development of young children. Drawing on the child development ideas of Jean Piaget, it emphasizes that children are **active learners,** who learn best from activities that they themselves plan, carry out, and then review. The role of adults is to observe, support, and extend children's activities in the following ways: by arranging and equipping interest areas in the learning environment; by maintaining a daily routine that permits children to plan, carry out, and review their own activities; and by joining in children's activities, asking appropriate questions that extend their plans and help them to think about their activities. Using as a framework a set of active learning **key experiences*** derived from child development theory, adults encourage children to engage in play activities that involve making choices and solving problems and that otherwise contribute to their intellectual, social, and physical development.

The High/Scope Curriculum does not include defined subject matter that adults must "teach" children. Instead, with the key experiences in mind, adults listen closely to what children plan and then actively work with and question them to extend their activities to developmentally appropriate experiences. The questioning style adults use is important. It emphasizes **open-ended questions** that initiate conversations with children and help them to participate. Adults rarely ask questions that test children's specific knowledge of letters, numbers, or colors. Instead, they ask children to generate descriptions or ideas: *What happened? How did you make that? Can you show me? Can you help another child?* This questioning style permits free conversation between adult and child and serves as a model for conversations among children. Such an approach permits the adult and the child to interact as thinkers and doers rather than to assume the traditional school roles of the teacher who initiates and the pupil who responds. Both adult and child share and learn as they work.

To create a setting in which children engage in active learning, a consistent **daily routine** is maintained. The routine varies only when the child has fair warning that things will be different the next day: Field trips are not surprises; special visits or events are not initiated in the classroom on the spur of the moment. This adherence to routine gives the child the control necessary to develop a sense of responsibility and to enjoy the opportunities for independence. The daily routine includes a **plan-do-review** sequence as well as large- and small-group activities. The plan-do-review sequence is the central device that gives children opportunities to express and act on their intentions while keeping the adult intimately involved in the process.

As already mentioned, in the High/Scope approach, adults use a set of active learning key experiences as a framework for their interactions with children. Key experiences help teachers not only to support and extend children's activities but also to monitor children's progress. In short, the key experiences provide a way of thinking about education that frees the teacher from the resource books of themes and activities that characterize some early childhood programs and from the scope-and-sequence charts, workbooks, and standardized tests that dominate behavioral approaches. Not culture-specific, the key experiences are crucial to children's development the world over; they are also very simple and practical. Ten categories of preschool key experiences are identified:

- Creative representation

- Language and literacy

- Social relations and personal initiative

- Movement

- Music

- Classification (recognizing similarities and differences)

- Seriation (creating series and patterns)

- Number

- Space

- Time

Each category includes several specific key experiences. For example, the category of *social relations and personal initiative* includes

- Making and expressing choices, plans, and decisions

- Solving problems encountered in play

- Taking care of one's own needs

- Expressing feelings in words

- Participating in group routines
- Being sensitive to the feelings, interests, and needs of others
- Building relationships with children and adults
- Creating and experiencing collaborative play
- Dealing with social conflict

The category of *creative representation* includes

- Recognizing objects by sound, touch, taste, and smell
- Imitating actions and sounds
- Relating pictures, photographs, and models to real places and things
- Role play and pretending
- Making models out of clay or blocks
- Drawing and painting

High/Scope's early childhood educational approach provides explicit theoretical justification for what are often implicit, experience-based intuitions about how to deal with children. The approach grew out of the constructive give-and-take of teachers and researchers who held strong convictions but were nonetheless open to new ideas and practices. Since its early development at the Perry School, the High/Scope Curriculum has continued to evolve (Hohmann, Banet, & Weikart, 1979; Hohmann & Weikart, in press) and has been widely accepted. By the end of 1992, the High/Scope Foundation had certified over 1,100 High/Scope Curriculum trainers in 11 countries, who had in turn trained an estimated 28,500 teachers and assistant teachers serving over a quarter-million children annually (Epstein, 1993). The original High/Scope Curriculum textbook *Young Children in Action* (Hohmann et al., 1979) has been translated from English into Spanish, Portuguese, Dutch, Flemish, Norwegian, Finnish, and Chinese; it is currently being translated into Turkish, French, Arabic, and Thai.

---

*The idea of key experiences was a part of the curriculum from the first years of the High/Scope Perry Preschool Project; the term *key experiences*, however, was introduced later.

Study Data Collection

The High/Scope Perry Preschool study has accumulated an unusually rich and comprehensive data set on young people growing up in poverty, with variables representing their status from birth through childhood and adolescence and into adulthood. The many variables encompass demographic characteristics, test performance throughout childhood and adolescence, school success, delinquent and criminal activity, socioeconomic success, and personal development. Table 5 on the next page lists the study's instruments and principal variables. The study phases at ages 19 and 27 verified information from records against information from study-participant interviews and vice versa.

Low Attrition

One of the High/Scope Perry Preschool study's special strengths is that attrition in the study sample has been extraordinarily low. The median percentage of missing data across all measures was 4.9%, and the mean was 8.7%. Rates of missing data averaged 8.1% across the 28 administrations of intellectual tests (as listed in Table 5); 18.0% across the six administrations of school achievement tests; 8.6% across the parent interviews at study entry and at youth's age 15; 8.7% across the three study-participant interviews at ages 15, 19, and 27 (4.9% for the age-27 interview); 8.9% for the school records; and 0.0% for the crime and social services records, since the names of all the study participants were included in these searches.[8] These low rates of missing data mean that attrition usually had a negligible effect on sample representativeness or group comparisons. When attrition was greater, as on the age-14 school achievement tests, analyses revealed no attrition effect on the analyses (Schweinhart & Weikart, 1980).

The study's low attrition is largely attributable to the persistence of research staff in finding study participants. The wave design meant that data collectors had to find and assess only about 25 persons (one wave) each year, which permitted careful attention to each study participant. The study interviewers, who were involved in the life of the community, went to great lengths to locate study participants. The tenacity of the interviewers was extraordinary. One of them, Van Loggins, endured a strip-search at a prison in order to obtain one interview; while obtaining another interview, Loggins had to take cover to avoid some neighborhood gunfire. The continued collaboration and good will of schools, courts and police, social services providers, and the study participants themselves also contributed to successful data collection.

Another factor in the study's low attrition was the geographic stability of the study participants through age 27, which was a little higher

---

[8]It is possible, however, that some records in other agencies were not found by these searches.

Table 5

MEASURES AND PRINCIPAL VARIABLES

Measure	Age of Study Participants (Years)	Principal Variables
Initial parent-interview	3[a]	Parents' schooling, employment; persons, rooms in household; siblings
Stanford-Binet Intelligence Scale (Terman & Merrill, 1960)	3–9[b]	Intellectual performance
Adapted Leiter International Performance Scale (Arthur, 1952)	3–9	Nonverbal intellectual performance
Illinois Test of Psycholinguistic Abilities (ITPA, experimental version; McCarthy & Kirk, 1961)	3, 5–9	Psycholinguistic abilities
Peabody Picture Vocabulary Test (PPVT; Dunn, 1965)	3–9	Vocabulary
Wechsler Intelligence Scale for Children (WISC; Wechsler, 1974)	14	Intellectual performance
California Achievement Tests (CAT; Tiegs & Clark, 1963, 1971)	7–11, 14	Reading, language, mathematics, and total school-achievement
Adult APL Survey (American College Testing Program, 1976)	19, 27	General literacy
Pupil Behavior Inventory (PBI; Vinter, Sarri, Vorwaller, & Schafer, 1966)	6–9	School misconduct, school motivation
Ypsilanti Rating Scale (YRS; Weikart et al., 1970)	6–9	School potential, social maturity
Age-15 Interview (from Bachman, O'Malley, & Johnston, 1978)	15	Commitment to schooling, homework, school misconduct, employment history, delinquent behavior, memberships, peer relations, activities, health, parent relations, general attitudes, life objectives
Parent interview at youth's age 15	15	Parent on youth's schooling, parent-youth relationship, parent time-use
Age-19 Interview (from Freeberg, 1974, 1976)	19	High school satisfaction, employment history, employment, income, savings, ownership, job satisfaction, plans, self-reported crime and delinquency, arrests, memberships, help-seeking, people problems, pregnancies, family relations; activities, health, self-esteem
Age-21 case-study interview	21	Parental role in discipline and education, role models, attitudes towards money, goal orientation, church and religion, sense of responsibility

Table 5 (continued)

MEASURES AND PRINCIPAL VARIABLES

Measure	Age of Study Participants (Years)	Principal Variables
Age-27 interview	27	Schooling, postsecondary programs, employment history, income, car ownership, health, health services, reproductive history, rearing of oldest child, people problems, self-reported crimes and arrests, welfare, marital status, living arrangements, community activities, ease in everyday activities, personal influences, life frustrations and positive aspects, interviewer ratings
School records	15, 19, 27	Highest year of schooling, special services; grades, suspensions, expulsions
Police and court records	19, 27	Juvenile and adult arrests, convictions, sentences
Social services records	19, 27	Welfare assistance, use of social services

Note. Copies of the Pupil Behavior Inventory, the Ypsilanti Rating Scale, and the interview forms at ages 15, 19, and 27 are available on request from the High/Scope Educational Research Foundation.

[a]Age 3 for Waves One to Four, age 4 for Wave Zero.

[b]A dash indicates annual assessments between the indicated ages.

than is typical in the U.S. The age-27 study found that of the Perry study participants, 56% had remained in Ypsilanti, 71% had remained in Washtenaw County, and 86% had remained in Michigan. These latter two percentages reveal slightly greater stability in this sample than in the nation. Estimates from the University of Michigan's Panel Study of Income Dynamics[9] (PSID; Duncan, 1992) indicate that nationally, 54% of people remain in their childhood counties and 76% remain in their childhood states as young adults. Sixteen of the 117 Perry study participants (14%) interviewed at age 27 lived outside Michigan: 4 in California, 3 in Massachusetts, 2 in Texas, and 1 each in Alabama, Arizona, Colorado, Georgia, Louisiana, Nebraska, and Pennsylvania.

The Age-27 Data

This age-27 report presents findings that are based on data from four sources—an interview of study participants at age 27, school records, crime records, and social services records.

---

[9]Based on 1,117 children aged 3–6 in 1968 who were interviewed again in 1988.

The Age-27 interview When the 123 longitudinal study participants were about 27 years old, staff interviewed 95% (117) of them—31 of the 33 program-group males, all 25 of the program-group females, all 39 of the no-program-group males, and 22 of the 26 no-program-group females. The high percentage interviewed was largely due to the efforts of the principal locator and interviewer of study participants, Van Loggins—a long-time, well-known black resident of the Perry School neighborhood in Ypsilanti. Because he was a coach at Ypsilanti High School when the study participants were attending high school, Loggins knew many of them and had even coached several of them. He was able to locate many participants by obtaining information from their families and friends. Loggins was not, however, informed about whether individual study participants belonged to the program group or the no-program group. All 123 study participants were subject to the various searches of data in public records, and earlier data were available for all the study participants.

Modal age for the interview was 27, the age at which 53% of interviewees were questioned; 27% of interviewees were questioned at age 28; 12%, at age 26; 4%, at age 29; 2%, at age 30; and 1%, at age 33 (the oldest interviewee was a special case who had been undergoing personal problems). The mean age for the interview was 27.7; the program group and the no-program group did not differ significantly in the mean ages at which they were interviewed. Despite the variations in interview age, for editorial simplicity, this interview is referred to throughout this report as the age-27 interview.

Six study participants did not take part in the age-27 interview: Two males in the program group could not be found; both had been interviewed at age 19 and had records of school suspensions and a few arrests. Also, 4 females in the no-program group were not part of the age-27 interview. Two were sisters and had also not been interviewed at either age 15 or age 19. The other 2 females were deceased, both victims of drug-related murders. The body of one, a high school dropout and welfare recipient, was found in an apartment building that was burned in 1983, when she was 21 years old; the fire was suspected to be drug-related arson. The other, a high school dropout with an arrest record, was stabbed to death in 1984 at age 24; she left behind two daughters on Aid to Families with Dependent Children (AFDC). Despite the lack of interviews with these study participants, staff did find and include relevant information on them from public school, police, and social services records and from the age-19 interview.

The age-27 interview lasted 1½–2 hours and included questions on the following topics:

- Respondent identification

- General literacy (APL Survey, American College Testing Program, 1976)

- Schooling completed and planned, secondary and postsecondary programs, parent schooling and expectations, frequency of reading activities

- Health, use of health services, sick days in previous year, smoking and drinking
- Employment status and plans, unemployment in previous 24 months, employment in previous 5 years, job characteristics and satisfaction
- Marital status, spouse's schooling and employment, times married
- Income of respondent, spouse, and others in household in previous month and year from all sources, financial emergencies, bank accounts, alimony and child support, years on welfare in previous 10 years
- Living arrangements and household dwelling
- Reproductive history
- Rearing of oldest child, learning opportunities and practices before and since age 7, preschool program enrollment, child's school performance and behavior, respondent's support for schooling
- Getting along with others, respondent's family of origin, hassles with others (Freeberg, 1976)
- Self-reported crimes (Bachman & Johnston, 1978), drug use, school suspensions and expulsions, arrests, time in jail or on probation
- Car ownership, traffic tickets, wearing a seat belt
- Community activities, importance of religion, group memberships, voting, civic meetings or volunteer activities
- Ease in everyday activities, such as learning new skills and getting along with people at work
- Personal influences
- 5-year goals, frustrations and positive aspects of life (open-ended questions)
- Interviewer ratings of the respondent's behavior during the interview

The interviewer asked each respondent to sign consent forms for release of personal information from school, police, and social services records and also paid each respondent $50 for being interviewed.

When questions were asked in several ways (for example, concerning employment, earnings, and income), study participants often gave inadequate or inconsistent answers. Data processing staff—who had no knowledge of whether the study participants affected were in the program group or the no-program group—reviewed each interview and filled in missing answers when it was possible to do so from other available information. For example, if a study participant reported having been in the same job for the previous 3 years but did not report the number of months unemployed during the previous 24 months, then the response to the latter item was changed from "missing" to 0; or if a study participant reported having never been employed in the previous

2 years, the missing report of the number of months unemployed was changed to 24. Despite these efforts, however, it was not possible to provide totally consistent or complete data in all cases.

School records through age 27   Public school records regarding special education services were found for 91% of the study participants. Data on high school graduation status were obtained for all the study participants: 94% from public school records, 3% from adult high school records, and 3% from unverified self-reports on the age-27 interview. The Ypsilanti school district had the records of 63% of the study participants; other Washtenaw County school districts had the records of 24% of the study participants; and school districts outside Washtenaw County had the records of 8% of the study participants. Staff of adult high school programs in Ypsilanti, Willow Run, and Ann Arbor conducted records searches; 10 study participants were identified in the Ypsilanti program, while none were identified in the other programs.

The Michigan Department of Education and the Washtenaw Intermediate School District searched their General Educational Development (GED) records for the 56 study participants with no record of high school graduation, including 8 who claimed GED certification. For 5 participants (2 in the program group and 3 in the no-program group), GED certificates were found. Nine other study participants took but did not pass the national GED test or took the preparatory course but did not take the test; some of these nevertheless reported in their age-19 and age-27 interviews that the GED was their highest level of schooling, probably because they took GED coursework after dropping out of high school. Since the high school graduation rates reported at age 19 (Berrueta-Clement et al., 1984) were based on only 112 cases (rather than all 123) and included 8 unverified reports of GED certification, the rates reported in the age-27 study are based on more-complete data.

Requests and signed consent forms for records were sent to all post-secondary education programs identified by study participants in their age-27 interview—18 schools in 6 states. Responses came from 11 schools, at which 31 study participants were enrolled; there were no responses from 7 schools, at which 8 study participants reported their enrollment.

Crime records through age 27   The analysis of data from crime records included all 123 study participants, since adult crime records are public information and the crime records of all 123 were subject to search. Because 86% of the study participants interviewed at age 27 lived in Michigan, 71% of them in Washtenaw County, the searches of crime records concentrated on these locations. In addition, searches were requested from state police in other states identified in the age-27 interview as residences of study participants.

At our request in August of 1990, the Michigan State Police Law Enforcement Information (LEIN) system conducted a computer search for all 123 study participants. During the summer and fall of 1990,

High/Scope staff searched the paper records of local courts, including the Washtenaw County District and Circuit courts and several courts in Detroit. A search of Washtenaw County social services records in March 1991 turned up a few additional criminal incidents. Additional data came from the age-19 study's search of the records of Washtenaw County Juvenile Court in May 1982. Finally, in 5 cases, self-reported arrests and adjudications not identified by the records search were added to the file.

Project staff also requested criminal histories from criminal records agencies in the states, other than Michigan, in which 16 of the Perry study participants were living when interviewed at age 27. Six of the states—California, Georgia, Massachusetts, Nebraska, Pennsylvania, and Texas—complied with the request for information. Criminal records were found for only 3 of the study participants in California and for none of the study participants in the other states. The criminal records authorities in Alabama and Louisiana replied that they were unable to release any records, but only 2 study participants were located in these states, both of them high school graduates and employed when interviewed, with no previous juvenile or adult criminal records in Michigan. Based on the other information on the 2 study participants living in Alabama and Louisiana, it seems unlikely that they had engaged in criminal acts in their states of current residence.

After a computer search for all of the study participants, the Michigan Department of Corrections supplied information on the prison records of 15 of them; 2 others had county jail records in the Washtenaw County Sheriff's Office. Only 1 study participant had a prison record in a state other than Michigan; the California Department of Justice supplied information on this individual, and he was interviewed in prison. Overall, 12% of the males (9 of 72) and none of the females completed the age-27 interview in prison.

Every effort was made to obtain complete criminal histories on each of the 123 study participants, but the sources and the data collection process had inherent limitations. Local police and courts supply information to the Michigan State Police LEIN system. System administrators say that LEIN information is most complete for arrests, less complete for charges, and even less complete for adjudications. Moreover, local police and courts vary in their levels of compliance in sending complete information to the state LEIN system. The local court records searched by High/Scope staff members were often confusing and incomplete; it was difficult to track cases from arrest through sentencing. Finally, although most study participants remained in Michigan, and records were requested and obtained from known states of residence at age 27, other states of temporary residence between ages 19 and 27 were unknown. Also, it is not known whether the 2 study participants who were not found committed crimes outside of Michigan. Criminal histories from the national record system of the Federal Bureau of Investigation, which might have provided additional information, were requested several times but not obtained. For these reasons, the full extent of arrests could be slightly understated.

Social services records through age 27 Information was obtained from computer searches of official state and county social services records by the Michigan Department of Social Services and its Washtenaw County branch. In addition, High/Scope staff carried out a manual search of the Washtenaw County Department of Social Services paper files. Since the names of all 123 study participants were searched for, the sample size for social services records was 123. Even if study participants were not currently living in the county or the state, they probably lived there during some of the time covered by the searches.

The Michigan Department of Social Services computer search in March 1991 provided 5-year social services histories of the study participants. The data provided by this search included current types of program participation, total number of times that social services were received during the previous 5 years, and total months of each type of service during the previous 5 years.

The Washtenaw County branch of the department conducted two computer searches. The first, in January 1991, provided information on any given participant's social services status and county of record and also indicated whether the study participant was currently receiving Aid to Families with Dependent Children (AFDC), food stamps, General Assistance, or protective services. The second, in March 1991, provided data on dollar amounts received in total for that month; on specific dollar amounts received as AFDC, food stamps, or General Assistance; and on whether Medicaid was being received.

Project staff conducted a paper search of Washtenaw County social services records in March 1991. Sizable files were examined, although, unfortunately, they were somewhat fragmented and difficult to decipher. However, besides presenting some information on program amounts and individual histories, these records did provide illuminating anecdotal details about the lives of some of the study participants.

By these searches, social services records were found on 87 of the 123 study participants (including the 2 deceased females); 51 of those with social services records reported on the age-27 interview that they had been on welfare or public assistance at some time during the previous 10 years. (The social services referred to here do not include any categories of services besides welfare and public assistance.) When information on a study participant was available from both records and the interview, a claim of service took precedence over no claim of service, and a larger claim of service took precedence over a smaller claim.

Methods of Analysis

The analytic techniques presented in this report are based on simple comparisons of the program group and the no-program group, without statistical adjustments to compensate for the effects of background covariates. In general, the study's experimental design and the initial similarity of groups inspire scientific confidence that the performance of the no-program group represents what the performance of the program group would have been if they had not attended the preschool program. The next section of this chapter looks at certain background covariates on which groups did differ and examines the effects of these covariates on outcome variables.

Throughout this report, a group difference is identified as **significant** and printed in boldface in tables if it is *statistically significant with a two-tailed probability of chance occurrence of less than .05* (that is, less than 1 in 20). When the two-tailed probability of a group difference is between .05 and .10, the difference is mentioned in the text as **nearly significant.** When the two-tailed probability of a group difference is between .10 and .25, the difference, if mentioned in the text, is characterized as **noticeable.** The noticeable differences are mentioned not because they reliably distinguish between groups, but because they round out the picture that the data present by suggesting a noticeable, albeit unreliable, tendency for the groups to be different on the variable.

This strategy might be considered unnecessarily conservative, because the study's hypotheses are clearly **directional** (the obvious hypothesis was that the program group would do better than the no-program group), and directional hypotheses call for **one-tailed** tests. A one-tailed probability is half the size of the corresponding two-tailed probability; for example, a finding with an exact two-tailed probability of .068 has an exact one-tailed probability of .034. Therefore, those readers who prefer to assign statistical significance to findings in this report based on one-tailed tests should regard findings that we call "nearly significant" as fully statistically significant, with a probability half the size of the probability we report. To put it another way, they should interpret all findings with probabilities of up to .10 as statistically significant (see the discussion of this point by Locurto, 1991; Schweinhart & Weikart, 1991).

This report presents analyses of normally distributed continuous variables and categorical variables. For each **normally distributed continuous variable,** such as scores on a test, tabular column entries present

- The numbers of cases (given in the table note if numbers of cases are the same for all variables in the table), means, and standard deviations of the program group and the no-program group

- The exact, two-tailed probability of the *t* statistic comparing the two groups (with probabilities of less than .05 shown in boldface)

- The effect size (marked negative when the program mean was clearly less desirable than the no-program mean), defined as the quotient obtained by dividing the difference between the program-group mean and the no-program-group mean by the standard deviation of the whole sample

For each **categorical variable,** tabular columns of entries present

- The numbers of cases (given in the table note if numbers of cases were the same for all variables in the table) and percentages in each category of the program group and the no-program group

- Means, but not standard deviations, for count variables or other ordered categorical variables (since the standard deviation has little meaning when the distribution is highly skewed)

- The exact, two-tailed probability of the chi-square statistic comparing the two groups (with probabilities less than .05 shown in boldface)

- The effect size (marked negative when the program percentage is clearly less desirable than the no-program percentage), defined as the quotient obtained by dividing the difference between the program percentages and the no-program percentages by the sample's standard deviation (Fitz-Gibbon & Morris, 1987)

The **chi-square** statistics presented are either (a) the Pearson chi-square statistic for variables with nominal categories or (b) the Mantel-Haenszel chi-square statistic for linear association of variables with ordinal categories, which is the Pearson correlation coefficient squared times 1 less than the sample size (Mantel & Haenszel, 1959).

The analysis f count variables presented a special challenge. A count variable is measured in whole numbers (e.g., the number of years of special school services, the number of arrests, the number of incidents of self-reported misconduct, the number of dollars earned, or the number of births). Typical count variables have L-shaped distributions, with a substantial percentage of study participants at "0" (or no) participation and the rest spread over a large range (see Figures 7 and 9 for examples). Parametric statistics that assume a normal distribution are inappropriate for analyzing such variables. After examining several options, we decided to use the Mantel-Haenszel test for linear association, because it did not assume that the variables being analyzed were normally distributed.[10] Prior to this analysis, some variables were truncated to fit the distributions presented in the tables and to reduce the skew of their distributions. Typically, the percentage of study participants having no participation was set; an effort was made to divide the remaining study participants into categories of equal percentages. Arrest variables, for example, were divided into no arrests, 1–4 arrests, 5–9 arrests, 10–15 arrests, and so on. Earnings variables were divided at $1,000 intervals.

To assess whether the preschool program had different effects on males than it had on females, for all the variables that were subject to analyses by groups with different preschool experience, we performed two-way preschool-experience-by-gender analyses—two-way analyses of variance for parametric variables and two-way chi-square analyses for nonparametric variables. Some tables in each chapter present preschool experience differences for males and females for all the variables with significant preschool-experience-by-gender interactions or significant gender main effects, when the latter seemed important to the interpretation of significant preschool experience effects.

---

[10]In fact, the *p*-values for the Mantel-Haenszel chi-square analyses in this study were quite similar to the *p*-values for *t* tests of the same variables.

Throughout the chapters of this report that present statistical findings, short vignettes of study participants are used to bring a sense of reality to the statistical presentation. The names used are not participants' real names. To remove the temptation of regarding the preschool program, or the lack of it, as the cause of isolated events, these brief stories do not identify individuals as belonging to the program group or the no-program group.

Assessment of Potential Threats to the Study's Internal Validity

Background Comparisons at Study Entry

The study's group-assignment procedures make it highly probable that group comparisons reflect the effects of the preschool program. Comparisons indicating that groups were not significantly different on various background characteristics make it even more likely.

The continuous and categorical background variables   As shown in Table 6, the two groups were neither significantly nor nearly significantly different at study entry on Stanford-Binet IQ (Terman & Merrill, 1960), family socioeconomic status, mother's or father's highest year of schooling, number of children in the family, number of siblings older than the study participant, number of siblings younger than the study participant, child's age, mother's and father's age, or number of rooms in home. The program group averaged nearly significantly fewer persons per room in their homes at study entry than did the no-program group (1.2 vs. 1.4 persons), a rather small difference on a variable that was only weakly related to the outcome variables measured later.

As shown in Table 7, at study entry the two groups were neither significantly nor nearly significantly different on percentages of males and females, family configuration (single-parent vs. two-parent, nuclear vs. extended), father's employment level, family welfare status, family in public housing, region of mother's birthplace (in the South vs. elsewhere), population of mother's birthplace, or family religion. Most of the fathers of the study participants had unskilled jobs—as janitors, construction laborers, and in a few cases, as automotive assembly line workers; the two with managerial jobs were a laundry supervisor and a local union president. All of the employed mothers had unskilled jobs—as maids, laundry workers, domestics; a few were store clerks, uncertified nurses' aides, cooks, waitresses, and dishwashers.

The difference in employed single mothers   *At study entry, the program-group members had significantly more single mothers employed away from home than the no-program-group members had (22% vs. 4%).* This was partly because of the transfer of 2 children of employed single mothers from the program group to the no-program

Table 6

CONTINUOUS BACKGROUND VARIABLES AT STUDY ENTRY,
BY PRESCHOOL EXPERIENCE

Variable	Program Group		No-Program Group			
	Mean	SD	Mean	SD	p	Effect Size
Stanford-Binet IQ at study entry	79.6	5.9	78.5	6.9	.378	0.16
Family socioeconomic status	8.0	1.3	7.9	1.2	.729	0.36
Mother's years of schooling	9.5	2.4	9.4	2.0	.839	0.05
Father's years of schooling[a]	8.4	2.3	8.8	2.5	.579	−0.02
Children in family	4.9	2.5	4.8	2.8	.739	0.06
Older siblings	2.8	2.4	3.0	2.8	.817	0.08
Younger siblings at study entry	1.1	1.0	0.8	1.6	.262	0.10
Child's age in months at study entry	42.7	6.2	41.9	5.9	.437	0.14
Mother's age in years at study entry	29.6	6.2	28.7	6.9	.449	0.13
Father's age in years at study entry[b]	31.5	5.0	34.0	8.2	.168	−0.31
Rooms in home at study entry	5.2	1.2	5.2	1.6	.925	0.01
Persons per room at study entry	1.2	0.3	1.4	0.6	.060	−0.33

Note. Program group $n = 58$, no-program group $n = 65$, except as noted; data source is the initial parent-interview; the p-values are based on t tests.

[a]Program group $n = 38$, no-program group $n = 34$.

[b]Program group $n = 28$, no-program group $n = 31$.

group.[11] However, as shown in Table 8, *program and no-program groups did not differ noticeably in their percentages of single mothers employed when study participants were 15 years old.* In short, the difference between groups at entry was limited to a temporary difference in the employment rates of single mothers.

Since maternal employment is more widespread today than it was in the 1960s, this solitary initial group-difference has become a matter of interest. In fact, in the program group, the 16 children of employed single mothers did not differ noticeably from the 42 children of unemployed single mothers on IQ, school achievement, regular high school

---

[11]If the 2 children of employed single mothers had not been transferred from the program group to the no-program group, the program versus no-program group difference in children with employed single mothers, although still noticeable, would have been neither significant nor nearly significant (7% vs. 19%, $p = .141$).

Table 7

CATEGORICAL BACKGROUND VARIABLES AT STUDY ENTRY,
BY PRESCHOOL EXPERIENCE

Variable	Program Group	No-Program Group	p	Effect Size
Participant's gender				
Male	57%	60%	.869	0.06
Female	43%	40%		
Family configuration at study entry				
Two-parent	55%	51%	.625	0.09
Single-mother	45%	49%		
Nuclear	15%	20%	.433	0.14
Extended	85%	80%		
Employment status of parents				
Father and mother employed	5%	9%	**.018**	0.44
Father alone employed	44%	35%		
Single mother employed	4%	22%		
No parent employed	47%	34%		
Father's employment level[a]				
Managerial or skilled	3%	2%	.279	0.29
Semiskilled	9%	3%		
Unskilled	28%	40%		
Family welfare status at study entry				
On welfare	58%	45%	.230	−0.25
Not on welfare	42%	55%		
Family in public housing	40%	32%	.396	−0.15
Mother's birthplace region[b]				
Southern U.S.	83%	75%	.293	0.19
Elsewhere in the U.S.	17%	25%		
Mother's birthplace population[c]				
Population under 10,000	38%	39%	.407	0.16
Population 10,000–100,000	33%	43%		
Population over 100,000	29%	18%		
Family religion				
Baptist	80%	72%	.557	−0.20
Other Protestant	18%	21%		
Catholic	0%	4%		
None claimed	2%	4%		

Note. Program group $n = 56$ to 58, no-program group $n = 63$ to 65, except as noted; data source is the initial parent-interview; the p-values are based on Pearson chi-square statistics.

[a]Program group $n = 26$, no-program group $n = 29$; employed mothers reporting were at the unskilled level.

[b]Program group $n = 48$, no-program group $n = 55$.

[c]Program group $n = 42$, no-program group $n = 56$.

graduation rate, rate of high school graduation or the equivalent (adult high school graduation or GED certification), employment at some time in the 5 years before the age-27 interview, receipt of social services or AFDC in the previous 10 years, or marital status at age 27. As compared with the children of single mothers who were *unemployed* at study entry, children of single mothers who were *employed* at study entry were nearly significantly more likely to be employed at age 27 (81% vs. 55%, $p = .071$) and had noticeably fewer lifetime arrests (44% ever arrested vs. 69% ever arrested, $p = .179$). Thus, on the only outcome variables for which it made a difference, single mothers being employed *decreased* the size of group differences. This means that the differences reported, because they were not adjusted for maternal employment differences, are actually *underestimates* of these program effects.

Background Comparisons Over Time

As shown in Table 8, when study participants were 15 years old, the two groups did not differ noticeably in family configuration (two-parent vs. single-parent), parental employment status, parent's rating of neighborhood, number of family moves since study participant began school, or number of persons per room in household.

The age-19 and age-27 interviewers rated the study participants interviewed on these dimensions: cooperative, sociable, involved in the interview, talkative, attentive, active, relaxed, needs urging, keeps trying, self-confident, open, truthful, and warm. The program and no-program groups did not differ noticeably, at age 19 or at age 27, on any interviewer-rating item or on the total interviewer-rating scales.

Background Comparisons by Gender

While the program and no-program groups were intentionally matched on certain initial characteristics, this same characteristic-matching was not attempted for program-group and no-program-group males or for program-group and no-program-group females. However, because differences attributable to their preschool experience emerged later for program versus no-program males and for program versus no-program females, it is important to know if same-gender subgroups differed from each other at study entry. On employed single mothers, program males significantly differed from no-program males, and program females significantly differed from no-program females. On the following list of background variables, which are most of the variables in Tables 6–8, no significant or nearly significant differences were found either at study entry or at age 15 for program males versus no-program males or for program females versus no-program females:

- Binet IQ at study entry
- Family socioeconomic status
- Mother's or father's years of schooling completed

Table 8

BACKGROUND VARIABLES AT AGE 15, BY PRESCHOOL EXPERIENCE

Variable	Program Group	No-Program Group	p^a	Effect Size
Family configuration				
Two-parent	43%	47%	.685 (P)	0.08
Single-parent	57%	53%		
Employment status of parents				
Father and mother employed	15%	24%	.735 (P)	0.16
Father only employed	17%	14%		
Single mother employed	27%	24%		
No parent employed	42%	38%		
Neighborhood rating by parent				
Excellent	21%	15%	.539 (M)	0.12
Good	45%	46%		
Fair	13%	19%		
Not so good	13%	7%		
Poor	9%	13%		
Number of family moves, school-entry to age 15				
Mean	1.3	1.3	.972 (M)	0.01
0	15%	17%		
1	58%	54%		
2–4	27%	30%		
Number of persons per room at youth's age 15				
Mean	0.84	0.86	.753 (t)	0.07
(SD)	(0.32)	(0.32)		

Note. Program group $n = 48$, no-program group $n = 54$; the data source is the parent questionnaire at youth age 15.

[a](P) indicates that the *p*-value is based on the Pearson chi-square statistic. (M) indicates that the *p*-value is based on the Mantel-Haenszel chi-square statistic on the truncated distributions presented. (*t*) indicates that the *p*-value is based on the *t* test.

- Number of children in the family
- Numbers of older or younger siblings at study entry
- Child's age
- Mother's or father's age
- Total rooms or persons per room in the home at study entry
- Total rooms or persons per room in the home at age 15
- Family configuration at age 15
- Father's employment status at study entry

- Parental employment status at age 15
- Family welfare status at study entry
- Nuclear or extended family at study entry
- Mother's birthplace (region or population)
- Family religion
- Parent's neighborhood rating at age 15

While the program males and the no-program males did not differ even noticeably on any of the background variables in Tables 6–8, the program females did differ nearly significantly from the no-program females on the percentages in single-parent families at study entry (32% vs. 58%, $p = .065$) and on the number of family moves from school entry through age 15 (1.0 vs. 1.4, $p = .095$). To assess whether such differences affected the comparisons between program females and no-program females presented in Chapters 3–6, these comparisons were also made with analyses of covariance controlling for family configuration at study entry, family moves, and maternal employment at age 15 (another powerful predictor of outcome variables). The significant, nearly significant, and noticeable differences between program-group females and no-program-group females reported in Chapters 3–6 remained in the same category of statistical significance, except for the following:

- The significance levels for two comparisons reported as significant dropped to nearly significant or noticeable—-years in EMI programs went from .029 to .076, and monthly earnings at age 27 went from .046 to .136
- The significance levels for three comparisons reported as nearly significant or as noticeable rose to significant—-years retained in grade went from .051 to .007; lifetime arrests went from .053 to .003; and General Assistance went from .499 to .032

Since these were only three of the many possible covariates that might have been chosen, and since the p-values of any comparisons by preschool experience would be different for each set of covariates chosen, the p-values obtained from these analyses of covariance will, with one exception, not be reported in subsequent chapters. The exception will be our noting of the largest change, which regards monthly earnings at age 27.

Aggregation Across Waves

The analyses in this report combine the five waves to achieve a larger sample size; however, the group differences that were significant across all waves were in the same direction in each wave, with only two very slight exceptions. In these two exceptions the two groups were not noticeably different.

Participation or nonparticipation in the preschool education program was the only differential treatment of study participants by the investigators. Regardless of which group they were in, all study participants received the same schedule of tests and interviews. Although, almost inevitably, testers knew to which group study participants belonged during the preschool program, project staff did not inform testers, interviewers, or subsequent teachers of the group membership of study participants. If subsequent teachers did learn on their own who attended the preschool program, such knowledge may be considered a natural extension of the preschool program experience. Thus, it is reasonable to regard the differences between the program group and the no-program group that will be reported in Chapters 3–6 as evidence of the effects of the preschool program.

III Educational Performance

The findings for educational performance through age 27 focus on the highest year of schooling completed and the rate of high school graduation. The program group (especially program females as compared with no-program females) significantly[12] outperformed the no-program group on these measures. The graduation-rate differences for program versus no-program females were found to be related to their earlier differences in rate of placement in programs for educable mental impairment (EMI) and in grade retention. Other educational measures on which the program group significantly outperformed the no-program group include a literacy test at age 19, a school achievement test at age 14, and various tests of intellectual and language performance from after the first preschool year up to age 7. The program group also had significantly better attitudes towards school than the no-program group had on measures at ages 15 and 19, and program-group parents had better attitudes towards their 15-year-old children's schooling than did no-program-group parents.

By age 27, the program group on average had completed a significantly higher level of schooling than the no-program group had (11.9 vs. 11.0 years, including postsecondary education[13]). In addition, as compared with the no-program group, the program group had a significantly higher rate (66% vs. 45%) of regular high school graduation and a nearly significantly higher rate (71% vs. 54%) of regular high school graduation or the equivalent (adult high school graduation or General Educational Development [GED] certification).

Findings over time for special school services indicated that compared with the no-program group, the program group on average spent significantly fewer years in EMI programs (1.1 vs. 2.8 years) but significantly more years in compensatory education programs (1.0 vs. 0.4 years); this may be because the school problems of the program group were reduced from the EMI-program level to the less serious, compensatory-program level. While the percentages of program males and no-program males ever enrolled in EMI programs were only noticeably different (20% vs. 33%), the percentages of program females and no-program females ever enrolled in EMI programs were significantly different (8% vs. 37%), and the percentages of program females and no-program females retained 2–4 times in grade were nearly significantly different (8% vs. 36%).

The group differences in high school graduation rates were due primarily to a graduation-rate difference for the females in the two groups. As compared with the no-program females, the program females completed, on average, a significantly higher level of schooling (12.2 vs. 10.5 years) and had a significantly higher rate (84% vs. 35%) of regular high school graduation or the equivalent. A major factor accounting for this

---

[12]This report describes a group difference as **significant** if it has a two-tailed probability of less than .05, as **nearly significant** if it has a two-tailed probability between .05 and .10, and as **noticeable** if it has a two-tailed probability between .10 and .25. Since the hypotheses of this study are clearly directional, readers who prefer one-tailed tests of significance may interpret "nearly significant" findings as significant.

[13]Scored as grade of dropout for dropouts, 12 for high school graduation or equivalent, 12.5 or more for any postsecondary schooling (including basic), 14 for an associate's degree, 16 for a bachelor's degree, and 18 for a master's degree.

latter difference appears to be that nearly significantly fewer program females than no-program females (29% vs. 55%) had been assigned to EMI programs or retained in grade, and significantly fewer assigned/retained females graduated from high school or the equivalent (26% of those assigned/retained vs. 85% of those not assigned/retained). Program males and no-program males did not differ noticeably on rate of high school graduation or the equivalent.

The program group significantly outscored the no-program group on various tests over the years. On the Adult Performance Level Survey (APL; American College Testing Program, 1976), the program group significantly outscored the no-program group in problem solving and health information at age 27, as well as in health information, occupational knowledge, reading, and general literacy at age 19. On the California Achievement Tests (CAT; Tiegs & Clark, 1963, 1971), the program group outscored the no-program group significantly on reading, mathematics, language, and total school achievement at age 14, and nearly significantly on total school achievement at ages 7–9. On the Stanford-Binet Intelligence Scale (Terman & Merrill, 1960), the program group scored significantly higher than the no-program group from the end of the first preschool year to age 7. Immediately after the preschool program, the program group scored significantly higher on the Arthur Adaptation of the Leiter International Performance Scale (Arthur, 1952), the Peabody Picture Vocabulary Test (PPVT; Dunn, 1965), and the Illinois Test of Psycholinguistic Abilities (ITPA; experimental version, McCarthy & Kirk, 1961). Ironically, the school achievement difference did not appear until after the intellectual performance difference disappeared.

At age 19, the program group had a significantly better attitude than the no-program group towards the last high school they had attended. Findings at age 15 on the attitudes of the study participants and their parents indicated the following: Significantly more of the program group than of the no-program group spent time on homework. Significantly more program parents than no-program parents found their children willing to talk about school, said their children had done as well in school as they would have liked, and hoped their children would get college degrees. Significantly fewer program parents than no-program parents went to conferences at the invitation of their children's teachers, but about the same proportion of parents in each group got in touch with their children's teachers on their own.

This chapter will present and interpret group comparisons in educational performance—-including schooling completed, special school services over time, performance on various tests over time, and attitude towards school expressed by parents and study participants over time. Group comparisons by gender are also examined, with special attention to the difference between program females and no-program females in high school graduation rates.

Figure 4

HIGHEST YEAR OF SCHOOLING, BY PRESCHOOL EXPERIENCE

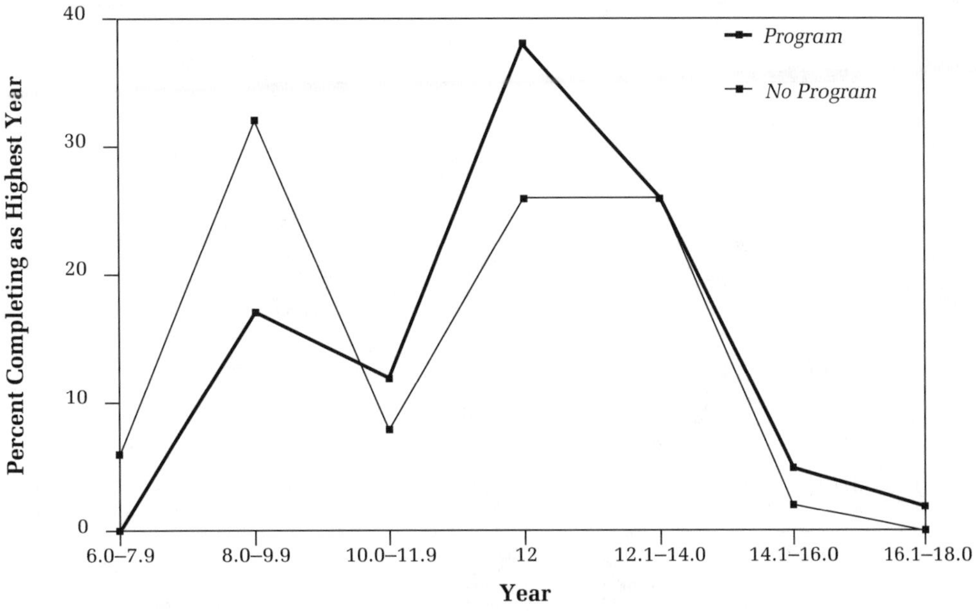

Note. Whole-group comparison, $p = .016$, Mantel Haenszel chi-square statistic.
See Table 9 for details.

Schooling Completed

Table 9, and Figure 4 above, present the highest years of schooling completed by the program and no-program groups.[14] **On average, if postsecondary education, adult education, and GED programs are included,
the program group completed almost a year more of schooling than the
no-program group did (11.9 vs. 11.0 years), which is a significant difference.** Even after deletion of the values of the 2 program-group members with college degrees (one a bachelor's, one a master's), which
changes the respective schooling-completed means to 11.7 years and
11.0 years, the group difference on this variable remains significant
($p = .042$). The program group's average of 11.9 years of schooling completed was 2.8 years more than their parents' average of 9.1 years at
study entry; the no-program group's average of 11.0 years was 1.8 years
more than their parents' 9.2 years at study entry.

---

[14]Actual values for *highest year of schooling* were as follows: program-group males—3 at
8.5, 3 at 9.5, 4 at 10.5, 1 at 11, 1 at 11.5, 1 at 11.9, 12 at 12, 1 at 12.5, 3 at 13, 1 at 13.5, 1 at
14, 2 at 14.5; program-group females—2 at 8.5, 2 at 9.5, 10 at 12, 5 at 12.5, 3 at 13, 1 at 14,
1 at 16, 1 at 18; no-program-group males—1 at 6.5, 3 at 8.5, 6 at 9.5, 2 at 10.5, 1 at 11.5, 15
at 12, 5 at 12.5, 4 at 13, 1 at 14, 1 at 15; no-program-group females—3 at 7.5, 2 at 8.5, 10 at
9.5, 2 at 10.5, 2 at 12, 1 at 12.5, 3 at 13, 1 at 13.5, 2 at 14.

Table 9

SCHOOLING COMPLETED, BY PRESCHOOL EXPERIENCE

Variable	Program Group	No-Program Group	p^a	Effect Size
Highest year of schooling[b]				
Mean	11.9	11.0	**.016** (M)	0.43
16.0–18.0	3%	0%		
12.5–15.0	29%	28%		
12.0	38%	26%		
6.5–11.9	29%	46%		
Postsecondary education				
Earned postsecondary degree[c]	3%	2%	.539 (P)	0.11
Earned postsecondary credits	33%	28%	.759 (P)	0.11
Types of postsecondary credits earned				
4-year	5%	6%	.815 (P)	0.04
2-year transferable to 4-year	12%	11%	.821 (P)	0.04
2-year non-transferable basic	19%	19%	.943 (P)	0.01
Secondary education				
High school graduation or equivalent[d]				
Graduate or equivalent by age 27	71%	54%	.055 (P)	0.35
Not graduate or equivalent by age 27	29%	46%		
High school graduation equivalent[e]				
Adult high school graduate	2%	5%		
GED-certified	3%	5%		
Regular high school graduation				
Graduate	66%	45%	.020 (P)	0.43
Nongraduate	34%	55%		
Grade of regular high school dropout				
11–12	14%	14%	.214 (M)	0.22
9–10	21%	31%		
7–8	0%	6%		
Grade of dropout unknown	0%	5%		

Note. Program group $n = 58$, no-program group $n = 65$; data sources are 116 high school records, 2 adult high school records indicating regular high school dropout, 5 unverified self-reports of high school graduation status (2 graduates, 3 nongraduates), college transcripts of 29 study participants, and unverified self-reports of college attendance by 8 study participants. Numbers differ slightly from those reported at age 19 because additional data are included.

[a](M) indicates that the p-value is based on the Mantel-Haenszel chi-square statistic, and (P) indicates that the p-value is based on the Pearson chi-square statistic.

[b]Scored at age 27 by grade of dropout, 12 for high school graduation or equivalent, 12.5 or more for any postsecondary schooling (including basic), 14 for associate's degree, 16 for bachelor's degree, and 18 for master's degree; the p-value is based on the analysis of the untruncated variable, although the analysis of the truncated variable had the same results.

[c]The program group had one member with a master's degree and another with a bachelor's degree; the no-program group had one member with an associate's degree.

[d]Of black 19- and 20-year-olds in the U.S. in 1979, 66% had graduated from high school or obtained a GED (Berrueta-Clement et al., 1984).

[e]Local adult education program records were requested for every study participant with no record of high school graduation. The Ypsilanti Adult Education Program found enrollment records for 10 study participants; the Willow Run and Ann Arbor programs found none.

Secondary Schooling

As shown in Table 9, the program group had a nearly significantly higher rate of high school graduation or the equivalent (adult high school graduation or GED certification) than the no-program group had (71% vs. 54%). Comparable recent rates for U.S. young adults 4 years after the time of expected regular high school graduation were 78% for black 22-year-olds and 83% for all 22-year-olds (Frase, 1989). The no-program group's 54% rate is what might be expected from a group at grave risk of school failure and dropout. The program and no-program graduation rates, however, differed substantially by gender, as will be described later in this chapter.

The variable *high school graduation or the equivalent* involves four possibilities: (a) graduating from a regular high school, (b) dropping out of a regular high school but graduating from an adult high school, (c) dropping out of a regular high school but passing the examination for the GED certificate, or (d) dropping out of a regular high school and not pursuing either adult high school or the GED. Ypsilanti's adult-education representatives say that employers regard adult high school graduation almost as highly as regular high school graduation; they regard the GED certificate less highly because it is based only on a test of written skills and provides no evidence of other desirable school and workplace behaviors, such as perseverance, regular attendance, compliance with rules, acceptance of authority, and ability to get along with others.

As shown in Table 9, **the program group had a significantly higher regular high school graduation rate than did the no-program group (66% vs. 45%).** The dropout rates of the program group and the no-program group were noticeably different by 10th grade (21% vs. 37%). The program group and the no-program group did not noticeably differ in their minimal rates of adult high school graduation or GED certification.

Ypsilanti's **adult high school programs** offered various daytime and evening courses and provided students with transportation. A particular incentive to enrollment in adult-education programs was that young parents had to be enrolled in either regular or adult education in order to continue to receive Aid to Families with Dependent Children (AFDC). Of

YVONNE,[*] a woman who barely graduated from high school, with C's and D's on her record, recalls, "I passed through, but I also did a lot of hanging out. I was skipping all the time. I'd do my work, I passed—that's one thing. You know, I'd do my work, and then after I got the grade for that one semester, or that week, then I knew it would be time to hang out." Yvonne had a history of disciplinary problems in school and has 15 misdemeanors on her adult criminal record.

---

[*]Brief stories like this throughout this report describe real study participants but do not use their real names.

> Talking about his lack of a high school diploma and vague plans to go back and get it, **BOB** says: "I think about things today. I know I need to go back to school—at least get a GED or something. Because things are getting worse and worse every day. The skills I know I have, I can go back to school and just use any one of them. The cab . . . I can be a plumber, or an electrician, or something like that. I also do hair. I can do any one of them, but I just don't have the paper." Bob, who dropped out after 11th grade, was unemployed at age 27, but did odd jobs and collected worker's compensation for an injury he received while he was a luggage handler at the airport.

the 54 study participants who dropped out of high school, 10 (2 in the program group, 8 in the no-program group) registered for adult-education courses.[15] However, only 4 of them (1 in the program group, 3 in the no-program group) earned adult high school diplomas. The **GED certificate** is another alternative to high school graduation; persons who do well enough on adult-education screening tests are often advised to take the GED test, perhaps after a GED preparation course. Five study participants (2 in the program group, 3 in the no-program group) received GED certification.

Postsecondary Schooling

Despite the poverty and high risk associated with their backgrounds, by age 27, 30% of the study participants had earned postsecondary credits of some kind (33% of the program group, 28% of the no-program group). From the age-19 self-report alone, we obtained data indicating that 38% of the program group and 21% of the no-program group had at some time enrolled in what appeared to be academic or vocational post-secondary programs (Berrueta-Clement et al., 1984). The different percentages for postsecondary credits in this age-27 report are based on more-precise categorization of information from both self-report and school records; some of the programs we previously categorized as post-secondary now appear to have been adult-education programs.

Similar percentages of the program group and the no-program group earned basic 2-year-college credits (remedial work in basic academic skills), 2-year-college credits transferable to 4-year colleges, and credits at 4-year colleges. Two members of the program group (but none of the no-program group) received bachelor's degrees, and 1 of these received a master's degree as well.

---

[15]Of these 10 participants, 4 were required to register for (and 2 of these 4 successfully completed) basic reading and mathematics courses to prepare them for high school completion courses; the successful 2 and another 6 of the original 10 registered for adult high school credit courses; of the original 10, 6 earned credits and 4 earned adult high school diplomas; 1 additional study participant earned a GED without earning credit.

CAROL, married and attending school at age 27, says: "I'd like to become a warden for the Department of Corrections. The main thing that I want to accomplish in the next 5 years is to have my doctorate from the university. I'm presently working on my master's degree in guidance and counseling, which will be completed next summer, and then I'm going on for my doctorate. I'm proud of those things."

Special School Services Over Time

Table 10 presents the placements in all types of special school services identified on study participants' school records. Some of these services involved programs in self-contained classrooms that were alternatives to the regular classroom, while others involved students receiving part-time assistance that only periodically pulled them out of the regular classroom. Grade retention is regarded here as a special school service, even though it does not involve an alternative or part-time program outside the regular classroom.

Assignment to special school services means two things. First, it means that the assigned student has been identified as someone who needs and could profit from the service. Second, it means that the student's subsequent school experience will be different from what it would have been if the student had not been assigned to the service.

In the final accounting, **the program group spent, on average, significantly fewer school years in EMI programs than did the no-program group—1.1 versus 2.8 years per study participant,** which is a difference of 1.7 years. Fewer program-group members than no-program-group members were ever placed in EMI programs (15% vs. 34%), and fewer spent 6 or more school years in these programs (9% vs. 27%).

Groups did not noticeably differ in their years spent in special programs for emotional impairment, learning disability, or discipline, or in years retained in grade. **On average, the program group spent significantly more school years in compensatory education programs than did the no-program group (1.0 vs. 0.4 years)** and noticeably more school years in programs for speech and language impairment (0.13 vs. 0.05 years). Taking these services together, in comparison with the no-program group, the program group on average spent *less* time (by 1.7 years) in EMI programs, *more* time (by 0.6 year) in compensatory education, and *more* time (by 0.08 year) in speech and language programs—all of which totals *less* time (by 1.02 years) receiving one or another of these three kinds of services. Overall, the program group spent, on average, 1.3 fewer school years than the no-program group (3.9 vs. 5.2 years) in some kind of special program. This pattern of findings suggests that the preschool program improved the school performance or conduct of some study participants enough so that, instead of being placed in the EMI programs (as one would have expected on the basis of their

Table 10

SPECIAL SCHOOL SERVICES, BY PRESCHOOL EXPERIENCE

School Years Spent, by Type of Special Service	Program Group	No-Program Group	p^a	Effect Size
Educable mental impairment				
Mean	1.1	2.8		
1–5 yr	6%	7%	**.009**	0.49
6–13 yr	9%	27%		
Emotional impairment				
Mean	0.7	0.5		
1 yr	9%	12%	.638	−0.09
2–9 yr	13%	9%		
Learning disability				
Mean	0.3	0.3		
1 yr	2%	0%	.713	0.07
2–6 yr	7%	10%		
Speech and language impairment				
Mean	0.13	0.05		
1 yr	7%	3%	.150	−0.27
2–5 yr	6%	2%		
Compensatory education				
Mean	1.0	0.4		
1 yr	20%	12%	**.045**	−0.38
2–8 yr	20%	10%		
Disciplinary				
Mean	0.2	0.4		
1 yr	11%	10%	.437	0.15
2–4 yr	6%	10%		
Grade retention				
Mean	0.5	0.7		
1 yr	19%	16%	.437	0.15
2–4 yr	17%	24%		
Any of these special services				
Mean	3.9	5.2		
1 yr	17%	10%	.512	0.12
2–5 yr	28%	14%		
6–10 yr	11%	22%		
11–18 yr[b]	9%	14%		

Note. Program group $n = 54$, no-program group $n = 58$; data source is school records; percentages of groups with 0 years were included in the analyses but not the table.

[a]p-values are based on the Mantel-Haenszel chi-square statistic for the truncated distributions of the variable.

[b]Highest numbers exceed 13 because some children received more than one type of special service in a given school year.

intellectual-performance test scores at study entry), they were placed in the less intensive and less costly compensatory education programs.

Since the study participants were originally selected because they were at special risk of school failure, it is not surprising that members of both groups—program and no-program—spent quite a few years receiving special school services. Despite the many criticisms of intelligence tests, IQs continue to be a major determinant of placement in EMI programs; the American Association on Mental Deficiency identifies IQs between 70 and 85 as *borderline mental impairment* and IQs below 70 as *mental impairment* (Grossman, 1973). In the Perry study, EMI programs served 25% of the study participants; at age 3, 13% of the study participants had IQs below 70, and 72% had IQs between 70 and 85; at age 14, 16% of the study participants had IQs below 70, and 56% had IQs between 70 and 85.

Differences in school placements first appeared 5 years after the preschool program. At that time, it was reported that **significantly fewer program-group than no-program-group children had been placed in special school programs or retained in grade by grade 4 (17% vs. 38%;** Weikart et al., 1978).

Schooling Variables, by Gender

Schooling Completed, by Gender

As shown in Table 11, **in comparison with no-program-group females, program-group females, on average, completed a significantly higher level of schooling (12.2 vs. 10.5 years) and had a significantly higher rate of high school graduation or the equivalent (84% vs. 35%)**—a 49 percentage-point difference. Of the program females, 5 out of 6 achieved graduation or the equivalent, as compared with 2 out of 6 of the no-program females. Since 72% of the 25 program females and 81% of the 26 no-program females attended Ypsilanti High School, this phenomenon essentially took place in this one high school, wherein the graduation rates were 89% for program females and 29% for no-program females. Program-group and no-program-group males did not differ noticeably on either high school graduation (Barnes, 1989) or highest level of schooling. Figure 5 contrasts the percentages of program and no-program males, as well as the percentages of program and no-program females, graduating from high school or the equivalent.

Perry study males' 64% rate of high school graduation or the equivalent compares with a 76% rate for all U.S. black males; the program-group females' 84% rate and the no-program-group females' 35% rate compare with an 83% rate for all U.S. black females (Fine & Zane, 1989). Also, the generational improvement in high school graduation rates was substantial and should not be overlooked. A generation earlier, mostly in the South, only 11% of the fathers of study participants had graduated from high school; this compares with 64% of their sons. A genera-

64

Table 11

SCHOOLING, BY PRESCHOOL EXPERIENCE AND GENDER

Variable	Program Group	No-Program Group	p^a	Effect Size
Males				
Highest level of schooling[b]				
Mean	11.6	11.4		
12.5–15.0	24%	28%	.646 (M)	0.11
12.0	36%	39%		
6.5–11.9	39%	33%		
High school graduation or equivalent[c]	61%	67%	.594 (P)	−0.12
No. of years in programs for mental impairment[d]				
Mean	1.3	2.5		
1–5	10%	8%	.133 (M)	0.37
6–13	10%	25%		
No. of years retained in grade[e]				
Mean	0.7	0.6		
1	23%	22%	.465 (M)	−0.18
2–4	23%	17%		
Females				
Highest level of schooling[f]				
Mean	12.2	10.5		
16.0–18.0	8%	0%		
12.5–15.0	36%	27%	**.005** (M)	0.85
12.0	40%	8%		
7.5–10.5	16%	65%		
High school graduation or equivalent[g]	84%	35%	**.000** (P)	1.14
No. of years in programs for mental impairment[h]				
Mean	0.8	3.4		
1–5	0%	5%	**.029** (M)	0.68
6–13	8%	32%		
No. of years retained in grade[i]				
Mean	0.3	0.9		
1	13%	5%	.051 (M)	0.73
2–4	8%	36%		

Note. Data source is school records; the table includes all the schooling variables with significant preschool-experience-by-gender interactions, except for one listed in Table 16.

[a](M) indicates that the *p*-value is based on the Mantel-Haenszel chi-square statistic for the truncated distributions of the variable unless otherwise indicated. (P) indicates that the *p*-value is based on the Pearson chi-square statistic.

[b]Program males n = 33, no-program males n = 39; scored by grade of dropouts through age 27, 12 for high school graduation or equivalent, 12.5 or more for any postsecondary schooling (including basic), 14 for associate's degree, 16 for bachelor's degree, and 18 for master's degree; the p-value is based on the analysis of the untruncated variable, although the analysis of the truncated variable had the same results.

[c]Program males n = 33, no-program males n = 39; the equivalent of regular high school graduation is adult high school graduation or GED certification.

[d]Program males n = 30, no-program males n = 36.

[e]Program males n = 30, no-program males n = 36.

[f]Program females n = 25, no-program females n = 26; see footnote b for explanation of variable.

[g]Program females n = 25, no-program females n = 26; see also footnote c.

[h]Program females n = 24, no-program females n = 22.

[i]Program females n = 24, no-program females n = 22.

Figure 5

HIGH SCHOOL GRADUATION OR THE EQUIVALENT,
BY PRESCHOOL EXPERIENCE AND GENDER

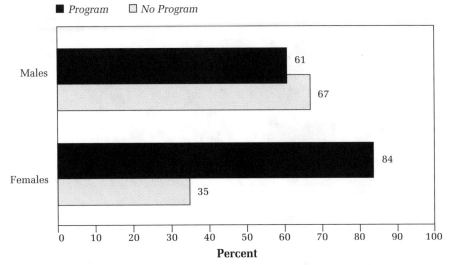

Note. Male comparison, *p* = .594, female comparison, *p* = .000; based on
Pearson chi-square statistics. See Table 11 for details.

tion earlier, only 21% of the mothers of study participants had graduated
from high school; this compares with 35% of their daughters in the no-
program group and 84% of their daughters in the program group.

Special School Services, by Gender

Table 11 shows that significantly fewer program-group females than no-
program-group females spent time in EMI programs (8% vs. 37%), and
nearly significantly fewer were retained in grade (21% vs. 41%). For
females (n = 46), the Pearson product-moment correlation coefficients
with high school graduation or the equivalent were as follows:

- −.415 for years in EMI programs (*p* = .002)
- −.559 for years retained in grade (*p* = .000)
- −.565 for years receiving any special school services (*p* = .000)

Nearly significantly fewer program males than no-program males spent
6–13 years in EMI programs, but there was no noticeable difference
between these groups in years retained in grade. Figure 6 contrasts the percentages of program males and no-program males, as well as the percentages of program females and no-program females, placed in EMI programs.

Figure 6

PLACEMENTS FOR EDUCABLE MENTAL IMPAIRMENT,
BY PRESCHOOL EXPERIENCE AND GENDER

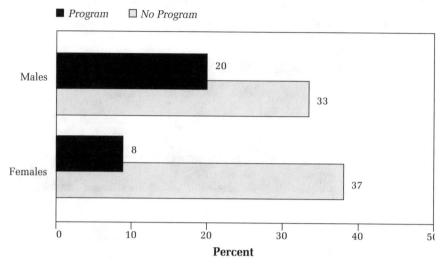

Note. Male comparison, $p = .133$, female comparison, $p = .029$; based on
Mantel-Haenszel chi-square statistics. See Table 11 for details.

School Achievement and Literacy Test Performance at Age 27 and Earlier

Table 12 presents the age-19 and age-27 findings from the APL Survey
(American College Testing Program, 1976), a test of general literacy with
various subtests. Except for the test material designated to assess the
respondent's reading ability, items of the APL Survey could be read
aloud and repeated by the interviewer at the respondent's request; so for
study participants for whom reading was a problem, the test was able to
assess abilities other than reading. At age 27, only 4 study participants (2
in each group) declined to complete the APL Survey; the 4 included 1
who had trouble reading, 1 who was in a hurry to buy drugs, 1 who had
a mental-health problem, and 1 who gave no specific reason. At age 19,
12 study participants (6 in each group) had declined to complete the
APL Survey; 8 said they could not read; others gave no specific reason.

On the age-27 APL Survey, the program group significantly
outscored the no-program group in health information and problem
solving, but not in general literacy (indicated by total score), despite a
noticeable trend in this direction. According to the test's national norms,
47% of the program group, as compared with 53% of the no-
program group, scored "below average" (0–23) at age 27.

On the age-19 APL Survey, the program group significantly outperformed the no-program group in general literacy. According to the test's
national norms, 39% of the program group, as compared with 62% of

Table 12

LITERACY AT AGES 19 AND 27, BY PRESCHOOL EXPERIENCE

Variable	r_t^a	r_α	Program Group		No-Program Group		p	Effect Size
			Mean	(SD)	Mean	(SD)		
Age 27								
Total (general literacy)	.501	.836	24.8	(6.5)	23.1	(6.3)	.149	0.28
Community resources	.380	.510	5.2	(1.6)	5.3	(1.6)	.599	−0.15
Occupational knowledge	.441	.470	5.1	(1.6)	4.7	(1.6)	.188	0.27
Consumer economics	.369	.480	4.7	(1.7)	4.3	(1.7)	.211	0.23
Health information	.491	.678	5.4	(2.0)	4.4	(2.1)	**.016**	0.49
Government and law	.423	.365	4.5	(1.6)	4.4	(1.4)	.569	0.15
Facts and terms	.378	.574	4.0	(1.4)	3.9	(1.6)	.779	0.06
Reading	.466	.586	5.2	(2.0)	4.8	(1.8)	.282	0.20
Writing	.361	.414	5.8	(1.5)	5.4	(1.5)	.179	0.25
Computation	.338	.417	3.9	(1.9)	3.8	(1.7)	.661	0.05
Problem solving	.418	.511	6.1	(1.3)	5.2	(1.8)	**.003**	0.54
Age 19								
Total (general literacy)		.903	24.6	(6.5)	21.8	(6.2)	**.025**	0.43
Community resources		.656	5.3	(1.6)	4.9	(1.6)	.211	0.24
Occupational knowledge		.680	5.3	(1.7)	4.4	(1.7)	**.007**	0.51
Consumer economics		.597	4.7	(1.6)	4.3	(1.7)	.302	0.20
Health information		.699	4.8	(1.9)	4.0	(1.9)	**.028**	0.42
Government and law		.576	4.5	(1.7)	4.1	(1.6)	.209	0.24
Facts and terms		.536	3.7	(1.3)	3.2	(1.3)	.064	0.36
Reading		.682	5.8	(1.7)	4.9	(1.9)	**.011**	0.48
Writing		.696	5.5	(1.8)	4.9	(1.6)	.056	0.37
Computation		.700	4.2	(2.3)	3.8	(2.0)	.354	0.18
Problem solving		.693	5.4	(1.7)	5.0	(1.8)	.211	0.24

Note. At age 19, program group $n = 52$, no-program group $n = 57$; at age 27, program group $n = 54$, no-program group $n = 59$; data source is the APL Survey (American College Testing Program, 1976) at ages 19 and 27; 40 items total, 8 per subscale except facts and terms (6), reading (9), and computation (9); all p-values in this table are based on t tests.

[a]Pearson correlation coefficients between same scales at age 19 and age 27; all obtained values were significant at $p < .001$.

the no-program group, scored "below average" (0–23) at age 19. **The program group significantly outscored the no-program group in the content areas of occupational knowledge and health information. The program group significantly outscored the no-program group in reading skill,** and nearly significantly outscored them in writing and identification of facts and terms.

Comparing the age-19 and age-27 APL Surveys, as shown in Table 12, the program-group mean remained at virtually the same level in general literacy, while the no-program-group mean rose about 1 point to partially close the gap between the two groups. Perhaps the no-program group's educational and general life experiences from ages 19 to 27 helped them close this gap. In general, the mean scores were remarkably stable from age 19 to age 27. Both program-group and no-program-group means went up for health information, identifying facts and terms, writing, and problem solving; both went down for reading. The Pearson product-moment correlation between the age-19 and age-27 total scores was .501 (df = 108, p = .000), and the correlations between same subscales at age 19 and age 27 ranged from .338 to .491 (df = 108, p < .001).

As shown in Table 13, earlier findings on tests of educational performance include study participants' high school grade point averages; numbers of failing grades; and CAT raw scores for total school achieve-

Table 13

SCHOOL ACHIEVEMENT AND GRADES, BY PRESCHOOL EXPERIENCE

Variable	Age	Program Group			No-Program Group			p	Effect Size
		n	Mean	(SD)	n	Mean	(SD)		
High school grade point average	27	42	2.09	(0.65)	44	1.68	(0.74)	**.008**	0.58
Failing grades per year, K–12	19	48	0.72	(1.07)	53	1.08	(0.93)	.073	0.31
Total school achievement	7	53	97.1	(39.9)	60	84.4	(37.7)	.085	0.33
	8	49	142.6	(48.0)	56	126.5	(45.7)	.082	0.34
	9	54	172.8	(69.8)	55	145.5	(76.5)	.054	0.37
	10	49	225.4	(72.2)	46	199.3	(84.1)	.106	0.33
	11	42	252.4	(70.2)	46	242.4	(71.1)	.507	0.14
	14	49	122.2	(41.6)	46	94.5	(35.5)	**.001**	0.68
Reading achievement	7	53	39.7	(15.1)	60	35.3	(13.7)	.109	0.30
	8	49	56.0	(17.6)	56	51.2	(16.3)	.150	0.28
	9	54	48.7	(21.2)	56	41.9	(19.7)	.086	0.33
	10	49	60.6	(21.6)	46	52.3	(23.6)	.078	0.36
	11	42	68.3	(19.8)	46	63.4	(19.9)	.249	0.25
	14	49	31.5	(12.1)	46	25.7	(9.9)	**.013**	0.51
Arithmetic achievement	7	53	32.6	(18.0)	60	27.0	(17.8)	.099	0.31
	8	49	53.0	(18.9)	56	45.3	(21.4)	.053	0.37
	9	54	93.8	(40.2)	56	79.0	(45.7)	.074	0.34
	10	49	124.2	(36.4)	46	112.4	(49.2)	.191	0.27
	11	42	137.3	(35.4)	46	136.5	(37.7)	.920	0.02
	14	49	31.5	(13.2)	46	25.0	(12.4)	**.014**	0.49
Language achievement	7	53	24.9	(12.1)	60	22.5	(11.2)	.282	0.21
	8	49	33.5	(16.3)	56	30.0	(12.9)	.226	0.24
	9	53	31.0	(16.0)	55	24.8	(15.0)	**.039**	0.40
	10	49	40.9	(18.5)	46	34.6	(15.9)	.076	0.36
	11	42	46.0	(18.5)	46	42.4	(17.6)	.357	0.20
	14	49	46.5	(16.0)	46	34.8	(12.6)	**.000**	0.76

Note. This table reports statistics for raw scores of the California Achievement Tests Lower Primary Form at ages 7–8, Upper Primary Form at ages 9–11, and Level 4 Form at age 14 (Tiegs & Clark, 1963, 1971); r_α coefficients of internal consistency for the age-14 CAT were .966 for the total, .879 for reading, .911 for arithmetic, and .917 for language; r_α for the CAT total across all occasions was .953; grades come from school records; all p-values in this table are based on t tests.

ment, reading, arithmetic, and language at ages 7–11 and 14—when study participants were scheduled to complete first through fifth grades, and eighth grade, respectively.

On a 4.0 scale (A = 4, B = 3, C = 2, D = 1, F = 0), the program group's mean high school grade point average significantly exceeded that of the no-program group (2.1 vs. 1.7). During their time in school, the program group averaged nearly significantly fewer failing grades per school year than the no-program group.

The mean **CAT total school achievement score** of the program group was nearly significantly higher than that of the no-program group at ages 7, 8, and 9, and it was noticeably higher at age 10; **the program group scored significantly and substantially higher than the no-program group at age 14. Arithmetic achievement had the same pattern of differences. For reading achievement,** nearly significant differences appeared at ages 9–10, and **a significant difference, at age 14. For language achievement,** a nearly significant difference appeared at age 10, and **significant differences, at ages 9 and 14.** On average at age 14, the program group scored at the 13th percentile and the no-program group scored at the 6th percentile on total achievement, with similar differences on the subtests (15th vs. 9th percentile on reading, 13th vs. 8th percentile on arithmetic, and 17th vs. 7th percentile on language). The reader should keep in mind that both groups were at special risk of school failure and that the proper comparison is between groups rather than between the program group and the overall population.

The large achievement-test differences at age 14 (effect size of 0.68 for total school achievement) may be partly due to the greater task persistence demanded by the group-administered test as opposed to the individually administered intellectual and language tests. At age 14, the program group failed to complete an average of 11% of the test items, whereas the no-program group failed to complete an average of 18% of the items.

Earlier Intellectual and Language Test Performance

Table 14 presents the findings for children's intellectual and language performance from study entry to age 10, and at age 14.

The intellectual performance (mean Stanford-Binet IQ) of the program group was significantly higher than that of the no-program group at the end of the first preschool year (95.5 vs. 83.3); at the end of the second preschool year, at age 5 (94.9 vs. 83.5); at age 6 (91.3 vs. 86.3); and at age 7 (91.7 vs. 87.1), 2 years after the preschool program. The mean IQs of the two groups differed by 12.2 points after one program year; by 11.4 points after two program years, at age 5; by 5.0 points at age 6; and by 4.6 points at age 7. The mean IQs of the two groups did not differ even noticeably prior to the preschool program or again at ages 8, 9, and 10, or on the WISC at age 14. **Within 3 months of program entry and immediately after the preschool program, the program group**

Table 14

INTELLECTUAL AND LANGUAGE PERFORMANCE, BY PRESCHOOL EXPERIENCE

Variable	Age[a]	Program Group			No-Program Group			p	Effect Size
		n	Mean	(SD)	n	Mean	(SD)		
Intellectual performance	P0	58	79.6	(5.9)	65	78.5	(6.9)	.378	0.16
(Stanford-Binet IQs)	P1	58	95.5	(11.5)	65	83.3	(10.0)	.000	0.99
	P2	44	94.9	(13.0)	49	83.5	(10.2)	.000	0.89
	6	56	91.3	(12.2)	64	86.3	(9.9)	.017	0.44
	7	58	91.7	(11.7)	61	87.1	(10.2)	.022	0.42
	8	55	88.1	(13.1)	62	86.9	(10.7)	.569	0.11
	9	56	87.7	(10.9)	61	86.8	(12.5)	.666	0.08
	10	57	85.0	(11.3)	57	84.6	(11.2)	.861	0.03
Nonverbal intellectual	P¼	58	69.6	(21.9)	64	59.0	(18.0)	.004	0.52
performance (Leiter	P1	37	97.0	(15.7)	41	72.0	(20.6)	.000	1.12
International	P2	44	89.8	(14.0)	49	77.9	(14.6)	.000	0.77
Performance IQs)	6	56	86.3	(11.7)	63	83.7	(13.1)	.242	0.22
	7	58	88.6	(12.0)	61	87.2	(11.3)	.536	0.11
	8	54	88.4	(10.4)	62	88.0	(13.1)	.892	0.03
	9	54	89.3	(10.0)	60	84.8	(12.3)	.036	0.39
Vocabulary (PPVT)	P¼	58	66.8	(12.1)	60	62.4	(8.2)	.022	0.42
	P1	37	74.5	(15.6)	41	63.6	(13.1)	.001	0.72
	P2	44	81.0	(20.9)	49	62.9	(15.1)	.000	0.90
	6	56	80.8	(15.7)	64	75.8	(14.2)	.070	0.33
	7	58	83.8	(12.9)	61	80.6	(12.5)	.167	0.25
	8	55	83.0	(14.7)	61	82.0	(10.3)	.701	0.07
	9	56	81.7	(13.6)	61	80.4	(14.3)	.624	0.09
Psycholinguistic	P¼	55	2.83	(0.78)	65	2.62	(0.72)	.127	0.28
abilities (ITPA)[b]	P2	44	4.75	(0.70)	47	3.95	(0.56)	.000	1.08
	6	55	5.17	(0.69)	62	5.05	(0.54)	.282	0.20
	7	54	6.09	(0.80)	54	5.86	(0.60)	.104	0.31
	8	48	6.74	(0.94)	54	6.52	(0.80)	.187	0.26
	9	54	7.45	(1.07)	56	7.22	(0.92)	.235	0.23
Intellectual performance (WISC full IQ)	14	54	81.0	(11.2)	56	80.7	(10.9)	.885	0.03

Note. All *p*-values in this table are based on *t* tests.

[a]P0 = study entry at age 3 or 4; P¼ = within 3 months of study entry; P1 = end of first preschool year; P2 = end of second preschool year; 7–14 = ages in years, at the ends of normative grades, e.g., 7 = end of grade 1.

[b]The program group also significantly (*p* < .05, two-tailed) outscored the no-program group on ITPA auditory-vocal association subscores at P¼, P2, 7, 8, and 10.

significantly outscored the no-program group on nonverbal intellectual performance (on the Leiter), on vocabulary (on the PPVT), and on psycholinguistic abilities (on the ITPA, especially on its auditory-vocal association subtest). The program group significantly outscored the no-program group on the Leiter at age 9; also, the program group nearly significantly outscored the no-program group on the PPVT at age 6 and noticeably outscored the no-program group on the ITPA at age 9. There were not even noticeable group differences, however, on administrations of these three tests at ages 7–8. The effect sizes associated with these significant group differences ranged from 0.39 to 1.12 standard deviations. Effect sizes exceeded 0.70 standard deviation on the Stanford-Binet at the end of the first and the second preschool years and on the Leiter, PPVT, and ITPA at the end of the second preschool year.

Test Performance Over the Years, by Gender

No significant preschool-experience-by-gender-interaction effect was found at any testing on any of the test scores—Stanford-Binet, Leiter, PPVT, ITPA, WISC, CAT total or subtests, or APL Survey or subtests. This lack of significant interactions presents a strong argument that the preschool program did not affect the tested educational performance of females much more than that of males, even if it did affect females', more than males', school placement and highest year of schooling.

Regardless of their preschool experience, study males either matched or outscored study females on intellectual tests; they significantly outscored females in vocabulary (on the PPVT) after 2 years of the preschool program and at ages 7, 8, and 9; in psycholinguistic abilities (on the ITPA) at ages 8 and 9; and in intellectual performance (on the WISC) at age 14. However, females either matched or outscored males on school achievement and literacy tests; they significantly outscored males on the CAT total, reading, and language at age 8; on the APL community resources subtest at age 19; and on the APL government and law subtest at age 27. In other words, study males significantly surpassed study females in some of the intellectual abilities that they brought to their schooling, but they scored the same as or significantly worse than the females on measures of what they gained from schooling.

SAM says he attended six different schools from 5th to 10th grade. The preschool program's home visitors had found the home visits to go well and described Sam's mother as very cooperative. But Sam's testers covered the tests with remarks such as "untestable," "hostile," and "difficult." His second-grade teacher described him as not reading and just beginning to learn letters: "He will not be forced to do anything. If you hold him in any way, he just goes wild. He likes to fight." Other comments: "He has a speech hesitation when he tries to talk." "He cannot function at all in a group." His second-grade teacher, who had him repeat the grade, said, "Sam is an emotionally disturbed child." His mother said that he was bused to an integrated school in third grade but misbehaved in school. He was taken to a child guidance clinic, then went back to Perry Elementary School and seemed okay. But by grade 10, he was in an EMI program.

Attitudes Towards Schooling at Age 27 and Earlier

The program and no-program groups differed neither significantly nor nearly significantly in any of the attitudes towards school measured at age 27. However, noticeably larger percentages of the program than of the no-program group reported the following:

- They were satisfied with the last high school they had attended ($p = .100$).

- Their parents considered their high school education important ($p = .134$).

- Their parents emphasized the importance of homework ($p = .149$).

- They had received special recognition for achievement during high school or since ($p = .243$).

It is interesting that at age 27, 90% of the study participants said they planned to complete more schooling.

Table 15 presents indicators of teacher-reported and self-reported attitudes towards school for study participants from age 6 through age 19. Teachers K–3 rated the program group nearly significantly higher than the no-program group in school motivation, with a noticeably higher mean rating on school potential, as well. The difference in average number of days absent from elementary school (11.9 for the program group vs. 16.3 for the no-program group) was nearly significant.

On average, the program group at age 15 placed nearly significantly greater importance on high school than the no-program group did (scoring 24.1 vs. 22.7 on a 7-item scale with 4 points per item, developed by Bachman, O'Malley, and Johnston [1978]). **On average, the program group at age 19 expressed a significantly better attitude towards their high school experience than the no-program group did (scoring 22.3 vs. 18.9 on a 16-item scale with 3 levels per item, modeled after a job-satisfaction scale developed by Freeberg [1974]).[16] At age 15, significantly more of the program group than of the no-program group (68% vs. 40%) reported that their schoolwork required preparation at home,** and this agreed with the proportions of each group reporting that they spent time each week on homework. Noticeably more of the program group than of the no-program group said they had ever thought of going to college (77% vs. 60%).

Study participants at age 15 were fairly accurate predictors of what level of schooling they would complete in the future: Of those who attended college, 91% (49 of 54) had thought of doing so at age 15, whereas of those who did *not* attend college, 60% (26 of 43) had *not* thought of doing so at age 15 ($r = .365$, $df = 96$, $p = .000$). Similarly, although, of those who dropped out of high school, only 33% (14 of 43)

[16]This finding differs from the one reported at age 19 (program-group mean = 21.3, no-program-group mean = 20.2, $p = .083$) because, this time, the interpretation of one item's numerical score was reversed from positive to negative. ("How often did you try to change something you didn't like about your school?") The interpretation previously focused on the positive aspect of trying to change a situation; the current interpretation focuses on the negative aspect of the school needing to be changed.

Table 15

ATTITUDES TOWARDS SCHOOL THROUGH AGE 19, BY PRESCHOOL EXPERIENCE

Variable	Age	Program Group				No-Program Group				p^a	Effect Size
		n	%	Mean	(SD)	n	%	Mean	SD		
School motivation[b]	6–9	46		3.17	(0.80)	49		2.88	(0.74)	.075 (t)	0.37
School potential[c]	6–9	50		4.09	(1.30)	55		3.68	(1.37)	.115 (t)	0.30
Days absent per year, K–6	13	48		11.9	(7.4)	45		16.3	(15.8)	.088 (t)	-0.04
Value placed on schooling[d]	15	44		24.1	(3.2)	54		22.7	(3.6)	.052 (t)	0.39
Schoolwork requires home preparation	15	44	68%			55	40%			.010 (P)	0.54
Days/week doing some homework	15	44		1.9		55		1.1		.023 (M)	-0.47
0			39%				62%				
1–2			29%				20%				
3–6			32%				18%				
Do parents talk with teacher about your schoolwork?	15	44	52%			53	79%			.009 (P)	-0.54
Ever thought of going to college	15	44	77%			53	60%			.119 (P)	0.31
Attitude towards high school[e]	19	58		22.3	(7.6)	63		18.9	(8.8)	.026 (t)	0.40

Note. Data sources: two scales on which teachers rated children—the Ypsilanti Rating Scale for school motivation and the Pupil Behavior Inventory for school potential; the age-15 and age-19 interviews for attitudes at these ages; and school records for days absent.

[a](M) indicates p-value is based on Mantel-Haenszel chi-square statistic. (P) indicates p-value is based on Pearson chi-square statistic. (t) indicates p-value is based on t test.

[b]Mean of 9 items scored 1 = very infrequently, 2 = infrequently, 3 = sometimes, 4 = frequently, 5 = very frequently (or the reverse) for at least 3 of 4 years from K–3, r_α over time = .829. Examples: Shows initiative, alert and interested in schoolwork, learning retained well, completes assignments, motivated towards academic performance.

[c]Mean of 3 items scored 1 = worst to 7 = best on at least 3 of 4 occasions, r_α over time = .839. Degree of imagination and creativity shown in handling materials and equipment, academic readiness, predicted future academic success.

[d]Sum of 7 items scored 1 = not at all, 2 = a little, 3 = pretty much, 4 = very much (or the reverse), r_α = .634. Examples of items: A real education comes from your own experience and not from things you learn in school; even if I could get a very good job at present, I'd still choose to stay in school and get my education.

[e] Sum of 16 items scored 1 = worst response to 3 = best response, individually worded; r_α = .799. Examples: What are your feelings about the high school you went to? How much studying did you do? Did you feel you were really part of the school, really belonged? How often did you try to change something you didn't like about your school?

Recalling his family emphasis on doing homework, **JERRY** says: "They pressured me, when I got home, to do my homework before I could go outside and play." But Jerry looks back on this pressure as a positive thing: "Through the years, if you put it in your mind that you don't have to do homework, then later on you just don't know anything. A lot of them drop out, a lot of them don't graduate; that's one of the big reasons why." At age 27, Jerry has an associate's degree and is working full-time and saving money to return to school for a bachelor's degree.

GERALD says: "[My mother] reinforced my self-motivation; and now that I look back, I can conclude that my mother always knew I had that motivation, and she encouraged it. She was always there in my corner." At a state university, on a football scholarship, Gerald nearly completed a bachelor's degree. At age 27 he is working full-time and hoping to enroll at another nearby state university to complete a bachelor's degree and then a master's degree.

said at age 15 that they considered their graduation chances slim or even, of those who graduated from regular high school, 87% (47 of 54) said at age 15 that they were certain or fairly certain that they would graduate ($r = .269$, $df = 96$, $p = .004$).

Table 16 presents indicators of parents' attitudes towards school when their children were age 15. As shown, **significantly more program-group parents than no-program-group parents**

- **Said that their 15-year-old children enjoyed talking about what they were doing in school (65% vs. 33%)**

- **Said that their 15-year-old children had done as well in school as they would have liked (51% vs. 28%)**

- **Hoped that their 15-year-old children would get college degrees (55% vs. 35%)**

This last finding contained a preschool-experience-by-gender-interaction effect: While noticeably more parents hoped for college degrees for program-group males than for no-program-group males, **significantly more parents hoped for college degrees for program-group females than for no-program-group females (63% vs. 33%)**. It is interesting how these parental hopes, however developed, foreshadowed the preschool-experience-by-gender pattern for highest year of schooling completed.

Table 16

PARENTS' ATTITUDES TOWARDS THEIR CHILDREN'S SCHOOLING
AT AGE 15, BY PRESCHOOL EXPERIENCE

Variable	Program Group	No-Program Group	p^a	Effect Size
Is your child willing to talk about school?				
Enjoys it	65%	33%	**.004** (P)	0.58
Talks when asked	29%	56%		
Doesn't like to or refuses	6%	11%		
Has your child done as well in school as you would have liked?	51%	28%	**.034** (P)	0.43
How much schooling would you hope your child would get?				
All children[b]				
College degree	55%	35%	**.027** (M)	0.45
Some college	30%	29%		
High school	16%	35%		
Males[c]				
College degree	50%	38%	.207 (M)	0.33
Some college	29%	24%		
High school	21%	38%		
Females[d]				
College degree	63%	33%	**.033** (M)	0.73
Some college	31%	33%		
High school	6%	33%		
Over the years, have you gone to parent-teacher conferences when invited by a teacher?				
Mean	2.8	3.4		
Always (4)	42%	61%	**.018** (M)	−0.48
Most of the time (3)	29%	22%		
Sometimes (2)	10%	9%		
Once in awhile (1)	6%	7%		
Never (0)	13%	0%		
How often have you gotten in touch with teacher *on your own* to talk about your child's progress?				
Mean	0.9	1.0		
Often (2)	19%	25%	.631 (M)	−0.09
Occasionally (1)	51%	47%		
Never (0)	30%	28%		

Note. Program group $n = 48$, no-program group $n = 54$, except as noted; data source is the parent interview at youth's age 15.

[a](M) indicates that the *p*-value is based on the Mantel-Haenszel chi-square statistic. (P) indicates that the *p*-value is based on the Pearson chi-square statistic.

[b]Program group $n = 44$, no-program group $n = 50$; numbers of cases are lower than for other items because the category "as far as he or she wants" was treated as missing data in the analysis.

[c]Program males $n = 28$, no-program males $n = 29$.

[d]Program females $n = 16$, no-program females $n = 21$.

More generally, parents were fairly accurate predictors of whether their 15-year-old children would graduate from regular high school: 60% of parents (53 of 88) expecting their children to graduate from high school predicted accurately, and 83% of parents (10 of 12) expecting their children to drop out of high school predicted accurately ($r = .266$, $df = 100$, $p = .004$).

Significantly *fewer* program-group parents than no-program-group parents said that they went to parent-teacher conferences when *invited* by their children's teachers (42% vs. 61%); however, groups did not differ even noticeably in how often they got in touch with teachers *on their own*. Corroborating this finding, **only 52% of the program-group members, as compared with 79% of the no-program-group members, said their parents talked with their teachers about their schoolwork** (Table 15). Although this pattern of findings could be due to program-group parents wanting to be less involved in the schools, it seems more likely that it is due to their children having fewer problems with schoolwork or discipline.

Explaining the Female Graduation Difference

School Placements

Some of the difference between program-group females and no-program-group females in graduation rates appears to have been due to the difference in percentages of program females and no-program females assigned to EMI programs or retained in grade (29% vs. 55%, $p = .088$)—a 26 percentage-point difference. The percentages of program males and

BONITA'S father, a minister, emphasizes the importance of the home environment in establishing a positive attitude towards education: "They get that base from home; the most important part is that home environment. All of us were involved in the school from the beginning of Day One until she completed it. As the parents, we always stood behind Bonita and encouraged her. She was into books and things, and we would always buy the books and read them and give her the ideas as much as we could. If there were troubles at the school (and we never had too many), I was the man that solved the problems. It's hard to get the black parents involved. If the parents don't seem to be interested in it and they don't even participate, well, then they can say they don't care, but they couldn't say that about us. They know that I was there." At age 27, Bonita has completed a bachelor's degree and master's degree in special education.

no-program males assigned/retained (53% vs. 50%) were not noticeably different (only 3 percentage points). As noted earlier, assignment/retention both identifies school problems and attempts to remedy them. In the study sample, graduating from high school or the equivalent were

- 85% of the 27 not-assigned/retained females but only 26% of the 19 assigned/retained females ($p < .001$)—a 59 percentage-point difference

- 81% of the 32 not-assigned/retained males but only 44% of the 34 assigned/retained males ($p < .001$)—a 37 percentage-point difference

For each gender, the product of the placement-status and graduation-status differences may be construed as an estimate of the effect of preschool experience on the rate of high school graduation or the equivalent that was mediated by the assigned/retained variable. For females, the mediated effect was 26% x 59%, or about 15 percentage points. For males, the mediated effect was 3% x 37%, or about 1 percentage point. Thus, about one third of the 49 percentage-point difference between the graduation rates of program-group females and no-program-group females appears to have been due to their placements in EMI programs or their retentions in grade (or due to the factors that led to these placements/retentions).

As shown in Table 17, 100% of the 17 program-group females who were never EMI-assigned or retained in grade graduated from high school or the equivalent. In contrast to this, only 17% of the 12 no-program-group females who were at some time EMI-assigned or retained in grade achieved high school graduation or the equivalent.

Teen Parenthood

Graduating from high school or the equivalent were

- 44% of the 16 teen fathers, as compared with 70% of the 56 males who were not teen fathers ($p = .057$)—a 26 percentage-point difference (not in table)

- 42% of the 24 teen mothers, as compared with 76% of the 25 females who were not teen mothers ($p = .005$)—a 34 percentage-point difference

However, as shown later in Chapter 6 (Table 30), program males did not differ noticeably from no-program males in their rates of teen fatherhood (18% vs. 26%); neither did program females differ noticeably from no-program females in their rates of teen motherhood (44% vs. 58%). Based on the procedure described earlier, the indirect effect of preschool experience through teen motherhood on high school graduation or the equivalent would be the product of the two differences for females—34% times 14%, or about 5 percentage points. So teen motherhood does not

Table 17

HIGH SCHOOL GRADUATION OR THE EQUIVALENT BY PRESCHOOL EXPERIENCE,
GENDER, SCHOOL PLACEMENT, AND TEEN MOTHERHOOD

| | Program Group | | | No-Program Group | | | |
| | | Graduates in Category | | | Graduates in Category | | |
	No. in Category	n	%	No. in Category	n	%	p^a
Males[b]	33	20	61%	39	26	67%	.774 (P)
Neither in EMI program nor retained in grade	14	12	86%	18	14	78%	.326 (P)
In EMI program or retained in grade	16	5	31%	18	10	56%	.154 (P)
Females[c]	25	21	84%	26	9	35%	**.001 (P)**
Neither in EMI program nor retained in grade	17	17	100%	10	6	60%	**.005 (P)**
In EMI program or retained in grade	7	3	43%	12	2	17%	.211 (P)
Not teen mothers[d]	14	13	93%	11	6	55%	.149 (P)
Teen mothers	11	8	73%	13	2	15%	**.011 (P)**
Not EMI/retained, not teen mother	11	11	100%	5	4	80%	.313 (F)
EMI/retained, not teen mother	2	1	50%	5	2	40%	.714 (F)
Not EMI/retained, but teen mother	6	6	100%	5	2	40%	.061 (F)
EMI/retained, teen mother	5	2	40%	7	0	0%	.151 (F)

Note. Data sources are the school records and the age-19 interview. *n* refers to the number of male or female study participants graduating from high school or the equivalent out of the total number in the category.

[a](F) indicates that the *p*-value is based on the Fisher exact test. (P) indicates that the *p*-values are based on the Pearson chi-square statistic.

[b]School placement was unknown for 3 program males who graduated, 2 no-program males who graduated, and 1 no-program male who did not graduate.

[c]School placement was unknown for 1 program female who graduated, 1 no-program female who graduated, and 3 no-program females who did not graduate.

[d]See Table 30 in Chapter 6 for additional information on teen pregnancies and births.

appear to have had a large role as a mediator between preschool experience and high school graduation or the equivalent.

Nonetheless, teen motherhood does illustrate a striking difference between program-group females and no-program-group females. As shown in Table 17, of the female study subjects who became teen mothers, **significantly more program-group than no-program-group subjects graduated from high school or the equivalent (73% vs. 15% of teen mothers).** Some of this difference may be traced to the program-group/no-program-group difference in EMI assignment and grade retention. As can be calculated from the information in Table 17, regardless of preschool experience, 73% of teen mothers who were not assigned/retained graduated from high school or the equivalent (8 of 11), while only 17% of the teen mothers who were assigned/retained did so (2 of 12).

This extraordinary difference provides evidence of strong commitment to schooling that is more compelling than any similarly large difference one might find on some attitudinal scale. Teen motherhood is a substantial obstacle to be overcome on the path to graduating from high school, even if the school provides special programs for teen mothers. The entire pattern of findings about preschool-experience-by-gender influence on schooling variables suggests that females benefited more than males in terms of the effects of the preschool program on their elementary and secondary school experience. One interpretation of this pattern is that the preschool program's improvement of males' school ability was not noticed or responded to by school staff; the pattern of findings on arrests, presented in Chapter 4, suggests that instead, the attention of school staff was on males' acceptable versus unacceptable conduct. By this interpretation, the preschool program's improvement of females' school ability was sustained and amplified by the attention of school staff to this improvement, particularly by the tracking of females according to their school ability (keeping higher ability females in the upper track of regular classes, on grade, while placing lower ability females in the lower track of EMI classes or grade retention). Subsequently, females in the upper track developed higher school achievement and commitment to schooling than did females in the lower track. Then, when teen motherhood stood in the way of high school graduation for some females, most of those in the upper track, because of their stronger commitment to schooling, graduated anyway, while most of those in the lower track did not.

Similar Findings in Another Study

Gray and others, in a 1982 report of their study of the Early Training Project, described a similar pattern of findings for males and females. The project provided 2 or 3 years of summer preschool programs, as well as weekly home visits during the school year, for a group of young children living in poverty. In addition to the program group ($n = 41$), the study had a local no-program group ($n = 21$) and a distal no-program group ($n = 24$) in a nearby community. Various findings reported in this chapter for the High/Scope Perry Preschool study are paralleled by these findings of the Early Training Project study at the last follow-up (Gray et al., 1982):

- Slightly **fewer** program males than local-no-program males graduated from high school.
- Slightly **more** program males than local-no-program males had been placed in EMI programs or retained in grade.
- Significantly **more** program females than local-no-program females graduated from high school.
- Noticeably **fewer** program females than no-program females were placed in EMI programs or retained in grade.

- Significantly **more** program teen mothers than local-no-program teen mothers graduated from high school. The published report does not permit the calculation of whether this difference was mediated by EMI placement/grade retention.

In the decade after the preschool program, the principal expression of program effects was provided by variables having to do with the schooling of study participants—educational performance on tests and classroom assignments; school conduct; manifest dispositions and attitudes towards other people, tasks, and school itself. Thus, the effects presented in this chapter serve as precursors, or mediators, of the effects presented in the following chapters—on delinquency and crime, adult employment and earnings, and family formation and health.

IV Delinquency and Crime

As compared with the no-program group, the program group averaged a significantly[17] lower number of lifetime (juvenile and adult) criminal arrests (2.3 vs. 4.6 arrests) and a significantly lower number of adult criminal arrests (1.8 vs. 4.0 arrests). According to police and court records collected when study participants were 27–32 years old, significantly fewer program-group members than no-program-group members were frequent offenders—arrested 5 or more times in their lifetimes (7% vs. 35%) or as adults (7% vs. 31%). As compared with the no-program group, the program group had noticeably fewer arrests for adult felonies, significantly fewer arrests for adult misdemeanors, and noticeably fewer juvenile arrests. As compared with the no-program group, the program group had significantly fewer arrests for drug-making or drug-dealing crimes (7% vs. 25%), nearly significantly fewer arrests for property crimes, and noticeably fewer arrests for personal-violence crimes. As compared with the no-program group, the program group averaged significantly fewer undropped misdemeanor cases (0.8 vs. 1.4 cases) and was sentenced to significantly fewer months on probation or parole (3.2 vs. 6.6 months).

Since males were arrested more frequently than females, male group-differences involved more arrests than did female group-differences. As compared with no-program males, program males on average were arrested significantly fewer times over their lives (3.8 vs. 6.1 arrests, with 12% vs. 49% arrested 5 or more times) and as adults (3.0 vs. 5.4 arrests, with 12% vs. 43% arrested 5 or more times as adults). Nearly significantly fewer program males than no-program males were ever arrested for drug-making or drug-dealing crimes. As compared with no-program females, program females on average were arrested nearly significantly fewer times over their lives, nearly significantly fewer times as adults, and noticeably fewer times for crimes of drug making or drug dealing.

Self-reported misconduct differences over time were in the same direction but less pronounced. As compared with the no-program group, the program group themselves reported noticeably fewer acts of misconduct by age 27, noticeably fewer arrests or pickups by the police by age 27, and significantly less time spent on probation by age 27. As compared with the no-program group, the program group had also reported noticeably fewer acts of misconduct by age 19 and nearly significantly fewer acts of misconduct by age 15. When study participants were ages 6–9, teachers had rated the program group nearly significantly lower than the no-program group on personal misconduct and school misconduct.

The findings of group differences in social responsibility—as evidenced by differences in arrests and crimes—are quite strong and perhaps the most important of this study. This chapter presents details of the findings about study participants' arrests, criminal activity, and self-reported misconduct.

---

[17]This report describes a group difference as **significant** if it has a two-tailed probability of less than .05, as **nearly significant** if it has a two-tailed probability between .05 and .10, and as **noticeable** if it has a two-tailed probability between .10 and .25. Since the hypotheses of this study are clearly directional, readers who prefer one-tailed tests of significance may interpret "nearly significant" findings as significant.

Arrests

The categories of criminal behavior we examined included numbers of lifetime (including both juvenile and adult) arrests, juvenile arrests, and adult arrests. Criminal incidents leading to adult arrests were classified either as felonies (serious offenses) or misdemeanors (minor offenses), using the distinctions made by the State of Michigan, where most of the offenses occurred. (See insert on p. 85 listing categories of felonies and misdemeanors.) A few recorded misdemeanors led to detention by a police officer but not arrest.

The analysis of arrests presented in this chapter represents a compromise position in the criminological debate over whether to study crimes or criminals (e.g., Wilson & Herrnstein, 1985). The compromise, which utilizes what might be called *degrees of criminality*, consists of dividing arrests and crimes into these categories, based on maximum frequencies of occurrence: 0 incidents, 1–4 incidents, 5–9 incidents, 10–15 incidents, and so on. Thus, a single arrest does not make a noncriminal into a criminal, but rather moves the person into the category of offenders with 1–4 arrests. In arrests and crimes with high frequencies of occurrence (e.g., lifetime arrests, adult arrests, and adult misdemeanors), the group differences in this study were largest for offenders with 5 or more arrests—the ones who might be called frequent offenders. It can be argued that since most crimes are committed by frequent offenders, it makes sense to target prevention efforts on this category of offenders (Wilson & Herrnstein, 1985).

As shown in Table 18 and Figure 7, **the program group averaged significantly fewer *lifetime* arrests than the no-program group (2.3 vs. 4.6 arrests, only half as many).**[18] Over their lifetimes, 7% of the program group were frequent offenders (arrested 5 or more times), as compared with 35% of the no-program group. Compared with the no-program group, the program group averaged noticeably fewer juvenile arrests and **significantly fewer adult arrests (1.8 vs. 4.0 arrests, not even half as many).** As adults, 7% of the program group, as compared with 31% of the no-program group, were frequent offenders (arrested at least 5 times). As compared with the no-program group, the program group had noticeably fewer adult felony arrests and significantly fewer adult misdemeanors.

The program group averaged significantly fewer arrests than the no-program group for crimes of drug making or dealing (0.2 vs. 0.4 crimes, only half as many). Only 7% of the program group had ever been arrested for drug-related crimes; this compared with 25% of the no-program group. As compared with the no-program group, the program group also had nearly significantly fewer arrests for crimes against property and noticeably fewer arrests for crimes of violence against persons.

---

[18]Actual values for lifetime arrests were as follows: program-group males—8 at 0, 3 at 1, 6 at 2, 9 at 3, 3 at 4, 1 at 9, 1 at 15, 1 at 22, 1 at 27; program-group females—17 at 0, 5 at 1, 3 at 2; no-program-group males—7 at 0, 8 at 1, 2 at 2, 3 at 3, 2 at 5, 2 at 6, 2 at 7, 1 at 8, 1 at 9, 2 at 10, 1 at 11, 2 at 14, 2 at 15, 1 at 16, 1 at 17, 1 at 21, 1 at 23; no-program-group females—13 at 0, 6 at 1, 1 at 3, 2 at 4, 2 at 6, 2 at 15.

Categories of Felonies and Misdemeanors

Felonies

Assault
Aggravated assault (V)[*]
Aggravated child-abuse (V)
Assault with dangerous weapon (V)
Assault with intent of great bodily harm (V)
Assault with intent to murder (V)
Criminal sexual conduct—-rape (V)
Kidnapping (V)
Murder (V)

Drug-Related
Dangerous drugs (D)
Sale, possession, trafficking, or delivery of
    controlled substance (D)

Fraud
Embezzlement over $100 (P)
Forgery (P)
Fraudulent use of credit card over $300 (P)
Welfare fraud (some cases) (P)
Fraudulent activities (P)
Fraudulent uttering and publishing (P)
Hindering legal system
Escape
Flee-and-elude involving violence (V)
Habitual offender
Failure to stop at scene of serious accident (V)

Larceny (Robbery)
Armed robbery or felony (V)
Larceny from a person (V)
Vehicle theft (P)
Breaking and entering any building with
    intent (P)
Larceny over $100 (P)
Larceny in a building (P)

Property Violations
Arson (P)
Malicious destruction of property
    over $100 (P)
Receiving or concealing stolen property
    over $100 (P)
Armed trespass (P)

Weapons Offense
Carrying a concealed weapon

Misdemeanors

Status or Juvenile Crime
Runaway
Minor in possession of intoxicants
Pickup order
Truancy
Traffic violation
Turned over to boys' training school

Assault
Assault or battery, or assault and battery (V)
Child abuse or negligence (V)

Disorderly Conduct
Accosting and soliciting
Disorderly conduct or disturbing the peace
Indecent exposure
Public nuisance
Trespassing (P)
Frequenting place of illegal activity
Invasion of privacy
Gambling

Driving Offenses
Driving while license suspended
Driving while unlicensed
Impaired operating of vehicle while
    intoxicated or under the influence
    of liquor
Open intoxicant in a moving vehicle
Reckless driving
Failure to stop at accident with a moving
    or unattended vehicle
No insurance
Failure to provide child safety-seat

Drug-related
Possession of drug paraphernalia (D)
Possession of less than 20 grams of
    marijuana (D)

Fraud
Food stamp or welfare fraud (P)
Fraudulent use of credit card (P)
Embezzlement less than $100 (P)
Scheme to defraud (P)

Hindering or Obstructing Legal System
Failure to appear under bond
Fleeing or attempting to elude a law-
    enforcement officer (felony if violence
    involved, see felony list)
Hinder, obstruct, resist, interfere with
    police officer
Probation violation

Larceny or Burglary
Larceny from a building (P)
Larceny under $100 (P)
Larceny, specifically shoplifting
    under $100 (P)

Property Violations
Building code violation
Breaking and entering, illegal entry (P)
Malicious destruction of property
    under $100 (P)
Receiving or concealing stolen property
    under $100 (P)
Receiving or concealing stolen property
    over $100 (P)
Criminal mischief

Weapons Offense
Carrying or possession of firearm without
    license or concealed, or discharging
    or dangerous display

*Felonies and misdemeanors are coded as follows: P = property offense; V = offense involving personal violence; D = drug-related offense.

Table 18

ARRESTS, BY PRESCHOOL EXPERIENCE

Variable	Program Group	No-Program Group	p	Effect Size
Lifetime arrests				
Mean	2.3	4.6		
1–4	50%	34%	**.004**	0.54
5–9	2%	15%		
10–15	2%	14%		
16–27	3%	6%		
Juvenile arrests				
Mean	0.5	0.6		
1–4	12%	21%	.238	0.21
5–9	3%	5%		
Adult arrests				
Mean	1.8	4.0		
1–4	41%	26%	**.013**	0.46
5–9	2%	11%		
10–15	3%	17%		
16–21	2%	3%		
Adult felony arrests				
Mean	0.7	1.5		
1–4	24%	22%	.122	0.28
5–11	3%	14%		
Adult misdemeanors				
Mean	1.2	2.5		
1–4	36%	29%	**.032**	0.39
5–9	7%	17%		
10–15	0%	6%		
Property crimes				
Mean	0.6	1.3		
1–4	24%	23%	.073	0.33
5–12	2%	12%		
Personal-violence crimes				
Mean	0.4	1.1		
1–4	19%	23%	.147	0.26
5–10	3%	9%		
Crimes of drug making or dealing				
Mean	0.2	0.4		
1–4	5%	23%	**.022**	0.42
5–7	2%	2%		

Note. Program group n = 58, no-program group n = 65; data sources are criminal records supplemented by self-reports; findings do not include 10 arrests (4 in the program group, 6 in the no-program group) reported by juvenile court authorities without individual identification at age 19 (Berrueta-Clement et al., 1984). Percentages of groups with 0 incidents were included in the analyses but not the table; all p-values are based on Mantel-Haenszel chi-square statistics on the truncated distributions presented. The insert on page 85 lists the constituents of the crime categories used above.

Figure 7

LIFETIME ARRESTS BY AGE 27, BY PRESCHOOL EXPERIENCE

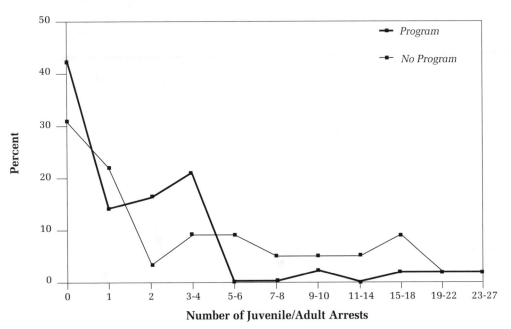

Note. Whole-group comparison, p = .004, Mantel-Haenszel chi-square statistic.
See Table 18 for details.

Arrests, by Gender

Table 19 presents the arrest, criminal sentence, and self-reported misconduct findings that had significant *main effects for gender;* none of
the arrest, sentence, or self-reported misconduct variables had a
preschool-experience-by-gender-interaction effect. In every category,
males had significantly more arrests and longer criminal sentences than
females had. As shown in Table 19 and Figure 8, **program males averaged significantly fewer lifetime arrests than did no-program males (3.8
vs. 6.1 arrests, with 12% vs. 49% arrested 5 or more times).** Program
males also averaged significantly fewer adult arrests than did no-
program males (3.0 vs. 5.4 arrests, with 12% vs. 43% arrested 5 or more
times). Program males had nearly significantly fewer drug-related arrests
than no-program males had (12% vs. 36% ever arrested). Since the effect
size (0.46) was similar to that of the overall group comparison (0.42), the
lack of a fully significant difference may be attributed to the fact that the
male comparison had only about half as many cases as the total sample.

Compared with no-program females, program females had nearly significantly fewer lifetime arrests,[19] nearly significantly fewer adult arrests,

---

[19]In addition to adult arrests, lifetime arrests of program-group females included three
other arrests; without these, the lifetime-arrest difference between program females and
no-program females would have been significant.

Table 19

ARRESTS, BY PRESCHOOL EXPERIENCE AND GENDER

Variable	Program Group	No-Program Group	p^a	Effect Size
Males				
Lifetime arrests				
Mean	3.8	6.1		
1–4	64%	33%	**.018**	0.58
5–9	3%	21%		
10–15	3%	18%		
16–27	6%	10%		
Adult arrests				
Mean	3.0	5.4		
1–4	58%	28%	**.045**	0.48
5–9	3%	15%		
10–15	6%	23%		
16–21	3%	5%		
Crimes of drug making or dealing				
Mean	0.3	0.6		
1–4	9%	33%	.053	0.46
5–7	3%	3%		
Females				
Lifetime arrests				
Mean	0.4	2.3		
1–4	32%	35%	.053	0.55
5–9	0%	8%		
10–15	0%	8%		
Adult arrests				
Mean	0.3	1.8		
1–4	20%	23%	.093	0.47
5–9	0%	4%		
10–15	0%	8%		
Crimes of drug making or dealing				
Mean	0.0	0.2		
1–4	0%	8%	.161	0.39

Note. Program-group males $n = 33$, no-program-group males $n = 39$, program-group females $n = 25$, no-program-group females $n = 26$; data sources are criminal records supplemented by self-reports where records were unavailable; findings do not include 10 previously reported records of juvenile arrest (4 in the program group, 6 in the no-program group) that had no individual identification (Berrueta-Clement et al., 1984). Percentages of groups with 0 incidents were included in the analyses but not the table. This table includes all arrest and criminal sentence variables with significant main effects for gender; none of the arrest and criminal sentence variables had significant preschool-experience-by-gender interactions.

[a]All p-values are based on Mantel-Haenszel chi-square statistics on the truncated distributions presented.

Figure 8

FIVE OR MORE LIFETIME ARRESTS BY AGE 27,
BY PRESCHOOL EXPERIENCE AND GENDER

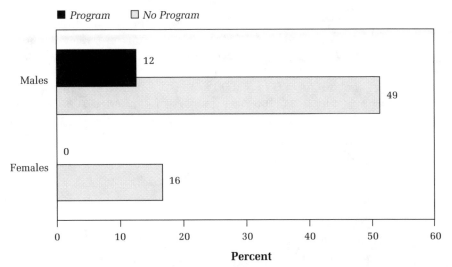

Note. Male comparison, $p = .018$, female comparison, $p = .053$; based on Mantel-Haenszel chi-square statistics. See Table 19 for details.

BARBARA[*] had a child at age 14, dropped out of school at age 15, and had another child at age 17. A known drug-user, she had been arrested 13 times for creating disturbances, interfering with the police, fighting, and malicious destruction of property. She was stabbed to death in a drug-related murder when she was 24. Her daughters, one with a child of her own, now live with her parents and receive Aid to Families with Dependent Children.

[*]Brief stories throughout this report describe real study participants but do not use their real names.

and noticeably fewer arrests for crimes of drug making or dealing. Although none of the preschool-experience-by-gender-interaction effects were statistically significant, the group differences in arrests favoring the program group were slightly stronger for males than for females.

Groups were not noticeably different in their mean ages of first offenses. On average, study participants who were offenders in each category were 15.4 years old at first juvenile offense, 21.3 years old at first adult felony, and 22.4 years old at first adult misdemeanor.

BOB's goals are a good job, buying a house, raising his children the best he can, and getting away from the neighborhood he grew up in. His day-to-day efforts are to stay sober, go to work, stay away from the crowd, and not sell drugs anymore. He is frustrated that drugs are so widespread and that they so often lead to violence. "This game of drugs ain't no joke," he says. "Drug dealers who do a lot of business make about $4,000 to $6,000 a week." The drug problem, he claims, comes from the politicians, police, and certain drug dealers who don't get touched by the police. Of the friends he grew up with, he says, about 10 are dead and about 20 are serving long-term to life sentences.

Glad that she did not succumb to peer pressure and get mixed up with drugs, **CHARLEEN** says: "I'm glad that I didn't follow the wrong crowd when I was in school. I don't smoke; I don't drink. That makes me feel good about myself, because I do have friends that went the wrong way. I'm glad that I was strong-minded enough to say no." At age 27, Charleen is a medical technician in a hospital and plans to go back to school.

Criminal Sentences

As shown in Table 20, **as compared with the no-program group, the program group averaged significantly fewer undropped misdemeanor cases (0.8 vs. 1.4 cases) and significantly fewer months on probation or parole[20] (3.2 vs. 6.6 months); fewer than half as many program group members were placed on probation or parole for 19 months or longer (9% vs. 20%).** All but one of the study participants placed on probation or parole were male. Nearly significantly fewer program-group members than no-program-group members served time on probation or parole.

The program group and the no-program group, on average, did not noticeably differ in numbers of felony convictions, in numbers sentenced to imprisonment for felonies, or in months sentenced to prison or jail. There was also no noticeable difference in percentages serving time in prison or jail. This lack of noticeable group differences probably reflects

---

[20]Probation is a type of sentence, an alternative to a prison sentence. Parole is an alternative way of completing a prison sentence, outside of prison. Both involve supervised conditional liberty.

Table 20

CRIMINAL SENTENCES, BY PRESCHOOL EXPERIENCE

Variable	Program Group	No-Program Group	p^a	Effect Size
Undropped misdemeanor cases				
Mean	0.8	1.4		
1	19%	9%	**.019** (M)	0.43
2–3	17%	17%		
4–6	2%	14%		
7–10	5%	6%		
11–15	0%	6%		
Convictions for adult felonies				
Mean	0.7	0.8		
1	7%	11%	.747 (M)	0.06
2	7%	2%		
3–5	2%	8%		
6–10	5%	5%		
Sentenced to prison for adult felonies	19%	22%	.897 (P)	0.02
Months sentenced to prison or jail				
Mean	8.6	9.4		
0.01–1	8%	12%	.307 (M)	0.18
1.01–48	6%	11%		
49–168	7%	9%		
Months placed on probation or parole				
Mean	3.2	6.6		
6–18	7%	9%	**.046** (M)	0.34
19–36	9%	20%		
Served time in prison or jail	22%	31%	.273 (P)	0.20
Served time on probation or parole	16%	29%	.070 (P)	0.33

Note. Program group $n = 58$, no-program group $n = 65$; data sources are criminal records supplemented by self-reports where records were unavailable; percentages of groups with 0 incidents were included in the analyses but not the table.

[a](M) indicates that the p-value is based on the Mantel-Haenszel chi-square statistic on the truncated distributions presented. (P) indicates that the p-value is based on the Pearson chi-square statistic.

- The lack of noticeable group differences in percentages of felony arrests (as opposed to misdemeanors)
- The incomplete information on convictions and sentences
- The variety of options available for disposition of persons arrested
- The factors other than the crime itself that enter into the determination of convictions and sentences

> Serving time for armed robbery, **JIM** talks not only about being cut off from society as a whole but also about losing all sense of family ties: "I have never had any children, not had any role in raising any. In the last 6 years I have had no contact with my family. My mother is not too happy about my behavior, and she knows I have been in and out of jail and prison. My family thinks I am not doing anything worth much and not doing as well as they expected. They didn't expect me to be a convict." Jim was the 7th of 10 children and lived in what a teacher described as a chaotic home situation. He was in special education a lot until he dropped out after ninth grade. He has spent a total of 6 years in prison.

Arrests Through Age 19

As might be expected, the findings based on data found in the search of criminal records for the age-19 study (see Berrueta-Clement et al., 1984) foreshadowed the findings at age 27. **By age 19, the program group and the no-program group differed significantly in all the following criminal-record categories:**

- **Fewer group members ever arrested (31% vs. 51%) and an average of fewer arrests per group member (1.3 vs. 2.3)**

- **Fewer arrests, on average, for crimes of property or personal violence (0.8 vs. 1.2)**

- **An average of fewer felony arrests per group member (0.7 vs. 2.0)**

- **Fewer members ever arrested for adult misdemeanors (2% vs. 16%) and an average of fewer adult misdemeanor arrests per group member (0.02 vs. 0.33)**

- **Fewer petition requests per group member submitted to juvenile court (0.2 vs. 0.4)**

- **Fewer members receiving fines (3% vs. 14%)**

BETTY had a history of violent behavior in her school career and was in several disciplinary programs. She attended an alternative high school program and was often in trouble there, once even intentionally burning her counselor: "Everybody was smoking, and he singled me out of the crowd and told me to put my cigarette out; so I did—on him." At 16, she and four other girls attacked and beat another girl in the school parking lot. At 17, she assaulted a classroom teacher, using a 7½-inch butcher knife. Betty attended a juvenile detention school but did graduate from high school.

Self- and Teacher-Reported Misconduct at Age 27 and Earlier

As shown in Table 21, when reporting their own misconduct, the program group scored noticeably lower than the no-program group on total misconduct by age 27 and serious misconduct by age 19, and nearly significantly lower on total misconduct by age 15. On scales of teacher ratings averaged across ages 6–9, the program group was rated nearly significantly lower than the no-program group on personal misconduct and school misconduct. These findings were obtained by the Mantel-Haenszel chi-square analysis that has been used on all the nonparametric variables in this report. Previous reports of this study indicated that when analyzed by median tests, the program group had a nearly significantly lower median on serious misconduct at age 19 ($p = .063$; see Berrueta-Clement et al., 1984) and **significantly lower medians than the no-program group on total misconduct at age 15 ($p = .022$) and on serious misconduct at age 15 ($p = .048$;** see Schweinhart & Weikart, 1980). The methodological tenuousness of this finding is due to the small size of the difference and the peculiarity of the distributions.

No significant group differences were found on any type of self-reported misconduct on the age-27 interview. Given the large number of arrests recorded in study participants' public records, it is surprising how few participants reported engaging in any misconduct at all. Fewer than 10% of study participants reported ever damaging property at work on purpose, setting fire to someone's property, getting into a serious fight at work or school, using a weapon to get something from someone, stealing a car or part of a car, or breaking into a building. However, these categories do not permit direct comparisons to arrests or crimes of record.

Program-group members did report spending significantly less time on probation than no-program group members reported (12% vs. 26% ever on probation), which corroborates the group difference found in the records. Study participants reported a mean of 5.7 months on probation, while the records indicate a mean sentence of 5.0 months. No group differences were found in study participants' reports of numbers of suspensions from work or school, school expulsions, traffic tickets, or

Table 21

SELF- AND TEACHER-REPORTED MISCONDUCT OVER TIME, BY PRESCHOOL EXPERIENCE

Variable	n	Program Group Mean (SD)	%	n	No-Program Group Mean (SD)	%	p^a	Effect Size
Self-Reports[b]								
Total acts of misconduct by age 27	55	18.8		61	19.4		.227 (M)	0.22
0–2			45%			36%		
3–5			31%			31%		
6–29			24%			33%		
Times picked up or arrested by police by age 27	55	0.5		61	0.9		.116 (M)	0.28
1–2			19%			23%		
3–5			5%			12%		
Months on probation by age 27	58	5.6		62	5.8		**.050** (M)	0.36
1–18			5%			8%		
24–257[c]			7%			18%		
Serious misconduct by age 19	58	12.4		63	15.3		.209 (M)	0.23
1–8			47%			40%		
9–145[d]			29%			41%		
Total misconduct by age 15	44	5.2		55	7.1		.100 (M)	0.33
1–6			43%			40%		
7–35			30%			44%		
Teacher ratings								
Personal misconduct, ages 6–9[e]	45	0.84 (0.49)		49	1.02 (0.51)		.080 (t)	0.36
School misconduct, ages 6–9[f]	46	1.36 (0.65)		49	1.61 (0.60)		.054 (t)	0.40

Note. Percentages of groups with 0 incidents were included in the analyses but not the table.

[a](M) indicates that the p-value is based on the Mantel-Haenszel chi-square statistic on the truncated distributions presented. (t) indicates that the p-value is based on the t test.

[b]Developed by Martin Gold of the University of Michigan's Institute for Social Research, the scales for misconduct at ages 15, 19, and 27 had 14–16 items, with alpha coefficients ranging from .774 to .863. The items were scored 0 = not at all, 1 = once, 2 = twice, 3 = 3 or 4 times, 4 = 5 or more times, with seriousness weightings (after Phillips & Votey, 1981) noted in parentheses. The age-19 items, for example, were as follows: Have you ever hurt someone badly enough to need bandages or a doctor (10), used a knife or a gun or some other thing like a club to get something from a person (9), set fire to someone's property on purpose (8), hit an instructor or supervisor (7), gotten into a serious fight at school or work (7), taken part in a fight where a group of your friends were against another group (7), taken a car that didn't belong to someone in your family without permission of the owner (6), gone into some house or building when you weren't supposed to be there (5), taken something not belonging to you worth under $50 (3), taken something not belonging to you worth over $50 (4), taken something from a store without paying for it (2), damaged school property on purpose (1), damaged property at work on purpose (1)?

[c]Means and t test excluded the maximum values, which were well above the rest of the distributions.

[d]Means and t test excluded the maximum values, which were well above the rest of the distributions.

[e]Six teacher ratings scored 1 = very infrequently, 2 = infrequently, 3 = sometimes, 4 = frequently, 5 = very frequently; $r_\alpha = .754$; absences or truancies; inappropriate personal appearance; lying or cheating; stealing, swearing, or using obscene words; poor personal hygiene.

[f]Twelve teacher ratings scored 1 = very infrequently, 2 = infrequently, 3 = sometimes, 4 = frequently, 5 = very frequently; $r_\alpha = .762$. Examples: Blames others for trouble, is resistant to teacher, attempts to manipulate adults, influences others towards troublemaking.

months spent in jail. Noticeably fewer program-group members than no-program group members reported having ever been picked up or arrested by age 27 (24% vs. 35%).

On age-19 misconduct scale items, as compared with the no-program group, the program group reported, on average, significantly fewer of three types of violent offenses—being involved in a serious fight (0.5 vs. 0.8 offenses), being involved in a group or gang fight (0.4 vs. 0.9 offenses), or causing someone an injury requiring bandages or a doctor (0.4 vs. 0.7 offenses). Also in the age-19 self-reporting, the program group averaged being involved with the police significantly fewer times than the no-program group did (0.6 vs. 1.0; see Berrueta-Clement et al., 1984). **On age-15 misconduct scale items, as compared with the no-program group, the program group reported significantly fewer of two types of violent offenses—taking something by force from a person (a mean of 0.0 vs. a mean of 0.5 offenses) and damaging institutional property (a mean of 0.0 vs. a mean of 0.3 offenses;** see Schweinhart & Weikart, 1980).

Although the group differences reflect those found in the criminal records, study participants reported fewer arrests than their criminal records indicated. In their interviews, 57% of them reported ever being arrested; their records showed that 69% had been arrested. In their interviews, 7% said they had 5 or more arrests, whereas records indicated that 35% of them had 5 or more arrests. Possible reasons for such underreporting are (a) memories that become imprecise as the years go by and, in some cases, as arrests accumulate; (b) cautiousness about revealing such information to the interviewer; and (c) eagerness to please or appear better than one is to the interviewer. Also, the criminal records are cumulative, whereas the interviews represent memories at single points in time; age 27, in particular, may have been well after the peak of individual criminal activity. Furthermore, individuals bring their own meanings to self-reported misconduct, whereas police making arrests are aware that the charges they make leading to the arrests must conform to strict legal definitions that will stand up in court.

The extraordinary central finding of this chapter is that members of the program group were arrested only half as often as members of the no-program group. Such a finding suggests basic lifestyle differences between the two groups. The next chapter reveals that such a lifestyle difference was also manifest in study participants' earnings and accumulation of property wealth.

V Economic Status

The most recent evidence of the High/Scope Perry Preschool Project indicates that compared with the no-program group, the program group at age 27 not only had higher earnings[21] but also had fewer members who had received social services in the previous 10 years. Specifically, at age 27 the program group reported

- *Significantly[22] higher monthly earnings (a whole-group mean of $1,219 vs. a whole-group mean of $766, with 29% vs. 7% earning $2,000 or more)*

- *Nearly significantly higher annual earnings (a whole-group mean of $13,328 vs. a whole-group mean of $11,186, with 29% vs. 15% earning $20,000 or more)*

- *Significantly higher monthly earnings for those group members who were employed (an employed-group mean of $1,556 vs. an employed-group mean of $1,251, with 36% vs. 11% earning $2,000 or more)*

- *Noticeably higher monthly earnings for all spouses of study participants (a mean of $1,307 vs. a mean of $845, with 35% vs. 5% earning $2,000 or more)*

- *Significantly higher monthly household earnings for all couples, i.e., study participants and their spouses (a mean of $2,762 vs. a mean of $1,859, with 47% vs. 17% earning over $3,000)*

The program group's employment rate was noticeably but not significantly higher than that of the no-program group (71% vs. 59%), but the groups did not differ noticeably in rate of employment over the previous 5 years or in months of unemployment in the previous 2 years.

At age 27, the program males reported significantly higher monthly earnings than did the no-program males (a whole-group mean of $1,368 vs. a whole-group mean of $830, with 42% vs. 6% earning over $2,000). The employment rates of program males and no-program males did not differ noticeably, but the monthly earnings of program males who were employed were significantly higher than those of no-program males who were employed (an employed-group mean of $1,816 vs. an employed-group mean of $1,310, with 53% vs. 8% earning over $2,000 per month). The program females reported significantly higher monthly earnings than did the no-program females at age 27 (a whole-group mean of $1,047 vs. a whole-group mean of $651), with 48% vs. 18% earning over $1,000 per

---

[21]In this report, *earnings* are restricted to income from employment.

[22]This report describes a group difference as **significant** if it has a two-tailed probability less than .05, as **nearly significant** if it has a two-tailed probability between .05 and .10, and as **noticeable** if it has a two-tailed probability between .10 and .25. Since the hypotheses of this study are clearly directional, readers who prefer one-tailed tests of significance may interpret "nearly significant" findings as significant.

month.[23] *Since the employment rate of program females at age 27 was significantly higher than that of no-program females (80% vs. 55%), when the monthly earnings of the program-group females and the no-program-group females were averaged over just the employed members in each group, the two means that were obtained did not noticeably differ.*

According to social services records and interviews at age 27, a significantly smaller percentage of the program group than of the no-program group had received social services sometime in the previous 10 years (59% vs. 80%); this was due to a significant difference for males (52% vs. 77%) and a noticeable difference in the same direction for females (68% vs. 85%). When interviewed at age 27, significantly fewer program-group members than no-program-group members reported they were receiving government assistance (15% vs. 32%); this was especially the case for females (with 26% vs. 59% on government assistance).

Significantly more program-group members than no-program-group members owned their own homes (36% vs. 13%, or almost three times as many), and significantly more program-group than no-program-group members owned a second car (30% vs. 13%, or over twice as many).

Earlier, when interviewed at age 19, significantly more in the program group than in the no-program group had said they were self-supporting (45% vs. 25%) and employed (50% vs. 32%). The age-19 interview revealed several other differences indicating that at age 19, the program group was economically better-off than the no-program group: Program group members reported significantly fewer months unemployed since leaving school (a mean of 4.9 vs. a mean of 10.3 months), significantly more months employed in their age-19 calendar year (a mean of 6.1 vs. a mean of 3.9 months), nearly significantly more months employed in their age-18 calendar year, and nearly significantly higher earnings in their age-19 calendar year. Also, in the age-19 interview, significantly fewer program group members reported receiving welfare (18% vs. 32%). Social services records around that time generally agreed with the self-report: They indicated fewer program-group members receiving General Assistance (19% vs. 41%) or receiving both General Assistance and food stamps (17% vs. 38%). The records also revealed that program-group members, on average, received a significantly lower annual welfare payment ($633 vs. $1,509).

This chapter examines the principal measures of study participants' economic productivity and self-sufficiency—their employment and earnings, independence from social services, and property wealth.

---

[23]As noted in Chapter 2, this comparison dropped from significant to noticeable ($p = .136$) when analyzed by analysis of covariance controlling for family configuration at study entry, family moves through age 15, and maternal employment at age 15.

Age-27 Employment and Earnings

As shown in Table 22 and detailed in Figure 9, **when interviewed at age 27, the program group reported monthly earnings[24] significantly higher than those of the no-program group (a whole-group mean of $1,219 vs. a whole-group mean of $766, with 55% vs. 37% earning $1,000 or more a month);** $1,000 a month is equivalent to a full-time job paying $6.00 an hour, which amounts to $12,000 per year. This annual income is $1,359 below the federally defined poverty level of $13,359 for a family of four in 1990.[25]

When asked about their annual earnings at age 27, the program group reported annual earnings that were nearly significantly higher than those of the no-program group. The fact that self-reported monthly earnings showed a *significant difference* but self-reported annual earnings showed just a *nearly significant difference* merits some additional scrutiny. If program-group members earned their stated monthly (whole-group) average of $1,219 for 12 months, this would be an average of $14,628 per year—$1,300 more than their stated annual (whole-group) average of $13,328. If no-program-group members earned their stated monthly (whole-group) average of $766 for 12 months, this would be an average of $9,192 per year—$1,994 less than their stated annual (whole-group) average of $11,186.

While it is conceivable that the group differences in monthly earnings were indeed unusually large in the month before the age-27 interview, it is more probable that study participants' earnings estimates for the previous month were more accurate than their estimates for the previous year. Remembering earnings over a year requires accurate recollection over 12 months rather than over just 1 month; practically, it would require having available either a statement of annual salary or a recent calculation of annual earnings (e.g., a pay stub or W-2 form). Further, some study participants worked at various jobs from time to time, some had a single job but worked irregular hours, and some had one or more part-time jobs at which they worked for varying numbers of hours from month to month. Such persons would find it almost impossible to

---

[24]The item was worded "What is the total income that you earned from work only, in the past month, before taxes?" Actual values for *monthly earnings at age 27* were as follows:
Program-group males—8 at $0, 1 at $654, 1 at $700, 1 at $750, 2 at $1,000, 1 at $1,040, 1 at $1,200, 1 at $1,400, 1 at $1,500, 4 at $2,000, 2 at $2,400, 1 at $2,500, 1 at $2,600, 3 at $3,000, 1 at $3,520
Program-group females—5 at $0, 2 at $500, 1 at $550, 1 at $600, 1 at $800, 1 at $900, 2 at $950, 1 at $1,000, 3 at $1,200, 1 at $1,280, 1 at $1,300, 1 at $1,600, 1 at $1,750, 1 at $2,000, 1 at $2,200, 1 at $2,700, 1 at $3,000
No-program-group males—11 at $0, 1 at $100, 1 at $250, 2 at $300, 1 at $500, 3 at $700, 1 at $800, 1 at $920, 1 at $1,000, 2 at $1,100, 3 at $1,200, 1 at $1,250, 3 at $1,300, 1 at $1,350, 1 at $1,360, 1 at $1,450, 1 at $1,500, 1 at $1,600, 1 at $1,700, 1 at $2,200, 1 at $4,000
No-program-group females—9 at $0, 3 at $500, 1 at $600, 1 at $700, 1 at $750, 1 at $800, 1 at $900, 1 at $976, 1 at $1,200, 1 at $1,916, 1 at $2,080, 1 at $2,900

[25]The findings on employment and earnings at age 27 do not include the 2 no-program-group females deceased before age 27. If they had lived and continued their earlier patterns, it is highly probable that they would be persistently unemployed, with no earnings.

Table 22

EMPLOYMENT AND EARNINGS AT AGE 27, BY PRESCHOOL EXPERIENCE

Variable	Program Group			No-Program Group			p^a	Effect Size
	n	Mean	%	n	Mean	%		
Previous month's earnings (whole group)	54	$1,219		61	$766			
$0			24%			33%	**.007** (M)	0.51
$1–$999			20%			31%		
$1,000–$1,999			26%			30%		
$2,000–$2,999			20%			5%		
$3,000–$4,000			9%			2%		
Previous year's earnings (whole group)	54	$13,328		59	$11,186			
$0			11%			22%	.069 (M)	0.35
$1–$9,999			24%			27%		
$10,000–$19,999			35%			36%		
$20,000–$29,999			20%			8%		
$30,000–$39,999			9%			5%		
$40,000–$48,000			0%			2%		
Previous month's earnings (employed only)	39	$1,556		36	$1,251			
$0			3%			0%	**.046** (M)	0.47
$1–$999			26%			39%		
$1,000–$1,999			36%			50%		
$2,000–$2,999			23%			8%		
$3,000–$4,000			13%			3%		
Previous month's earnings of spouse (all spouses)	26	$1,307		21	$845			
$0			27%			14%	.144 (M)	0.43
$1–$999			12%			52%		
$1,000–$1,999			27%			29%		
$2,000–$3,000			35%			5%		
Previous month's earnings of married couples (all couples)	28	$2,762		23	$1,859			
$0			4%			9%	**.029** (M)	0.63
$1–$999			4%			4%		
$1,000–$1,999			18%			44%		
$2,000–$2,999			29%			26%		
$3,000–$3,999			32%			13%		
$4,000–$4,999			4%			0%		
$5,000–$6,000			11%			4%		

Table 22 (continued)

EMPLOYMENT AND EARNINGS AT AGE 27, BY PRESCHOOL EXPERIENCE

Variable	Program Group			No-Program Group			p^a	Effect Size
	n	Mean	%	n	Mean	%		
Participant's employment status/history								
Currently employed	55		71%	61		59%	.181 (P)	0.25
Employed in previous 5 years	53		91%	61		84%	.273 (P)	0.21
Months unemployed in previous 2 years	54	5.7		61	8.0		.289 (P)	0.20
0			61%			48%		
1–12			16%			24%		
13–23			8%			10%		
24			15%			18%		

Note. Data source is the age-27 interview.

[a](P) means that the *p*-value is based on the Pearson chi-square statistic. (M) means that the *p*-value is based on the Mantel-Haenszel chi-square statistic for the truncated distributions.

Figure 9

MONTHLY EARNINGS AT AGE 27, BY PRESCHOOL EXPERIENCE

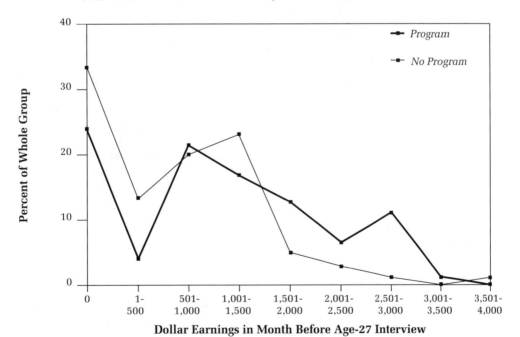

Dollar Earnings in Month Before Age-27 Interview

Note. Whole-group comparison, $p = .007$, Mantel-Haenszel chi-square statistic. See Table 22 for details.

accurately estimate their earnings of the past year in an interview, without any prior warning or opportunity for preparation.

The age-27 monthly earnings of the employed members of the program group, when averaged over *just the number employed,* were significantly higher than the comparable average for the no-program group ($1,556 vs. $1,251); 36% of the employed members of the program group, as compared with 11% of the employed members of the no-program group, earned over $2,000 in the month previous to their age-27 interview. Monthly earnings of $2,000 would mean $24,000 a year, or a full-time job at $10 an hour, probably with employee benefits—which is well above the poverty level for a family of four.

The monthly earnings of all the spouses of program-group members were on average noticeably higher than those of all the spouses of no-program-group members ($1,307 vs. $845). Thus, **the monthly earnings of all married couples with program-group members were significantly higher than those of couples with no-program-group members (a mean of $2,762 vs. a mean of $1,859);** 47% of couples with program-group members, as compared with 17% of couples with no-program-group members, earned $3,000 or more each month.

At the age-27 interview, noticeably more of the program group than of the no-program group reported being currently employed (71% vs. 59%). Also, though the group differences were not noticeable, the program group did report a somewhat higher percentage of employment in the previous 5 years (91% vs. 84%) and fewer months of unemployment, on average, in the previous 2 years (5.7 vs. 8.0 months).

For current employment, study participants reported various types of jobs. The following lists (see Occupations at Age 27 on p. 103) indicate how 55 program-group members and 61 no-program-group members identified their current occupations or employment status.

The information on earnings that has just been presented gives a more precise picture of the actual earning power of study participants than do the lists of occupations shown here. What is striking about the lists, however, is not the differences in the types of jobs held by the program group versus the no-program group, but rather the low status and low income-potential of most of the jobs listed. While the various occupations are not listed in strict order according to socioeconomic status, it is evident that only the top third or so of the jobs in the two lists have much status or income potential. Nevertheless, they can provide a living and enable their holders to be self-sufficient rather than dependent on welfare assistance.

Age-27 Employment and Earnings by Gender

As shown in Table 23 and Figure 10, **program males had significantly higher monthly earnings at age 27 than did no-program males (a whole-group mean of $1,368 vs. a whole-group mean of $830),** with 42% of program males but only 6% of no-program males earning $2,000 or more per month. Program males and no-program males reported

Occupations at Age 27

Program Group	No-Program Group
school teacher	social worker
small-business owner	reporter
purchasing agent or buyer	retail sales manager
cashier	manager
mail carrier	machinist
heavy-equipment mechanic	laboratory technician
printer	secretary
assembly-line worker	upholsterer
nurse's aide	assembly-line worker
legal secretary	gas station attendant
kennel owner	machine operator
equipment operator	clerk
switchboard operator	cab driver
inspector	groundskeeper
driver	stock handler
stock clerk	dishwasher
maid	waiter
waiter	housekeeper
3 laborers	guard
2 clerical workers	2 cooks
2 janitors	2 food service workers
2 health care workers	3 laborers
4 cooks	3 janitors
4 food service workers	3 maids
4 housekeepers	4 employed persons
16 unemployed persons	(job unknown)
	25 unemployed persons

about the same rates of current employment, but when monthly earnings were averaged over numbers employed, **the program males who were employed earned significantly more per month than the no-program males who were employed (a mean of $1,816 vs. a mean of $1,310, with 53% vs. 8% earning $2,000 or more per month).**

Program females had significantly higher monthly earnings at age 27 than no-program females (a whole-group mean of $1,047 vs. a whole-group mean of $651, with 20% vs. 41% earning $0 per month, and 48% vs. 18% earning $1,000 or more per month).[26] Whereas program males

---

[26]As noted in Chapter 2, this comparison dropped from significant to noticeable ($p = .136$) when analyzed by analysis of covariance controlling for family configuration at study entry, family moves through age 15, and maternal employment at age 15, but it is also the case that the comparison did not include the 2 deceased females in the no-program group, who would probably have had $0 in monthly earnings.

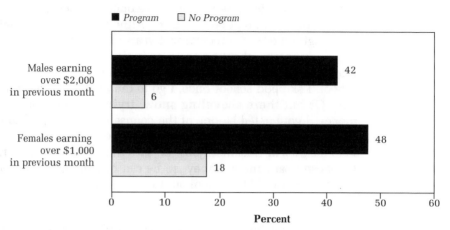

Figure 10

MONTHLY EARNINGS AT AGE 27,
BY PRESCHOOL EXPERIENCE AND GENDER

Note. Male comparison, $p = .035$, female comparison, $p = .046$; based on Mantel-Haenszel chi-square statistics. See Table 23 for details.

Use of Social Services

The findings for social services were based on several records searches and on the age-27 interview, as described in Chapter 2. As shown in Table 24, **significantly fewer members of the program group than of the no-program group had received social services sometime in the 10 years before the age-27 interview and records searches (59% vs. 80%).**[28] This finding is based on searches of the social services records, supplemented by the age-27 interview. The types of social services study participants received included mostly welfare assistance services, such as AFDC, food stamps, and General Assistance, plus, in a few cases, protective services, Medicaid, and public housing.[29] The program group averaged noticeably fewer months receiving welfare assistance than the no-program group did during the 10 years prior to the interview (18.2 vs. 26.3 months). During the 5 years before the age-27 interview and the records searches, the program group and no-program group did not noticeably differ regarding percentages who at some time received AFDC or food stamps. However, a nearly significantly smaller percentage of the program group than of the no-program group had received

---

[28]This finding includes data on 2 deceased no-program females. Before they died at ages 21 and 24, neither had ever been employed and both had consistently depended on welfare assistance, one on Aid to Families with Dependent Children (AFDC), the other on General Assistance.

[29]*Social services* do not include Supplemental Security Income disability payments.

Table 24

SOCIAL SERVICES THROUGH AGE 27, BY PRESCHOOL EXPERIENCE

Variable	Program Group	No-Program Group	p^a	Effect Size
Received any social services in previous 10 years[b]	59%	80%	**.010** (P)	0.44
Months on assistance in previous 10 years				
Mean	18.2	26.3	.137 (M)	0.27
0	55%	45%		
1–25	26%	24%		
26–120	19%	31%		
Types of assistance in previous 5 years				
AFDC	28%	26%	.858 (P)	0.00
Food stamps	29%	31%	.860 (P)	0.00
General Assistance	10%	23%	.061 (P)	0.30
Types of assistance at age-27 interview				
AFDC	8%	17%	.133 (P)	0.28
Food stamps	11%	20%	.194 (P)	0.25
General Assistance	2%	5%	.363 (P)	0.17
Receiving money from government at age-27 interview	15%	32%	**.039** (P)	0.40

Note. Program group $n = 58$, no-program group $n = 65$. Except for the variables noted "at age-27 interview," data sources were social services records found on 87 of the 123 study participants (including the 2 deceased females) combined with the age-27 interview on 55 of those with records who said that they had been on welfare or public assistance in the previous 10 years. On variables where the two sources differed, the larger amount or affirmative claim took precedence over the smaller amount or missing data. For variables noted "at age-27 interview," program group $n = 56$, no-program group $n = 61$; since data source is age-27 interview only, data do not include the 2 deceased females who consistently received social services before they died.

[a](P) indicates that the p-value is based on the Pearson chi-square statistic. (M) indicates that the p-value is based on the Mantel-Haenszel chi-square statistic for the truncated distributions.

[b]Includes AFDC, food stamps, General Assistance, protective services, Medicaid, and public housing.

NATALIE is someone who works at an established job but is also pursuing a dream: "I'm working in telemarketing and as a CRT [cathode-ray tube] operator for a distributor. I'm always into some kind of income—selling on the side. I'm also a musician. I sing and I'm in a group and direct the church choir. I'm also into fashion design. My main goal is being a musician and performing. I play drums, piano, and I also sing. I've formed a group in the past year. We've been singing in Michigan, Ohio. We're starting a demo cassette of gospel songs that we can send around to radio stations."

General Assistance sometime in the previous 5 years (10% vs. 23%). Although social services records provided no data on status at the time of the age-27 interview,

- **A significantly smaller percentage of the program group than of the no-program group reported currently receiving money from the government (15% vs. 32%).**

- Noticeably fewer members of the program group than of the no-program group reported currently receiving AFDC (8% vs. 17%).

- Noticeably fewer members of the program group than of the no-program group reported currently receiving food stamps (11% vs. 20%).

- The groups did not differ noticeably in their current receipt of General Assistance (which was limited to only 3% of all study participants).

Use of Social Services, by Gender

As shown in Table 25 and Figure 11, **significantly fewer program males than no-program males received social services sometime in the 10 years before the age-27 interview and social services records searches (52% vs. 77%).** Program males and no-program males did not noticeably differ in the number of months spent receiving public assistance in the previous 10 years, nor did they noticeably differ in the percentages receiving AFDC, food stamps, or General Assistance either sometime in the previous 5 years or at the time of the age-27 interview. There was, however, a noticeable difference in the percentages of males in the two groups receiving money from the government at the time of the age-27 interview.

Noticeably fewer program females than no-program females had received social services sometime in the previous 10 years (68% vs. 85%).[30] In those 10 years, program females, on average, spent nearly significantly fewer months receiving welfare assistance than did no-program females (32.0 vs. 50.7 months). Program females and no-program females did not differ noticeably in percentages receiving AFDC, food stamps, or General Assistance sometime in the previous 5 years. However, in the age-27 interview,[31]

- **Significantly fewer program females than no-program females said they were receiving money from the government (26% vs. 59%).**

---

[30]Findings for females include the 2 deceased no-program females who had received welfare assistance up to the times of their deaths at ages 21 and 24.

[31]Not included are the 2 deceased no-program females.

Table 25

SOCIAL SERVICES THROUGH AGE 27, BY PRESCHOOL EXPERIENCE AND GENDER

Variable	Program Group	No-Program Group	p^a	Effect Size
Males				
Received any social services in previous 10 years[b]	52%	77%	**.045** (P)	0.55
Months on assistance in previous 10 years				
Mean	7.8	10.1	.506 (M)	0.16
0	64%	59%		
1–13	21%	18%		
14–72	15%	23%		
Types of assistance in previous 5 years				
AFDC	12%	10%	.999 (P)	0.00
Food stamps	15%	23%	.580 (P)	0.20
General Assistance	12%	26%	.251 (P)	0.27
Types of assistance at age-27 interview				
AFDC	0%	3%	.372 (P)	0.22
Food stamps	3%	3%	.861 (P)	0.14
General Assistance	0%	3%	.372 (P)	0.22
Receiving money from government at age-27 interview	7%	16%	.250 (P)	0.28
Females				
Received any social services in previous 10 years[c]	68%	85%	.162 (P)	0.39
Months on assistance in previous 10 years				
Mean	32.0	50.7	.089 (M)	0.48
0	44%	23%		
1–43	32%	35%		
60–120	24%	42%		
Types of assistance in previous 5 years				
AFDC	48%	50%	.999 (P)	0.00
Food stamps	48%	42%	.899 (P)	0.03
General Assistance	8%	19%	.448 (P)	0.21
Types of welfare assistance at age-27 interview				
AFDC	17%	41%	.068 (P)	0.55
Food stamps	21%	50%	**.038** (P)	0.63
General Assistance	4%	9%	.499 (P)	0.20
Receiving money from government at age-27 interview	26%	59%	**.025** (P)	0.69

Note. Program males $n = 33$, no-program males $n = 39$; program females $n = 25$, no-program females $n = 26$. Except for the variables noted otherwise, data sources were social services records found on 87 of the 123 study participants (including the 2 deceased females) combined with the age-27 interview on 55 of those with records who said they had been on welfare or public assistance in the previous 10 years. On variables where the two sources differed, the larger amount or affirmative claim took precedence over the other. For variables noted "at age-27 interview," program males $n = 28$, no-program males $n = 34$; program females $n = 23$, no-program females $n = 22$; data source is age-27 interview only and thus excludes the 2 deceased females, persistent receivers of social services.

[a](P) indicates that the *p*-value is based on the Pearson chi-square statistic. (M) indicates that the *p*-value is based on the Mantel-Haenszel chi-square statistic for the truncated distributions.

[b]Included AFDC, food stamps, General Assistance, protective services, Medicaid, and public housing.

[c]See footnote b.

110

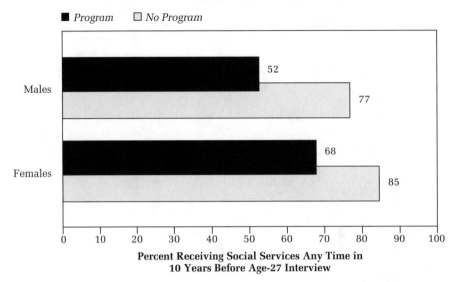

Figure 11

SOCIAL SERVICES RECEIVED IN PREVIOUS 10 YEARS,
BY PRESCHOOL EXPERIENCE AND GENDER

■ *Program*   □ *No Program*

Percent Receiving Social Services Any Time in
10 Years Before Age-27 Interview

Note. Male comparison, $p = .045$, female comparison, $p = .162$; based on Pearson chi-square statistic. See Table 25 for details.

- **Significantly fewer program females than no-program females reported currently receiving food stamps (21% vs. 50%).**

- **Nearly significantly fewer program females than no-program females reported currently receiving AFDC (17% vs. 41%).**

Overall, the pattern of findings presented in Tables 24 and 25 provides some evidence that the program group used social services less than the no-program group did. However, the finding of significant differences between the program group and the no-program group in use of social services in the 10 years before the age-27 interview and records searches is not consistently corroborated by findings of similar differences for numbers of months on assistance or types of assistance received. The age-27 interview *did* indicate that at that time, substantially fewer program females than no-program females were receiving government money, including AFDC and food stamps.

Home and Car Ownership at Age 27

As shown in Table 26, noticeably more program-group members than no-program-group members owned a car (71% vs. 59%), and **significantly more program-group members owned a second car (30% vs.**

ALEXANDER lives at home with his parents and three brothers. When he was 5 years old, his brother accidentally shot him in the stomach. The social services records describe him as "mentally slow" and as an addict who has frequent violent seizures and flies into rages that require restraint. Alexander has a history of alcohol abuse, which may have made him developmentally disabled or even brain damaged, but he says he does not abuse drugs. Records indicate that he has received welfare assistance and used protective services every month during the past 5 years. He has been hospitalized frequently and has never been employed.

Gaining material possessions is not the only reason to work; AGNES describes her motivation to help others and do something meaningful with her life: "I plan on going to college to become a registered nurse. I want to work with people that can't help themselves or that need help helping themselves. I'm taking some basic courses at [the community college], and they say that in about 2 years I can become a nurse. I try to help other people—like some friends getting high on crack, liquor, anything. I try to help them help themselves. If you get high on crack, after a while you have no other purpose in life except getting high on crack. And that's a waste of your life." Along with pursuing her nurse's training at the community college, Agnes is currently working and training to be a manager at a fast-food restaurant.

13%). The group difference for first-car ownership was 12 percentage points, as compared with 17 percentage points for second-car ownership, with both differences favoring the program group.

The two groups did not differ noticeably in the types of dwellings they lived in; of all study participants, 44% lived in houses, 5% lived in duplexes, 41% lived in apartments, and 10% lived in other types of dwellings. However, **significantly more of the program group than of the no-program group owned their own homes (36% vs. 13%, or almost three times as many).** When looked at by gender, as shown in Table 26 and Figure 12, **home ownership was significantly greater for program males than for no-program males (52% vs. 21%);** it was nearly significantly greater for program females than for no-program females (16% vs.

Table 26

HOME AND CAR OWNERSHIP AT AGE 27, BY PRESCHOOL EXPERIENCE

Variable	Program Group			No-Program Group			p^a	Effect Size
	n	Mean	%	n	Mean	%		
Own a car	56		71%	61		59%	.160 (P)	0.26
Own a second car	56		30%	61		13%	**.023** (P)	0.43
Dwelling type	52			58				
House			48%			41%	.853 (P)	0.17
Duplex			6%			5%		
Apartment			37%			45%		
Other			10%			9%		
Dwelling payment (all)	56			61				
Own home (mortgage or loan payment)			36%			13%	**.010** (P)	0.65
Rent			55%			74%		
Public subsidy			5%			2%		
Other			4%			12%		
Dwelling payment (males)	31			39				
Own home (mortgage or loan payment)			52%			21%	**.005** (P)	0.79
Rent			45%			67%		
Public subsidy			3%			3%		
Other			0%			10%		
Dwelling payment (females)	25			22				
Own home (mortgage or loan payment)			16%			0%	.105 (P)	0.76
Rent			68%			86%		
Public subsidy			8%			0%		
Other			8%			14%		
Monthly cost of dwelling	43	$358		43	$315			
Under $250			37%			37%	.292 (M)	0.23
$251–$500			37%			54%		
$501–$680			26%			9%		
Rooms in dwelling	49	6.7		54	6.6			
1–5			29%			37%	.877 (M)	0.03
6–8			61%			46%		
9–16			10%			17%		
Times moved	49	2.3		54	3.2			
0–1			45%			39%	.305 (M)	0.20
2–3			39%			35%		
4–30			16%			26%		

Note. Data source is the age-27 interview.

[a](P) indicates that the p-value is based on the Pearson chi-square statistic. (M) indicates that the p-value is based on the Mantel-Haenszel chi-square statistic for the truncated distributions.

0%). The program group and no-program group did not differ noticeably in monthly dwelling costs or in number of rooms in dwelling. The two groups also did not noticeably differ in frequency of moves from one dwelling to another.

Figure 12

HOME OWNERSHIP AT AGE 27,
BY PRESCHOOL EXPERIENCE AND GENDER

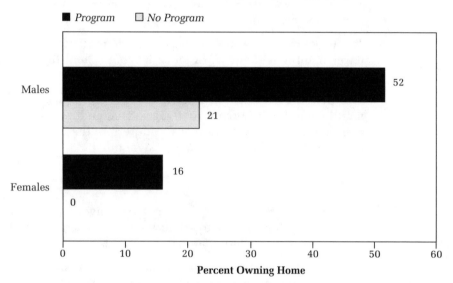

Note. Male comparison, $p = .005$, female comparison, $p = .105$; based on Pearson chi-square statistics. See Table 26 for details.

Talking about the frustrations of living on AFDC and being stuck with her children in a bad neighborhood, **KENRA** says: "The fact that I'm living on the South Side [of Ypsilanti] and that I'm on ADC—that's frustration. On ADC you can't get the things that you want to get, do the things that you want to do. On the South Side, you have friends that won't visit you because they're scared that they're going to be robbed or something like that." Kenra dropped out of high school in 11th grade; she enrolled in adult education but never completed it. Although she has never married, she has had five pregnancies, resulting in one abortion, two miscarriages, and two sons by different fathers. At age 27, she is collecting AFDC and food stamps and has been on welfare for 7 of the past 10 years.

Socioeconomic Characteristics at Age 19

The age-27 findings for earnings, employment, and social services extend the earlier findings of the age-19 study, listed in Table 27. **In the age-19 interview,**

- **Significantly more program-group members than no-program-group members said they were supporting themselves by their own and their spouse/partner's earnings (45% vs. 25%).**

- **Significantly more program-group members than no-program-group members said they were employed (50% vs. 32%).**

- **The program group, on average, reported spending significantly fewer months without work since leaving school than did the no-program group (4.9 vs. 10.3 months).**

- **The program group, on average, reported significantly more months employed during their age-19 calendar year (6.1 vs. 3.9 months)** and nearly significantly more months employed during their age-18 calendar year (2.5 vs. 1.5 months).

Social services records through ages 20–24 indicated that

- **The program group, on average, received significantly less money in annual welfare payments than the no-program group did ($633 vs. $1,509, which is less than half as much).**

- **Significantly fewer program-group members than no-program-group members received General Assistance (19% vs. 41%) or General Assistance and food stamps (17% vs. 38%).**

DAMON is an example of someone who not only wants material possessions but also has confidence that he can work and obtain them: "I definitely want to go forward. I work hard simply because there are things I feel I need. When I was coming up, my parents introduced me to the finer things. Times were tough, but my parents still shared the better things with me, so I guess I have that in my system. I don't see myself surviving in a scenario other than a nice place to live, nice car to drive, nice clothes to wear, well-maintained and groomed. This is just a stepping stone. I've traveled to the Caribbean, Puerto Rico. Eventually I hope to go further and be successful. I want all the finer things. They're not as far out of reach as one might imagine." At age 27, Damon is a carpet salesman with plans to own his own retail business.

Table 27

AGE-19 ASSESSMENT OF EMPLOYMENT, EARNINGS, AND SOCIAL
SERVICES, BY PRESCHOOL EXPERIENCE

Variable	Program Group	No-Program Group	p^a	Effect Size
Age-19 interview				
Self-supporting (own and spouse/partner's earnings)	45%	25%	**.040** (P)	0.41
Employment status at age-19 interview				
Employed	50%	32%	**.041** (P)	0.34
Unemployed, looking for work or not	50%	68%		
Months unemployed since leaving school				
Mean	4.9	10.3		
0	33%	18%	**.010** (M)	0.43
1–6	39%	26%		
7–12	15%	37%		
13–32	13%	19%		
Months employed, age-19 calendar year				
Mean	6.1	3.9		
0	23%	33%	**.020** (M)	0.32
1–6	26%	41%		
7–12	51%	26%		
Months employed, age-18 calendar year				
Mean	2.5	1.5		
0	53%	70%	.080 (M)	0.36
1–6	35%	22%		
7–12	12%	8%		
Earnings, age-19 calendar year				
Mean	$5,386	$4,347		
$0	21%	32%	.063 (M)	0.50
$100–$3,000	29%	34%		
$3,001–$31,000	50%	34%		
Receiving welfare assistance, age-19 interview	18%	32%	**.044** (P)	0.25
Social services records[b]				
Mean annual welfare payment (1981 dollars)	$633	$1,509	**.021** (t)	–
General Assistance	19%	41%	**.008** (P)	0.49
General Assistance and food stamps	17%	38%	**.011** (P)	0.47

Note. Program group n = 58, no-program group n = 63; unless otherwise noted, the data source is the age-19 interview.

[a](P) indicates that the p-value is based on the Pearson chi-square statistic. (M) indicates that the p-value is based on the Mantel-Haenszel chi-square statistic for the truncated distributions. (t) indicates that the p-value is based on the t test.

[b]Data source is September 1982, Michigan social services records, when all study participants were at least 20 years old.

A Final Thought on Economic Status

This chapter has provided considerable proof of significant but gradual change from poverty and welfare-dependence towards economic self-sufficiency based on earnings from legitimate employment. Together with the next chapter's evidence concerning family formation, the evidence of this chapter does not present a picture of a group's sudden transformation from poverty to the middle class. Despite the barriers of racial discrimination, the movement of blacks from poverty to the middle class seems to be a multigenerational process not totally unlike that faced by other ethnic groups. As this chapter and the next suggest, the preschool program experience seems to have contributed to and, for some, even hastened this multigenerational process.

VI Family Formation, Health, and Social Relations

At age 27, significantly[32] more program females than no-program females were married (40% vs. 8%). As compared with no-program females, program females averaged nearly significantly fewer out-of-wedlock births (1.0 vs. 1.7 out-of-wedlock births) and had a nearly significantly lower rate of abortions (4% vs. 23% ever had an abortion). At age 27, compared with no-program females, nearly significantly more program females were married and raising children (28% vs. 8%); only one-third as many program females were unmarried, cohabiting parents (4% vs. 13%), and substantially fewer were single parents (32% vs. 54%). Thus, as compared with no-program females, program females on average were raising about half as many children in single-parent homes. As for males, while equal percentages of program and no-program males were married, program-group husbands averaged significantly more years married than did no-program-group husbands (6.2 vs. 3.3 years).

The childrearing styles of the program group and the no-program group were similar in many ways. However, significantly more children of program-group parents than of no-program-group parents regularly used library cards (85% vs. 53%), and significantly fewer program-group parents than no-program-group parents said their children were turning out better than expected (28% vs. 55%), perhaps because the program-group parents had more-accurate expectations for their children in the first place.

Although program- and no-program groups did not differ significantly or nearly significantly in most measured aspects of health problems and health care, significantly more program-group than no-program-group members had been hospitalized in the 12 months prior to their age-27 interview (30% vs. 15%), possibly because of better financial access to health care. Nearly significantly more of the program-group than of the no-program-group reported usually or always wearing a seat belt (57% vs. 34%). In comparison with the no-program group, the program group also reported nearly significantly greater social ease and task persistence.

Inasmuch as the preschool program influenced participants' long-term performance and economic productivity, it is reasonable to expect that it might have affected other quality-of-life factors, such as family formation, health, and social relations. This chapter explores those areas of study participants' lives.

---

[32]This report describes a group difference as **significant** if it has a two-tailed probability of less than .05; as **nearly significant** if it has a two-tailed probability between .05 and .10; and as **noticeable** if it has a two-tailed probability between .10 and .25. Since the hypotheses of this study are clearly directional, readers who prefer one-tailed tests of significance may interpret "nearly significant" findings as significant.

Marital and Parental Status at Age 27

This section presents group comparisons on variables having to do with study participants' marital and parental status and pregnancy outcomes. Rather than considering whole-group comparisons, we look here at comparisons between program males and no-program males and comparisons between program females and no-program females. We make the comparisons on these variables in this way because marriage, parenthood, and pregnancy outcomes are so intimately bound up with gender. According to Table 28 and Figure 13, program males and no-program males did not differ noticeably in their marital status at age 27. About one fourth of them were married and living with their spouses; about one fourth were unmarried and living with girlfriends; and about half were single and not living with girlfriends (this includes 3% who were divorced). **Program-group husbands, on average, were married significantly longer than no-program-group husbands, in fact nearly twice as long (6.2 vs. 3.3 years).**

According to Table 28 and Figure 13, **program females differed significantly from no-program females in marital status at age 27, with five times as many program females married and living with their spouses (40% vs. 8%) and fewer program females unmarried and living with boyfriends (8% vs. 13%) or single and not cohabiting (52% vs. 79%).** On average, program-group wives had been married for about as many years as no-program-group wives.

Figure 13

MARITAL STATUS AT AGE 27,
BY PRESCHOOL EXPERIENCE AND GENDER

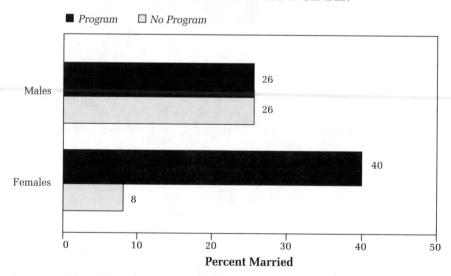

Note. Male comparison, $p = .856$, female comparison, $p = .036$; based on Pearson chi-square statistics. See Table 28 for details.

Table 28

MARITAL AND PARENTAL STATUS AT AGE 27,
BY PRESCHOOL EXPERIENCE AND GENDER

Variable	Program Group	No-Program Group	p^a	Effect Size
Males[b]				
Marital status				
Married cohabiting	26%	26%	.856 (P)	0.21
Unmarried cohabiting	26%	21%		
Single not cohabiting	48%	54%		
Years married (for currently married)[c]				
Mean	6.2	3.3		
Under 2	0%	50%	**.031** (M)	1.01
3–5	50%	20%		
6–8	40%	30%		
9–11	20%	0%		
Parents raising children	55%	56%		
Married cohabiting	3%	13%	.311 (P)	0.45
Unmarried cohabiting	16%	13%		
Single not cohabiting	10%	0%		
Marital status unknown	26%	31%		
Females[d]				
Marital status				
Married cohabiting	40%	8%	**.036** (P)	0.71
Unmarried cohabiting	8%	13%		
Single not cohabiting	52%	79%		
Years married (for currently married)[e]				
Mean	5.3	6.0		
Under 2	10%	0%	.999 (M)	0.00
3–5	40%	50%		
6–8	40%	50%		
9–11	10%	0%		
Parents raising children	64%	75%		
Married cohabiting	28%	8%	.088 (P)	0.63
Unmarried cohabiting	4%	13%		
Single not cohabiting	32%	54%		

Note. Program males $n = 31$; no-program males $n = 39$; program females $n = 25$; no-program females $n = 24$ unless otherwise indicated in footnotes; data source is age-27 interview.

[a](M) indicates that the p-value is based on the Mantel-Haenszel chi-square statistic on the truncated distributions. (P) indicates that the p-value is based on the Pearson chi-square statistic.

[b]*Single* includes 2 divorced program-group males (6%).

[c]Program males $n = 10$; no-program males $n = 10$.

[d]*Single* includes 2 divorced program-group females (8%) and 2 divorced (8%) and 1 widowed (4%) no-program-group females.

[e]Program females $n = 10$; no-program females $n = 2$.

Females' marital status at age 27 was strongly related to whether or not they graduated from high school or the equivalent and whether or not they had received welfare assistance in the past 5 years.

- Of the females who did not graduate from high school or the equivalent, only 5% (1 out of 20) were married at age 27, whereas of females who did graduate from high school or the equivalent, 38% (11 out of 29) were married at age 27 ($p = .008$, based on the Pearson chi-square statistic).

It appears that graduated females had the option of marriage, while this option was virtually closed off to females who dropped out of school. Another factor shaping females' marital options appears to be the policy of providing welfare assistance to females only if they are unmarried.

- Of females who had received AFDC sometime in the previous 5 years, only 8% (2 of 25) were married at age 27, whereas of females who had not received AFDC sometime in the previous 5 years, 42% (10 of 24) were married at age 27 ($p = .006$, based on the Pearson chi-square statistic).

- Of females who had received food stamps sometime in the previous 5 years, only 9% (2 of 23) were married at age 27, while of females who had not received food stamps sometime in the previous 5 years, 38% (10 of 26) were married at age 27 ($p = .016$, based on the Pearson chi-square statistic).

- None of the 7 females who had received General Assistance sometime in the previous 5 years were married at age 27; however, of the females who had not received General Assistance sometime in the previous 5 years, 29% (12 of 42) were married at age 27 ($p = .104$, based on the Pearson chi-square statistic).

Almost equal percentages of program males and no-program males—over half of each group—were raising children at age 27. Among those raising children, program males and no-program males did not differ noticeably in marital status. Also, among all program and no-program males, nearly equal percentages of the two groups reported they were making child-support payments (24% vs. 21%).

At age 27, program females differed nearly significantly from no-program females in parental status. In comparison with no-program females, more program females were nonparents (36% vs. 25%); more than three times as many were married cohabiting parents (28% vs. 8%); only one third as many were unmarried but cohabiting parents (4% vs. 13%); and considerably fewer were single parents (32% vs. 54%).

Earlier, at the time of the age-19 interview, 89% of the study participants were single and 69% were still living with their parents; 10% had married. One study participant had married at age 15 and divorced at age 18. The program group and no-program group did not noticeably differ on the variables related to marital status and living with parents.

Pregnancy Outcomes Through Age 27

As shown in Table 29, program males, on average, reported having about the same number of children as did no-program males (1.2 vs. 1.2 children), with fewer program males having 3–5 children (7% vs. 18%). Similarly, program males, on average, reported having about the same number of children born out of wedlock as did no-program males (0.8 vs. 0.9 children), with fewer program males having 3–5 children out of wedlock (3% vs. 13%). Overall, the male study participants reported that about two thirds of their children were born out of wedlock.

Program females and no-program females averaged almost the same number of pregnancies by age 27 (2.0 vs. 2.4 pregnancies); 28% of program females, as compared with 19% of no-program females, said they had never been pregnant. The two groups' average numbers of births were almost the same (1.8 vs. 2.0 births), but program females averaged nearly significantly fewer out-of-wedlock births than did no-program females (1.0 vs. 1.7 births), with the biggest difference in the percentages who reported 3–5 out-of-wedlock births (8% vs. 31%). **Only 57% of births to program females (26 of 46) were out-of-wedlock, as compared with 83% of births to no-program females (43 of 52); this was a significant difference ($p = .005$, 1 *df*, based on the Pearson chi-square statistic).**

Some out-of-wedlock births might be termed "premarital," because they occur just before the mother gets married and do not result in children being raised in single-parent families. In this study, 20% of program females and 4% of no-program females had premarital births but were married and cohabiting with their spouses at age 27. However, even if these premarital births are not counted as out of wedlock, it can still be said that nearly significantly fewer program females than no-program females had out-of-wedlock births (40% vs. 65%, $p = .069$).

Program females, on average, reported nearly significantly fewer abortions than no-program females did (0.04 vs. 0.23 abortions, with 4% vs. 23% having had an abortion). The program females and the no-program females did not differ noticeably in average number of miscarriages (0.16 vs. 0.33 miscarriages, with 12% vs. 33% reporting having had a miscarriage). These abortions and miscarriages help to explain why the group difference in numbers of pregnancies, especially teen pregnancies, was larger than the group difference in numbers of births.

As shown in Table 30, in the age-19 interview, program females reported nearly significantly fewer pregnancies than did no-program females (a mean of 0.6 vs. a mean of 1.2 pregnancies, with 48% vs. 67% being pregnant sometime during their teen years). Also at age 19, however, program females reported only slightly fewer births than did no-program females (a mean of 0.6 vs. a mean of 0.8 births, with 44% vs. 54% saying they were teen mothers). Similarly, program males reported only slightly fewer births than did no-program males (a mean of 0.30 vs. a mean of 0.38 births, with 18% vs. 26% saying they were teen fathers).

Table 29

PREGNANCY OUTCOMES BY AGE 27,
BY PRESCHOOL EXPERIENCE AND GENDER

Variable	Program Group	No-Program Group	p^a	Effect Size
Males				
Births				
Mean	1.2	1.2		
0	43%	41%	.901	0.03
1–2	52%	41%		
3–5	7%	18%		
Out-of-wedlock births				
Mean	0.8	0.9		
0	55%	54%	.712	0.09
1–2	42%	34%		
3–5	3%	13%		
Females				
Pregnancies				
Mean	2.0	2.4		
0	28%	19%	.492	0.41
1–2	40%	42%		
3–6	32%	38%		
Births				
Mean	1.8	2.0		
0	28%	17%	.414	0.23
1–2	44%	46%		
3–5	28%	37%		
Out-of-wedlock births[b]				
Mean	1.0	1.8		
0	40%	31%	.087	0.48
1–2	52%	38%		
3–5	8%	31%		
Abortions[c]				
Mean	0.04	0.23		
0	96%	77%	.058	0.57
1	4%	23%		
Miscarriages[d]				
Mean	0.16	0.33		
0	88%	67%	.243	0.36
1	8%	33%		
2	4%	0%		

Note. Program males $n = 33$; no-program males $n = 39$; program females $n = 25$, no-program females $n = 26$, unless otherwise indicated in footnotes; data source is the age-27 interview, an interview with the brother of 1 deceased study participant, and social services records of the other deceased study participant.

[a]All *p*-values are based on Mantel-Haenszel chi-square statistics on the truncated distributions.

[b]For 5 program and 1 no-program females, this includes premarital first births followed by marriage; thus these cases are listed as *married cohabiting* in Table 28.

[c]Ten no-program females who did not respond to this question were considered to have 0 incidents; program females $n = 25$, no-program females $n = 22$.

[d]Ten no-program females who did not respond to this question were considered to have 0 incidents; program females $n = 25$, no-program females $n = 18$.

Table 30

PREGNANCY OUTCOMES OVER TIME,
BY PRESCHOOL EXPERIENCE AND GENDER

Variable	Program Group	No-Program Group	p^a	Effect Size
Males				
Births by age 19[b]				
Mean	0.30	0.38		
0	82%	74%	.352	0.22
1	12%	13%		
2	6%	13%		
Age in years at birth of first child[c]				
Mean	21.0	20.8		
13–16	0%	9%	.865	0.05
17–19	35%	23%		
20–27	65%	68%		
Females[d]				
Pregnancies by age 19				
Mean	0.6	1.2		
0	52%	33%	.084	0.50
1	32%	38%		
2–5[e]	16%	29%		
Births by age 19				
Mean	0.6	0.8		
0	56%	46%	.399	0.24
1	28%	29%		
2–4	16%	25%		
Age in years at birth of first child[f]				
Mean	22.2	19.4		
14–16	17%	20%	.890	0.04
17–19	39%	45%		
20–27	44%	35%		

[a] All *p*-values are based on Mantel-Haenszel chi-square statistics on the truncated distributions.

[b] Program males $n = 33$; no-program males $n = 39$; data source is the age-19 interview.

[c] Program males $n = 17$; no-program males $n = 22$; data source is the age-27 interview. Data for this variable disagree with data for the *births by age 19* variable largely because of the smaller number of cases per group at the age-27 interview, as compared with the age-19 interview.

[d] For both pregnancies and births by age 19, program females $n = 25$; no-program females $n = 24$; data source is the age-19 interview.

[e] All females in this category had 2 children, except for one program female with 4 children and one with 5.

[f] Program females $n = 18$; no-program females $n = 20$; data source is the age-27 interview. Data for this variable disagree with data for *births by age 19* largely because of the smaller number of cases per group at the age-27 interview, as compared with the age-19 interview.

Table 30 indicates that program fathers did not differ noticeably from no-program fathers in average age at birth of the first child (21.0. vs 20.8 years of age). Likewise, program mothers did not differ noticeably from no-program mothers in average age at birth of the first child. If just those giving birth to their first child as teenagers are considered, we find also that program *teen* mothers were not noticeably different from no-program *teen* mothers in average age at birth of the first child (17.6 vs. 17.3 years of age).

Household Members at Age 27

As shown in Table 31, as compared with no-program-group members, program-group members, on average, reported at age 27 having in their households nearly significantly fewer adults (2.1 vs. 2.8 adults) and nearly significantly fewer children under age 18 (1.7 vs. 2.0 children).

Table 31

HOUSEHOLD MEMBERS AT AGE 27, BY PRESCHOOL EXPERIENCE

Variable	Program Group	No-Program Group	p^a	Effect Size
No. of adults in age-27 household				
Mean	2.1	2.8		
1	24%	23%	.083	0.34
2	52%	42%		
3–5	22%	28%		
6–14	2%	8%		
No. of children under age 18 in age-27 household				
Mean	1.7	2.0		
0	34%	26%	.088	0.34
1	24%	23%		
2–3	32%	32%		
4–9	10%	19%		

Note. Program group n = 48; no-program group n = 51; data source is the age-27 interview. These variables had no main effects of gender or of the interaction of gender and preschool experience.

[a] The *p*-values are based on Mantel-Haenszel chi-square statistics.

BRENDA* had this to say about having babies: "There was like six, well there was seven including me, that we all hung out with—all of them got babies, you know, before they even graduated. And one had hers on graduation day, you know, and I was the only one in the group that did not have one." When asked why not, she said, "That was not me. I didn't need no kid. Well, not back then, you know, plus I had no job." She said her parents "always say I am not going to get pregnant. I can't have no kids. I got to go ahead and go there and do this." And also, "Well, I guess it was just the way I was brought up. Because my mother, she was saved, you know. And by bringing me up in the church, I guess that was another way, you know. I wasn't really, like, going to parties and all that stuff, and smoking, and drinking. It wasn't my style. I tried it, but it was not me, so I just gave it up." Brenda, at age 27, recently gave birth to her first and only child, out of wedlock.

*Brief stories like this throughout this report describe real study participants but do not use their real names.

Childrearing Practices Through Age 27

Table 32 presents some of the group comparisons between 29 program-group parents raising children and 37 no-program-group parents raising children (those who responded to the childrearing questions in the age-27 interview). The following paragraphs also present additional childrearing findings, all of which concern variables on which the program and no-program parents reporting on childrearing did not differ noticeably. Of the children of reporting study participants, 94% were the respondents' biological children and 6% were their stepchildren; 42% were male and 58% were female; the children's average age was 7.5 years, with a standard deviation of 3.3.

Program-group parents did not noticeably differ from no-program-group parents regarding the broad categories of materials they made available to their children or regarding the availability of any specific materials. Of responding study participants, these percentages of parents reported that the following materials were available to their children at the time of the interview.

- 82%, crayons and other drawing materials
- 79%, age-appropriate children's books
- 78%, paper and writing materials

128

Table 32

CHILDREARING AT AGE 27, BY PRESCHOOL EXPERIENCE

Variable	Program Group			No-Program Group			p^a	Effect Size
	n	Mean	%	n	Mean	%		
Ever raised a child	56		55%	61		66%	.170 (P)	0.26
Having other children over to play	29	2.0		39	2.3			
Never (0)			0%			5%	.139 (M)	−0.36
Once in a while (1)			38%			15%		
Sometimes (2)			24%			21%		
Frequently (3)			38%			59%		
Child's use of library card	20	1.4		28	0.9			
Less than once a month (0)			15%			46%	**.033** (M)	0.64
1–3 times a month (1)			30%			21%		
Weekly or more (2)			55%			32%		
Child attended a preschool program	25		60%	34		74%	.272 (P)	0.29
Did this program provide child care?	16		50%	24		71%	.182 (P)	0.42
Child's current academic progress	24	1.2		28	1.3			
Below average (0)			8%			7%	.637 (M)	−0.13
Average (1)			63%			57%		
Above average (2)			29%			36%		
Child performing up to academic ability	23		39%	29		59%	.370 (P)	0.39
Child's behavior in school	24	1.5		28	1.7			
Never a problem (2)			46%			71%	.140 (M)	−0.41
Occasionally a problem (1)			54%			25%		
Constantly a problem (0)			0%			4%		
Child is turning out:	32	1.2		42	1.5			
Worse than expected (0)			13%			2%	**.010** (M)	0.62
As expected (1)			59%			43%		
Better than expected (2)			28%			55%		

Note. Program group n = 29; no-program group n = 37, except as noted; data source is age-27 interview. Numbers in parentheses indicate scores assigned to categories of the variable.

[a](M) indicates that the p-value is based on the Mantel-Haenszel chi-square statistic. (P) indicates that the p-value is based on the Pearson chi-square statistic.

- 75%, a dictionary

- 73%, children's records or cassettes

- 70%, craft materials

- 64%, musical instruments

- 51%, an encyclopedia

- 49%, a computer

- 6%, blocks or other educational toys

Most of the materials appeared to be readily available. Of parents responding to the childrearing questions, it seems that nearly two thirds provided their children with musical instruments; about half, with encyclopedias; and about half, with computers. It is surprising that only 6% reported the availability of blocks or other educational toys, but this may be because the children's average age was 7.5 years, which is beyond preschool age.

Program-group parents did not noticeably differ from no-program-group parents in the broad categories of activities or in any specific activities they engaged in with their children before age 7. Of study participants raising children, these percentages reported sometimes or frequently engaging in the following activities with their children before age 7:

- 94% ate meals together.

- 92% taught their children simple learning skills, such as counting, writing the child's name, or reciting the alphabet.

- 83% taught their children active skills, such as riding a bike, cooking, or sports.

- 80% discussed with their children the television programs that they watched together.

CATHY, who never married but at ages 21, 26, and 29 gave birth to three children, identifies a different father for each of the children. At the birth of her last child, she told a social worker that the father could have been any one of "20 or 30 different men." Having dropped out of high school at age 18, Cathy reports that she received public assistance during 84 of the 120 months previous to the age-27 interview. She once wrote the following note to one of her children's fathers: "Do you want your son for the summer? If not, I'll give him to anyone, even if it has to be the state. . . . I'm tired of him and I need some time away from him before I hurt him." She sent all three of her children away that summer; the note continued, "Sometimes I wish they were never born. . . . I just need some time for myself."

BONITA, who at age 27 is a teacher of second- and third-graders, says this about her students and the children she plans to have: "First, I want them to know who they are, how our people got over here, and to understand that black people are definitely treated differently. But I want them to have some self-respect, and I don't want them to take whatever the teacher says for granted. I want them to research things and know for themselves whether it's right or wrong, to challenge their teachers. I want them to be involved at a very young age and to be educated about their people."

On the importance of supporting education in the next generation, **RHONDA,** now a registered nurse, says: "I want to see my 6-year-old child having a happy and beneficial upcoming. I want her to live a happy life—the happiness and joy and education that I didn't have. I sit down and study with her. I read to her. We play games, and I think I'm giving her more now that I didn't have."

- 70% read books to their children.
- 38% went to museums or libraries with their children.

As shown in Table 32, significantly more children of program-group parents than of no-program-group parents regularly used library cards (85% vs. 53%). This difference reflects to some extent the program group's higher level of schooling, since the Pearson product-moment correlation between children's library card usage and their parents' highest year of schooling was .218 ($df = 47$, $p = .068$). However, the program group's children did not otherwise differ noticeably from the no-program group's children in reading habits (reading matter, frequency), nor did the two groups of parents. It is interesting to note that parents reported that their own daily reading emphasized newspapers, whereas children's daily reading emphasized books:

- 57% of the adult study participants and 39% of their children read the newspaper daily.
- 21% of the adult study participants and 33% of their children read magazines daily.

> **TOM** thinks that early childhood education has been important for his own children, aged 8 and 3. He keeps many educational materials in the house. He reads to his older daughter and says they visit museums and libraries sometimes. His daughter went to a day care program when she was 3–4 years old. "This program helped her do better in school. It taught her how to get along with other kids. She's reading. She does very well academically now, except that she wants to play instead of pay attention. That's her problem, but she knows it. I think she understands how important school is." Tom, a sergeant and section chief in the military, is married, has two children, and owns his own home.

- 22% of the adult study participants and 65% of their children read books daily.

Slightly fewer program-group than no-program-group parents had their children attend preschool programs (60% vs. 74%); this group difference reflected a similar group difference in those who said their children's preschool programs served as child care that permitted someone to be employed or attend school (50% vs. 71%). Overall, 84% of study participants said the preschool programs helped their children to do better in school.

A total of 53 study participants reported that their children were attending school. Program-group parents did not differ noticeably from no-program-group parents in their estimation of their children's current academic progress. Overall, 33% considered their children's academic progress as above average, 60% considered it average, and 8% considered it below average. Similarly, the program group did not differ noticeably from the no-program group in the percentages expecting their children to attend college—47% of the study participants had such hopes. The program parents did not noticeably differ from the no-program parents in how often they initiated talking with teachers about their children's progress. About two-thirds as many program parents as no-program parents considered their children to be performing up to their academic ability (39% vs. 59%). Noticeably more program parents than no-program parents saw their children's school behavior as occasionally a problem (54% vs. 25%), and **significantly fewer program parents than no-program parents said their children were turning out better than they (the parents) had expected them to (28% vs. 55%).** These group differences may signify that there are more behavior and academic problems among the children of program parents than among the children of no-program parents, or they may signify that program parents hold more-realistic social and scholastic expectations for their children.

On being a reverse role model for others—showing them what *not* to do by his bad example—**HENRY** says: "I would say I'm a big influence on my brother's life today, for the simple fact that he sees what I've been through in my life. And he's taking heed, because he's not following in my footsteps. He sees the mistakes that can lead him off the path, and it's taking him towards success. It's keeping him out of prison and keeping his head together. My little sister—the same. They listen to me just from my experience in life." Henry dropped out of high school in 11th grade and later earned a GED certificate while in prison; he wants to go back to school and earn a college business degree. So far he has spent 8 years in prison for crimes, including assault and armed robbery.

Family Relations

Both in the age-27 findings and in the age-19 findings, the program group and the no-program group did not differ noticeably in their estimates of how well they were getting along with their families, in their estimates of how their families felt they were doing, or in their estimates of whether they were turning out as their families expected. At age 15, the program group and the no-program group did not differ noticeably in their views of their parents' parenting skills; at the same time, parents' views of their own parenting skills were about the same for both groups.

Social Relations and Community Involvement

Findings from both the age-27 interview and the age-19 interview indicated that the program group and the no-program group did not noticeably differ in the broad categories of persons or in any specific persons they identified as "giving them a hassle." Interviewers had listed the following types of persons: work supervisors, coworkers, social or welfare workers, teachers, police or courts, people at church, friends, lawyers, collection agencies, storekeepers, family members, doctors or health care workers, neighbors, and others (in the age-27 interview, spouses and roommates were also listed).

At age 27, the program group and the no-program group did not noticeably differ on any measured aspect of community involvement. Of all the study participants at age 27,

- 27% belonged to a church (although 60% considered religion very important).

About discovering religion in his life while in prison, **JIM** says: "I am a Muslim. The Islamic religion has taught me a lot about being a strong individual. It teaches the individual to seek for knowledge and have a peaceful mind, and what you can do to better your life. I am supposed not to be a coward but to avoid confrontation and be humble." Jim dropped out of school after ninth grade and has spent 6 years in prison.

CARL, who works two jobs and holds an accounting degree, says he was saved about 6 months ago and wants to establish himself in the church. He says he wants to bring back churches and institutions on the South Side of Ypsilanti and to provide role models in the home. In this way, he believes, he can put something back into the community.

The mother of **MARLENE** talks about the importance of religion and discipline in her daughter's upbringing: "The best thing, I think, to make a good parent is to sit down and tell your child the most important things about life, and what to do, and how to do it. The first important thing I think a child should be told is to go to Sunday school and learn the truth about the church and the Lord. And then to obey their parents and to obey older people; you know, don't be talking back at older people. A bad parent don't care about what the child do."

FRANK, in the Marines, says that one of his 5-year goals is to be licensed as an Apostolic Faith minister and to do evangelical work. He says: "I have the love of God in me. I don't want to sound like a religious fanatic, but that's my life. I choose to live a straight and narrow path. I really like being in the church, where I get some joy and peace and inspiration to continue to go on day after day. Many times when things come up against me, I could have gone back to my old way of living. But when my family and people in the church see my stand and my firmness during suffering, it's an example to them. I'm solid. I want to be a light unto others. I'm seeking to be a leader."

- 65% belonged to no organizations.
- 62% were registered to vote.
- 39% had voted in the last presidential election.
- 19% had voted in the last state or local election.
- 13% had attended a school board or city council meeting.
- 29% did volunteer work.

Church attendance at age 15 was a good predictor of church membership at age 27: Of those who attended church regularly at age 15, 67% (14 of 21) belonged to a church at age 27, whereas of those who did not attend church regularly at age 15, 73% (51 of 70) did not belong to a church at age 27. Some study participants were active members of churches. A few of them sang in the choir, worked with youth groups, or taught Sunday school. One male served as deacon in his church, another played the bass guitar, and still another played the organ.

Health

As shown in Table 33, the program group and the no-program group did not differ noticeably in most measured aspects of health problems and health care. Of all the study participants at age 27,

- 77% had a routine physical examination annually.
- 68% had made a nonroutine health care visit in the previous 6 months.
- 57% had spent no days sick in bed in the previous 12 months.
- 37% had been treated for health problems in the previous 5 years.

At age 19, 11% of the study participants had reported having had health problems, and 44% had reported visiting a doctor in the previous 12 months.

Significantly more program-group than no-program-group members had been hospitalized in the 12 months prior to the age-27 interview (30% vs. 15%). Hospitalization involves both recognizing a health problem and having the means to pay for treatment. Since the program group and no-program group were much alike on other measures of health care but did differ significantly on current monthly earnings and ownership of a home and second car, the program-group's higher rate of hospitalization may be due to more of them having financial access to health care, possibly through employer-provided insurance.[33]

---

[33]Viewed in retrospect, it is unfortunate that data were not collected at age 27 on study participants' health insurance or other employee benefits.

Table 33

HEALTH AT AGE 27, BY PRESCHOOL EXPERIENCE

Variable	Program Group	No-Program Group	p^{a}	Effect Size
Routine health examinations				
Mean	1.6	1.6		
Hardly ever (0)	18%	13%	.535 (M)	0.11
Every 2–5 years (1)	7%	8%		
Annually (2)	75%	78%		
Months since last nonroutine health care visit				
1–6	71%	66%	.402 (M)	0.15
7–12	15%	15%		
13 or more	9%	10%		
Don't remember	5%	10%		
Days sick in bed in previous 12 months				
0	55%	59%	.594 (M)	0.10
1–2	25%	16%		
3–10	18%	15%		
11 or more	2%	10%		
Hospitalized in previous 12 months	30%	15%	**.043** (P)	0.38
Health problems treated in previous 5 years	36%	38%	.823 (P)	0.04
Smoke cigarettes	45%	56%	.231 (P)	0.22
Drink alcoholic beverages				
Mean	0.74	0.98		
Never (0)	44%	36%	.141 (M)	0.27
Once in a while (1)	40%	38%		
Several times a week (2)	14%	18%		
Daily (3)	2%	8%		
Wear a seat belt				
Mean	1.4	1.1		
Never (0)	17%	21%	.052 (M)	0.37
Sometimes (1)	26%	44%		
Usually or always (2)	57%	34%		

Note. Program group n = 55 to 56, no-program group n = 60 to 61; data source is the age-27 interview. Numbers in parentheses indicate scores assigned to categories of the variable.

[a](M) indicates that the p-value is based on the Mantel-Haenszel chi-square statistic on the truncated distributions. (P) indicates that the p-value is based on the Pearson chi-square statistic.

Nearly significantly more program-group members than no-program-group members said they usually or always wore a seat belt (57% vs. 34%); this could be evidence of a greater sense of social responsibility (as was also evidenced by their lower arrest rates). Noticeably fewer in the program group than in the no-program group smoked cigarettes, and the program group also drank alcoholic beverages noticeably less frequently.

Ease of Actions and Self-Image Over Time

Table 34 presents findings concerning how study participants at age 27 rated the ease with which they engaged in various actions. Although there was not a noticeable difference between the program and no-program groups on the ease of actions total scale, the two groups differed nearly significantly on the task persistence and social ease subscales.

- Nearly significantly more of the program group than of the no-program group said they found it very easy to persist at tasks. On the subscale's specific items, **significantly more of the program group than of the no-program group said they found it very easy to work (or study) hard all day (47% vs. 33%);** noticeably more said they found it very easy to keep a job (or stay in school). These findings are consistent with the finding about the program group's significantly higher monthly earnings at age 27, as reported in Chapter 5.

- Nearly significantly more of the program group than of the no-program group said they experienced ease in social relations. On the social ease subscale's specific items, **significantly more of the program group than of the no-program group said they found it very easy to feel close to family and friends (66% vs. 48%).** These findings are consistent with the findings on marital status and stability reported earlier in this chapter.

On another scale item, noticeably more of the program group than of the no-program group said they found it very easy to try out new experiences.

In earlier assessments, the program group and the no-program group did not differ noticeably on any measure of attitudes about self—at age 19 on self-esteem (Rosenberg, 1965) or at age 15 on perceived educational ability, self-confidence, locus of control, work ethic, or "the person you want to be" (Bachman, O'Malley, & Johnston, 1978).

Goals and Plans for the Next 5 Years

In their goals and plans for the next 5 years, the program group and the no-program group differed significantly on only one item. **Significantly**

Table 34

EASE OF ACTIONS AT AGE 27, BY PRESCHOOL EXPERIENCE

Variable	Program Group			Program Group			p^a	Effect Size
	Mean	(SD)	%	Mean	(SD)	%		
Task persistence: **It is very easy to**								
Keep a job (or stay in school)			69%			49%	.171 (M)	0.25
Work (or study) hard all day			47%			33%	**.043** (M)	0.38
Do well at work (or school) task			64%			57%	.759 (M)	0.06
Follow through on plans			36%			31%	.286 (M)	0.20
Keep working on a problem			38%			30%	.474 (M)	0.13
Task persistence total (possible 5–20 points)	16.6	(2.5)		15.7	(2.8)		.067 (t)	0.34
Social ease: **It is very easy to**								
Get along with people at work (or school)			66%			56%	.614 (M)	0.09
Feel close to family and friends			66%			48%	**.031** (M)	0.41
Help other people			58%			48%	.365 (M)	0.17
Social ease total (possible 3–12 points)	10.5	(1.7)		10.0	(1.7)		.096 (M)	0.13
Others: It is very easy to								
Learn new skills			34%			30%	.288 (M)	0.20
Do well in educational activities			20%			13%	.637 (M)	0.09
Try out new experiences			21%			34%	.143 (M)	0.27
Do what you know is right			55%			49%	.983 (M)	0.01
Ease of actions total (possible 12–48 points)	38.5	(6.5)		37.6	(5.7)		.438 (t)	0.14

Note. Program group $n = 55$, no-program group $n = 61$; data source is the age-27 interview. Each item was scored 1 = not easy, 2 = sort of easy, 3 = easy, 4 = very easy; the item percentages presented are for 4 = very easy. *Task persistence total* summarizes the 5 items above it; *social ease total* summarizes the 3 items above it; *ease of actions total* summarizes the 12-item scale.

[a](M) indicates that the *p*-value is based on the Mantel-Haenszel chi-square statistic. (t) indicates that the *p*-value is based on the *t* test.

more of the program than of the no-program group expressed a goal of travel, adventure, or changing residence in the next 5 years (16% vs. 5%, $p = .046$ by the Pearson chi-square statistic). Perhaps this difference occurred because the program group had higher monthly earnings and

ISAAC, working at an automobile plant, says that his goals include raising his son right. To accomplish his goals, he works every day, stays out of trouble, and lives right. He lists learning something new every day and watching his child grow up as positive aspects of his life.

HANNAH'S goals are to be financially set with a house and a car, to take care of herself, and to "raise my kids the way they should be raised." To accomplish these goals, she is going to school and working at a department store.

KEVIN, a housekeeper in a hospital, was on welfare for 7 out of the previous 10 years. He says that he has completed 2 years of community college in welding and hopes to get a bachelor's degree in the next couple of years.

LEROY identifies a 5-year goal of working for a private company or the government. Although his father is a university professor in another state, Leroy has been a janitor and now works in a grocery store for $4.25 an hour and part-time in a clothing store for $4.50 an hour. He hopes to become a store manager or owner.

MATTHEW has been frustrated watching Ypsilanti go down, watching fellow black people and friends who are unwilling to take low-paying jobs but want to drive luxury cars. Since they can't find jobs, he says, they waste their lives selling and using drugs and selling their bodies.

MARIA feels frustrated about being on AFDC, unable to pay her bills, and unable to feed and clothe her children. She wants to get completely off AFDC, have a home, and marry a man who will help with the children.

OSCAR knows about the drug and crime problems on the South Side of Ypsilanti but says that he had a wonderful mother and father, who taught him what was right, along with a large extended family. He is glad that the principal at Perry Elementary School was a firm disciplinarian who kept drugs and guns out of the school.

IRENE's mother describes how they lived on the South Side of Ypsilanti for 12 years, then moved away: "When I lived there, it was a nice neighborhood. There were nice children, and the parents were nice to me. They saw me going to church every Sunday, and so they respected me. And it was nice, it was nice over there, but now there has been a change—-the way I see how they tore the place up. They used to fix the houses real nice, and now the parents, I guess, let the children tear the houses up. The parents are just raising their children wrong. Most of the time, that's what it is. I see that the parents don't know what the children are doing when they are out in the street."

On the subject of prejudice, **PETER,** who has been in the military and is now a stock handler, says: "From time to time you have racial slurs. Those people are sick. They don't understand that we're all created equally. You see it all around the world. I've seen it in other countries. I've seen it regardless of who you are, how much money you have, you cannot enter a certain building. It still goes on to this day. Maybe one day the world will walk together."

could better afford to travel. Of the 115 respondents, the following percentages identified these specific **goals:**

- 30% wanted to own their own homes.
- 28% wanted to continue their educations.
- 22% wanted to get married.
- 14% wanted to achieve work success.
- 13% wanted to own cars or other major items.
- 12% wanted to have children.
- 10% wanted to achieve economic stability.
- 10% wanted to travel or change residence.
- 5% wanted to pursue their interests.
- 6% wanted to be good parents.

The following percentages identified these specific **plans,** or means, for achieving their goals:

- 46%, their current job
- 25%, saving money
- 18%, education or training
- 7%, improving their skills
- 7%, raising children
- 7%, setting goals
- 6%, considering their options
- 4%, looking for work
- 11%, doing nothing to achieve their goals

Positive and Negative Aspects of Lives

In identifying positive and negative aspects of their lives, the program group and the no-program group differed significantly on only one item. **Significantly more of the program group than of the no-program group identified work-related problems (23% vs. 7%, p = .012 by the Pearson chi-square statistic),** perhaps because the program group had a noticeably higher employment rate and jobs with significantly higher earnings, suggesting greater job responsibility. Of the 116 respondents, the following percentages identified these aspects of their lives as **positive:**

- 33%, their own children or families
- 28%, their jobs
- 15%, self-satisfaction
- 12%, their relationships with parents or siblings
- 9%, their marriages or spouses
- 9%, friends or a boyfriend or girlfriend
- 9%, religion or church
- 5%, independence
- 4%, staying out of trouble or off drugs or alcohol

The following percentages identified these aspects of their lives as **negative,** i.e., causing difficulty or frustration:

- 27%, financial problems
- 15%, work-related problems
- 12%, their own or the community's drug abuse
- 8%, raising children
- 7%, the neighborhood
- 6%, their spouses
- 5%, race-related problems
- 4%, current responsibilities
- 4%, personal or psychological problems
- 3%, unemployment or lack of a steady job

The most striking findings in this chapter are the two fifths of program females, as opposed to only a couple of no-program females, who were married at age 27 and the consequent group differences in the numbers of children being raised by single mothers. These findings suggest that the preschool program affected society, and in particular the early childhood experiences of the next generation, in a very basic way. In fact, *all* of the findings in Chapters 3–6 are important to society. One measure of their importance is their economic value, which is assessed in the next chapter.

VII Cost-Benefit Analysis

W. Steven Barnett*

From the perspective of human capital theory (e.g., Becker, 1964, 1981), the High/Scope Perry Preschool Project involved making an investment in the lives of young children who were predicted to have relatively poor educational outcomes. This investment in human capital can be evaluated by applying cost-benefit analysis to the preschool program and its consequences, both immediate and long-term. The goal of the cost-benefit analysis is to obtain answers to two questions: First, was the preschool program a sound investment for the society that sponsored it? Second, who incurred the costs and who realized benefits? More specifically, what did the program return to both those who invested in it (taxpayers) and those who participated in it?

Cost-benefit analysis has been a part of the High/Scope Perry Preschool Project for many years. Extensive cost-benefit analyses were conducted using data from the age-10 follow-up (Weber et al., 1978) and the age-19 follow-up (Berrueta-Clement et al., 1984). The cost-benefit analysis presented in this chapter has built directly on the cost-benefit analysis conducted with the age-19 data set. This newest analysis has extended to age 27 the period for which we can base cost/benefit estimates on actual observations. When no new data were available, this analysis incorporated estimates from the age-19 study, and when new data were available, this analysis provided new estimates.

The new data used here have at last eliminated the need to rely on any projections beyond the observed data to establish the preschool program's profitability. As this chapter will show, the preschool program is found to have been a sound investment, based on data through age 27 alone. However, to provide a complete estimate of costs and benefits over the participants' lifetimes, we also make projections beyond age 27.

Methodology

The process of conducting the cost-benefit analysis of the preschool program can be described as a series of steps that are standard procedures for the conduct of any cost-benefit analysis (Thompson, 1980). The steps are first listed, and then each is briefly described:

1. Define the scope of the analysis.

2. Obtain estimates of program effects.

3. Estimate the monetary value of costs and benefits.

4. Calculate present value and assess profitability.

5. Describe the distribution of costs and benefits.

6. Conduct sensitivity analyses.

---

*W. Steven Barnett, former Research Associate at High/Scope Educational Research Foundation, is Associate Professor of Economics and Policy in the Graduate School of Education and Senior Research Fellow at the Eagleton Institute of Politics, Rutgers—The State University of New Jersey.

Details of the estimation of the monetary value of costs and benefits for the program are described in later sections of this chapter and in a technical report that provides complete documentation for the analysis (Barnett, 1993).

1. Define the Scope of the Analysis

Cost-benefit analysis is always comparative. The first step in planning an analysis is to define the alternatives to be compared and identify the limits of the comparison. The design of the study determines the basic comparison: participation in the preschool program for one or two school years versus nonparticipation, with both groups entering kindergarten at age 5.

Although it would have been desirable to compare nonparticipation with one school year of participation and then with two school years of participation, the number of children experiencing only a single year of the program was too small ($n = 13$) to provide an adequate comparison. For the cost-benefit analysis, the 1-year and 2-year groups are pooled, and the resulting estimates of costs and benefits are essentially weighted averages of 1-year and 2-year preschool-program experiences. Because a considerably larger number ($n = 45$) had two school years of the preschool program, the weighted average is dominated by the 2-year results.

The cost-benefit analysis was conducted from the perspective of society as a whole. Ideally, the analysis should include every significant consequence of the preschool program, regardless of who received the benefit or bore the cost and regardless of whether the consequence was intended or unintended. However, as in every cost-benefit analysis, some potential effects could not be estimated, and some estimated effects could not be valued. These difficulties are discussed below, but as will be shown, they do not pose serious threats to the overall validity of the analysis.

2. Estimate Program Effects

Every cost-benefit analysis builds on an underlying evaluation of program effects and is only as strong as the underlying evaluation. The High/Scope Perry Preschool Project—because of its experimental design, length of follow-up, and wide range of potential outcomes examined—provides an unusually strong basis for estimating the preschool program's effects. For the cost-benefit analysis, all underlying effects were estimated as mean differences between the program and no-program groups for males and females. These separate estimates for males and females were then averaged together to produce an estimate for a population that was 50% male and 50% female. This procedure precluded the incidental imbalance in the gender composition of the sample from biasing the estimates.

Despite the Perry study's strengths, it has one limitation that is common to small-scale experimental studies. The study does not provide a complete basis for estimating effects on persons not in the sample—

indirect effects. Although certain kinds of effects on others can be estimated based on the effects on study participants, for some other kinds of indirect effects, such estimation is not possible. At least two general types of effects that could not be measured here might be important—*effects on siblings* and *global effects.*

Because detailed data on siblings were not collected, effects on brothers and sisters of the children in the preschool-program group cannot be estimated.[34] Such indirect effects are likely to be small in comparison with direct effects of the program, but they might not be negligible. Parents' interactions with all their children could have been altered by the home visits or as a result of one child's program participation. For example, the preschooler's requests for more parental reading might have led to a parent reading more not only to the preschooler but to the other children in the family as well. Also, having one child attend a preschool program might have allowed parents to redirect resources (including their own time) towards other children in the family, thereby causing indirect effects. It is also possible that a child who attended the preschool program might have affected siblings through interactions or as a role model.

Global effects are those that result from changing an entire environment. These can be estimated only in large-scale studies. For example, if the preschool program improved the school performance and behavior of large numbers of children, this effect might change the entire social climate of a school, boosting the performance of teachers and students, as well as enhancing their quality of life. A study like the Perry study affects so few children that effects on the social climate of their school would probably be too small to observe. The situation might have been quite different had all children in the Perry School neighborhood attended the preschool program.

3. Estimate Monetary Value

The heart of a cost-benefit analysis is the estimation of the monetary value of program effects. This step makes it possible to put all program consequences on an equal footing, so program costs, various positive outcomes, and any negative outcomes can be aggregated to provide a single measure of the program's impact on society and on particular subgroups of society (taxpayers, crime victims, and participants, in this case). Inevitably, this task is only partially accomplished. Although it is easy to assign monetary values to program costs, it is more difficult to accurately estimate the monetary value of program benefits. Fortunately, in the case of the Perry study, it was possible to produce reasonable estimates of monetary value for most of the preschool program's important effects.

---

[34]The few cases in which siblings were preschool program participants are exceptions that do not provide a firm basis for estimating indirect effects on siblings.

In this cost-benefit analysis, monetary values were estimated in eight categories:

1. Program costs

2. Child care provided by the program

3. Elementary and secondary education

4. Adult secondary education

5. Postsecondary education

6. Employment-related compensation

7. Delinquency and crime

8. Public welfare assistance

Although the categories just listed include most of the areas in which we found statistically significant differences favoring the program group over the no-program group, it was not possible to estimate the monetary value of all the effects identified in each category. Estimation of costs and benefits is discussed in greater detail later in this chapter, where each cost and benefit is discussed separately.

4. Calculate Present Value and Assess Profitability

When a cost-benefit analysis deals with costs and benefits that span more than a single year, adjustments must be made to dollar amounts from different years to make them comparable. One part of the adjustment removes the effects of inflation by translating nominal dollars from each year into dollars of equal purchasing power, or *real dollars.* The other part of the adjustment takes into account the time value of money by calculating the *present value* of real dollars from each year.

For all the years in which data were collected (through age 27), a real-dollar cost or benefit in any given year takes into account the effects of inflation over time (i.e., it takes into account that a dollar in 1965, near the beginning of the project, would purchase considerably more than a dollar in 1990). We have adjusted all nominal dollars for costs or benefits through age 27 to allow for inflation. This was done by using a price deflator to convert nominal dollars from various years into real dollars (dollars having the same purchasing power) in a single year. For ease of reference, we chose to convert all costs and benefits to 1992 dollars.

The second part of the adjustment, calculation of present value, takes into account the time value of money, (i.e., that even in the absence of inflation, $1,000 in hand is more valuable that $1,000 received next year, or in 25 years, because $1,000 in hand can be used now—to invest in a profitable enterprise or to purchase consumer goods or services for immediate enjoyment). The time value of money is specified by the *discount rate,* which can be thought of as the annual interest rate at which dollars from a given year can be fairly traded for dollars in another year. When dollars have already been adjusted for inflation, to calculate their present value, we use a *real discount rate,* constant across all years (as opposed to a nominal, or money, rate, which includes an inflation factor that varies from year to year).

The real discount rate is used to calculate the present dollar value of all costs and benefits. Present value of a cost or benefit in this analysis indicates the value of real dollars at study entry (age 3 or 4, depending on the wave).[35] The calculation of present value tends to reduce the real dollars of benefits more than it reduces the real dollars of costs, because benefits tend to come later than costs. For example, if the discount rate is 3%, a benefit's present value (for age-3 study entry) would be calculated by dividing the real-dollar benefit by 1.03 if the benefit occurred at age 4, by 1.03 squared (1.06) if it occurred at age 5, by 1.03 cubed (1.09) if it occurred at age 6, and by 1.03 to the 24th power (1.97) if it occurred at age 27. In this study, with a 3% discount rate, the present value of a real dollar of benefits occurring at age 27—that is, its actual worth when a 3-year-old entered the program—is only about 51 cents; the present value of a real dollar of benefits at age 65 is only 16 cents.

After present value has been calculated for each year, the present values of all costs and benefits across the years are summed together to yield net present value. If net present value is positive, then the program makes a positive economic contribution to society and has the potential of being a sound public investment.[36]

5. Describe the Distribution

Policies and programs vary in their distributional consequences—in who specifically gains and who specifically loses—as well as in their profitability for society as a whole. Although the net present value of a program can be the same regardless of whether it benefits everyone generally, benefits mainly low-income families, or benefits mainly high-

---

[35]Because it is not possible to accurately estimate benefits separately for those who had just a single year of the preschool program, the precise approach to discounting used was to calculate present value as a weighted average of costs or benefits discounted to age 3 and age 4, where the weights were the proportions of the sample entering at each age. The formula used to calculate net present value (benefits minus costs) at age 3 is this:

$$\text{net present value} = \sum_{t=e}^{65} \frac{\text{benefits}_t}{(1+\text{real})^{t-e+1}} - \sum_{t=e}^{65} \frac{\text{costs}_t}{(1+\text{real})^{t-e+1}}$$

In the formula, **benefits$_t$** are the benefits at age t (t ranges from 3 to 65) expressed in real (i.e., inflation-adjusted) dollars; **costs$_t$** are the costs at age t expressed in real dollars; **real** is the real discount rate; and e is the age (in years) at which children entered the study (either 3 or 4). We discount back to the start of the preschool program because we want to compare the value of costs and benefits at a single point in time, and the start of the program is the most logical time for the decision about whether to provide a program.

[36]We recognize that a positive net present value is not a sufficient reason for government to undertake an investment. Other investments may yield even higher rates of return, and other factors can complicate the decision about which programs to fund. However, it seems reasonable that programs that have proved to have positive net present value should have priority over programs, either proposed or in place, that lack such evidence.

income families, people and their political representatives are hardly indifferent about variations in distributional consequences. This cost-benefit analysis investigated the distribution of costs and benefits for three subgroups of society—program participants, taxpayers, and crime victims. We not only examined the extent to which the preschool program achieved its primary goal of improving the lives of young children at high risk of school failure but also assessed the extent to which the preschool program served the self-interest of taxpayers who paid for it and of potential victims of crime.

6. Conduct Sensitivity Analyses

To estimate costs and benefits, cost-benefit research invariably relies on some assumptions. At any given time, these assumptions may or may not prove to be valid, and changes in the assumptions can sometimes substantially alter the estimated costs and benefits. Thus, sensitivity analyses are conducted to identify critical assumptions and explore the effects of reasonable variations in them. From these analyses, it is possible to determine the extent to which the conclusions stand when alternative assumptions are employed and thus to determine what conditions must be met for the program to be a sound investment.

The sensitivity analyses conducted in this cost-benefit analysis were extensive and involved a wide range of alternative assumptions. Some were extremely specific (e.g., the analysis of impact on earnings beyond age 27 of alternative rates of productivity growth), while others were quite general (e.g., the analysis of effect on net present value and distribution if actual welfare reductions were only half the amount estimated). A complete discussion of the sensitivity analyses is beyond the scope of this chapter but is available in a separate technical report (Barnett, 1993). When the relevant benefit estimates are presented in this chapter, assumptions found to have important effects on the estimation of benefits are also discussed.

One assumption that is frequently a matter of contention in cost-benefit analysis is the choice of a real discount rate for the calculation of present value. To avoid becoming mired in a debate over the appropriate discount rate, we conducted this cost-benefit analysis using real rates ranging from 0% to 11%, a range greater than current disagreement spans. Since real rates are the amount above inflation, if inflation were 4% per year, this range would correspond to observed (nominal) interest rates of 4% to 15%. The specific analysis presented in this chapter employs a real discount rate of 3% (roughly 7% in nominal terms, assuming an inflation rate of 4%), which is consistent with the policy of the U.S. General Accounting Office (1992) for the choice of a discount rate in cost-benefit analysis of government programs. However, the conclusions of our analysis are unchanged by the use of real rates as high as 11%.

Estimated Costs and Benefits

Program Costs

The Perry Project's preschool program was operated by a public school district from October to June of the school year. It consisted of a daily $2\frac{1}{2}$-hour classroom session for children, held Monday through Friday mornings, and a weekly $1\frac{1}{2}$-hour home visit in which teachers worked with each child and mother. Children participated in the program at ages 3 and 4 (Wave 0 children were an exception because they participated only at age 4). All preschool program participants entered the public school's regular kindergarten at age 5.

The cost of the preschool program was estimated from a detailed description of the program and the resources it used. Basic data on the costs of the program were obtained from the Ypsilanti Public School District's records and budget reports for the years in which the preschool program operated. Operating costs (explicit costs) were calculated for these categories:

- Instruction
- Administration and support staff
- Overhead
- Supplies
- Psychological screening

Instruction costs include (a) teacher salaries, (b) fringe benefits, and (c) the employer's share of Social Security taxes. Administration and support staff costs include contributions by the staff of the special education department, which managed the preschool program. Overhead costs include (a) a share of general administration and other nonteaching staff of the school system, (b) maintenance, (c) utilities, and (d) a share of other school-wide and district-wide costs. Supplies include the costs of (a) equipping the classroom each year, (b) providing materials for the children to work with, and (c) providing daily snacks. Finally, screening costs were included because the testing was used to select children with a poor prognosis for educational success.

In addition to the explicit, basic operating costs, there were also the implicit, capital costs for the classrooms and other school district facilities. To provide an estimate of total implicit program-costs, imputed interest and depreciation were calculated for the program's fixed capital. *Imputed interest* was calculated to account for the income foregone when assets were employed by the preschool program. *Depreciation* was calculated to account for the decrease in value of assets due to wear, age, and other causes.

Table 35 presents specific costs for the various categories, the total cost for all categories, and the average cost per child for a typical year (1963–1964) of the preschool program. The costs given in Table 35 should be considered illustrative, because program costs varied somewhat from year to year. The primary source of cost variation was the number of children in each wave assigned to the program group. This number varied between 8 and 13 (with two waves combined to make up the number of children served in a given school year).[37] Table 36 presents the estimated cost per child for each wave and each school year, in the dollars that were current when costs were incurred and in 1992 dollars.

In addition to the program costs borne by the general public, preschool programs may impose other costs on participating children and parents. Such costs were negligible for the program in question. There were no fees, school supplies were provided, and transportation was merely a matter of walking to the neighborhood school. The only resource sought from parents was time for the home visits, and participation in the visits was voluntary. Parents could, and did, choose not to receive a visitor or not to participate in a visit, in which case the visiting teacher worked with the child alone. However, the visits did offer parents direct benefits in the form of positive social interactions with the teacher and information about parenting, education, and community services. On balance, parents' participation is taken to imply that they valued these immediate benefits (which are not included in the analysis) at least as much as the alternative activities they could have pursued in the 1½ hours taken up by each visit.

Thus, the costs in Table 36 can be taken to represent all the costs of the preschool program. In 1992 dollars, the estimated cost per child was $7,601 for one school year (Wave 0 only) and $14,415 for two school years (averaging Waves 1 to 4) of the program. Weighting the 1- and 2-year cost estimates by the percentage of children in each wave yields $12,888 as the average cost per child across the entire program group. This weighted-average cost estimate accurately represents what was spent on the entire program group and is the most appropriate figure for comparison with the benefit estimates across all waves. The present value (discounted at 3%) of this weighted-average cost per child is $12,356.

Compared with many other early childhood programs in operation today, the Perry study's preschool program is relatively expensive. The major reasons for this high cost were the program's highly qualified staff (who were paid public school salaries) and the small class-size. Each year's group of 20–25 children was taught by 4 experienced public school teachers. In comparison with the Perry preschool program, other preschool programs often have less-qualified staff and much larger classes and pay much lower salaries. The cost estimates given here were designed to represent as closely as possible the actual cost of the

---

[37]These calculations were based on the number of children attending the preschool program who completed the program, which is the appropriate measure of class size for estimating cost per person for comparison with benefits per person. Actual class size would have been slightly higher in some years, because 4 initial program participants moved away before completing the preschool program (see Chapter 2).

Table 35

COSTS FOR A TYPICAL SCHOOL YEAR OF THE PRESCHOOL PROGRAM

Category	Cost (1963–64 Dollars)
Explicit	
Instruction	$26,251
Administration and support staff	1,100
Overhead	1,600
Supplies	480
Screening	115
Implicit	
Interest and depreciation	2,326
Total	$31,782
Per-participant	$ 1,589

Table 36

PRESCHOOL PROGRAM COST PER PARTICIPANT, BY YEAR AND WAVE

Cost per Preschool Program Participant	School Year				
	1962–63 $n = 21$	1963–64 $n = 20$	1964–65 $n = 25$	1965–66 $n = 25$	1966–67 $n = 12$
	Wave 0 $n = 13$	Wave 1 $n = 8$	Wave 2 $n = 12$	Wave 3 $n = 13$	Wave 4 $n = 12$
Nominal dollars when incurred	$1,510	$1,583	$1,381	$1,472	$1,702
Real 1992 dollars	7,601	7,819	6,668	6,883	7,569
	Wave 1 $n = 8$	Wave 2 $n = 12$	Wave 3 $n = 13$	Wave 4 $n = 12$	
Nominal dollars when incurred	$1,516	$1,593	$1,389	$1,482	
Real 1992 dollars	7,632	7,869	6,707	6,930	

resources used by the program. This approach was judged to be fair and to require the fewest assumptions about extrapolation of costs.[38] Questions about what public preschool programs today should cost if they are to produce results similar to those of the Perry study's preschool program are deferred until later in this chapter.

Child Care Provided by the Program

It is now widely recognized that all early childhood programs, whether they are called preschool education or child care, simultaneously provide both education and care, with *care* defined as providing for children's health, safety, and comfort. However, the amount or quality of education and care provided by specific early childhood programs can vary considerably. The Perry preschool program was designed to provide high-quality education. However, it did incidentally also provide a certain amount of child care free of charge, which allowed parents to concentrate on other activities while their child attended the preschool program.

The value of child care provided by the Perry preschool program was estimated from survey data for hourly child care payments from the 1970s (Rodes, 1975; Rodes & Moore, 1975). Updated to 1992 dollars, the estimated payment for care would be roughly $1.50 per hour, which was about what the average family day care home or for-profit center charged in 1990 (Willer et al., 1991). At this rate, the program provided $435 in care per child each year, allowing for absences. The present value of the weighted-average benefit is $738 per child. This estimated child care benefit is quite small. However, it should be recognized that at the time of the Perry preschool program, full-time child care and full-time employment outside the home for mothers of young children were both less common.

---

[38]For example, this analysis estimates the Perry preschool program's personnel costs based on actual teacher salaries and benefits adjusted to 1992 dollars. Personnel costs could have been estimated based on national-average teacher-salary-and-benefit costs for 1992. This procedure would have produced a slightly higher cost estimate (real salaries and employee benefits have risen in recent years). However, actual personnel costs were also used to calculate program benefits, such as education cost savings. For comparability, personnel costs for all years of education (kindergarten through college) would have had to be estimated on the basis of current national personnel costs, which would have increased the program benefits as well. Because costs of special education have risen more than costs of regular education have over the years, the net effect probably would have been to increase program benefits more than program costs. Of course, teacher compensation and other costs vary considerably from time to time, and the exact results depend on the year from which cost data are taken. For a more detailed discussion of this issue, see the technical report of this cost-benefit analysis (Barnett, 1993). The use of actual salary figures for the years in question restricts the analyst's discretion and is not subject to producing different estimates, depending on the years from which salary levels are estimated (in the mid-1980s, real salaries were lower). Finally, it can be argued that the nature of people who are attracted into the field depends on the salaries offered, so the actual resources represented by "teachers" varies over time, as do salaries.

Elementary and Secondary Education

From an economic standpoint, a preschool program that improves the subsequent educational performance of children increases the efficiency of the educational process. This increase in efficiency may be observed as an increase in educational output or as a reduction in the cost of schooling. The Perry study provides both types of evidence of increased efficiency. Recall that the program group had higher achievement-test scores and greater educational attainment than the no-program group. The program group also had fewer placements in programs for educable mental impairment and less grade retention, which directly resulted in lower costs.

This section presents estimates for the benefits due to cost reductions in elementary and secondary education. It should be recognized that some of the program effects that increase educational output, such as reducing the dropout rate, actually *increase* educational costs. Thus, this section provides only a partial measurement of the benefits of increased educational efficiency. We do not include such direct benefits to children and their families as the increased enjoyment and satisfaction brought about by school success or the improved status and self-concept associated with educational placement or progress. Later sections of the chapter deal with less direct benefits from increased educational output, such as increased earnings.

To estimate the effects of the Perry preschool program on the costs of elementary and secondary education, it was necessary to link data on individual educational placements to data on school costs. Information on schooling experiences from entry through graduation or dropout was obtained from official public-school records for 112 study participants. These records specify the student's educational status each year, providing detailed information about school attended, grade level, educational program, special services, testing, and disciplinary incidents. The records data were used to construct individual school-placement and school-service histories.

School cost data were obtained from the Ypsilanti Public School District, which accounted for 80% of the years of schooling of study participants. Most of the study participants' remaining years of schooling were in three surrounding districts (Ann Arbor, Willow Run, and Van Buren), but it was not possible to obtain detailed cost data for all years (1963 to 1980) from these other districts attended by study participants.[39] Thus, the Ypsilanti cost data were used to estimate educational costs for the entire sample.[40] Information from district budgets, enrollment summaries, and personnel lists was combined to produce estimates of annual cost per child for each of seven types of educational placements: regular classroom, regular classroom plus speech and lan-

[39]Because Carol Weber had collected data through 1974 from the Ypsilanti school district for the first cost-benefit analysis of the Perry preschool program (Weber et al., 1978), detailed data were available for all years covered in the study.

[40]In the few instances in which students were placed in special residential schools, the costs for those schools were estimated on the basis of the amounts the state charged school districts for those placements.

guage services, regular classroom plus compensatory education, special education classroom, integrated special education, alternative (disciplinary) school, and special residential schools.

Costs were also estimated for psychological assessments, which were the only specific service, beyond the placements, that could be reliably determined from records.

The cost estimates for each placement and service were mapped onto the individual placement and service histories to produce 112 complete cost histories. The cost histories were used to compute the total inflation-adjusted cost (undiscounted, and discounted at 3% to calculate present value) of elementary and secondary education for each person. The preschool program's effect on total cost per person (which was a savings) was estimated as the difference between program-group and no-program-group mean costs, computed separately for males and for females. Table 37 presents these estimates.

Table 37

ESTIMATED SAVINGS PER PRESCHOOL PROGRAM PARTICIPANT DUE TO THE PROGRAM'S EFFECT ON ELEMENTARY AND SECONDARY EDUCATION

Savings per Program Participant	Males	Females	Total
1992 dollars	$13,520	$5,898	$9,709
Present value (1992 dollars discounted at 3%)	9,461	4,282	6,872

Because the preschool program's estimated effect on schooling costs is based on the individual cost histories, it incorporates considerably more information about schooling experiences than is summarized in the analyses of school placement and progression presented in Chapter 3. Not only do the numbers of years of special education and the number of years of grade retention enter in, but the differences in types of special placements matter, as well. Note that for program-group females, cost savings due to their improved progress were offset to some extent by their much greater propensity to stay in school through high school graduation.

Adult Secondary Education

The age-27 assessment revealed that some participants who did not complete high school by age 19 subsequently enrolled in adult-education courses (adult high school or GED preparation classes at the high school) as a means of completing their education. Therefore the cost of adult secondary education was estimated, based on adult-education records and an estimated cost of about $1,710 (in 1992 dollars) per adult-education class (Varden, 1982). Since the program group had a lower rate of adult secondary-education participation than the no-program group, the preschool program was estimated to have reduced the cost of adult education by \$532 per person in 1992 dollars (\$275 for males, \$789 for females). The present value (discounted at 3%) of this per-person savings on adult education is \$283.[41]

Postsecondary Education

It seems likely that the study participants, by age 27, had completed virtually all of their postsecondary, or higher, education. Only 2 study participants appeared to be continuing higher education at the time of the age-27 interview. However, since attendance patterns for the sample were highly erratic, no projections were made regarding future years of higher education. Thus, costs of higher education were estimated entirely on the basis of attendance data up to the age-27 interview. The primary source of information regarding higher education attendance was the official transcripts of study participants who reported having attended postsecondary institutions.

Transcripts were obtained from colleges for 30 of the 39 persons reporting higher education. For persons whose transcripts were not obtained (because the college did not respond or failed to find a transcript), attendance was estimated based on the ratio of actual credits enrolled to reported years of higher education for those for whom transcripts were available. This procedure was necessary because participants tended to report the number of years over which they had attended postsecondary institutions, but much of their attendance was only part-time.[42]

To produce an estimate of the postsecondary education cost for each study participant, data for each study participant on number of courses and credits and type of institution attended were combined with estimates of average cost per full-time-equivalent student for public 2-year colleges and public 4-year colleges. Given the large differences in costs between 2-year and 4-year institutions, it was essential to distinguish between them in cost estimation. However, no distinction was made between the costs of 2-year college classes that may have been taken in preparation for college enrollment and the costs of other 2-year college courses.

---

[41]Increased adult-education costs for the no-program group are not a "penalty" for returning to school and do not imply that their returning to school was bad for society. The benefits of adult education are obtained later, in increased earnings. To some extent, there was a shift in the timing of education costs and benefits: Students who dropped out of secondary school postponed some of the costs of education and postponed the benefits. It should be noted that the preschool program's reductions in the costs of K–12 education occurred despite the fact that program participants were less likely to drop out. Adding the savings on adult education to those on K–12 education provides an estimate of the preschool program's total impact on schooling costs.

[42]Two assumptions made in estimating postsecondary education costs tended to increase those costs more for the program group than for the no-program group: (1) No future costs were estimated for 2 no-program-group members who may have continued higher education beyond age 27, and (2) costs were estimated for all self-reported higher education, whether or not it was confirmed by official transcripts (unconfirmed higher education was greater for the program group than for the no-program group, either because of inaccurate reports or because of problems with obtaining the records).

The estimated effects of the preschool program on postsecondary education costs were, in 1992 dollars, a cost increase of $3,896 per person for females and a cost decrease of $747 per person for males. These results reflect differences in the number of classes attended (measured in terms of semester credits) and in the distribution of classes between 2-year and 4-year institutions. The estimated average effect across both genders is a cost increase of $1,575 per person. The present value (discounted at 3%) of this estimated effect is a cost increase of $868 per person.

Employment-Related Compensation

Data from both the age-19 and age-27 interviews provide evidence that the preschool program led to persistent improvements in earnings and employment for both females and males, with greater improvements for females than for males. The estimation of benefits from these improvements is limited to two pecuniary rewards of employment—earnings and fringe benefits.

Earnings   Self-report data from the two interviews on earnings and employment were sufficient to estimate earnings at ages 16 through 19 and ages 25 to 27. As might be expected, accuracy of recall declines over time, and the number of study participants who reported earnings and employment data for more than 3 years at the age-27 interview was too small to provide reasonable group-estimates. Moreover, those who recalled 4 years or more of earnings and employment data tended to be atypical (for example, people who over several years held the same job or had no job). Table 38 reports estimated earnings by preschool experience and gender. Clearly, participation in the preschool program appears to have increased earnings.

For females, the explanation of the earnings results is straightforward. Program females achieved substantially higher levels of educational attainment than did no-program females, and this would be expected to substantially increase their success in the labor market. Based on data for earnings and employment at the time of the age-27 interview (which, compared with data for longer periods of time, seems less likely to suffer from error due to imperfect recall), the program females earned more, because they were more likely to be employed (see Table 23 in Chapter 5).

For males, the results are somewhat more complicated. Program males attained about the same highest year of education as no-program males; so little or no difference in their earnings might be expected on this account. Thus, it is surprising that the preschool program appears to have had a large effect on males' monthly earnings at the age-27 interview (Table 23 in Chapter 5 shows a $538 difference between group means). This effect on earnings is entirely due to differences in earnings for those with jobs, because there is no noticeable difference in employment rates of program and no-program males at age 27. By contrast, the preschool program's estimated effect on annual earnings for males from age 25 to age 27 is quite small ($1,490 per year) and more consistent with expectations based on educational attainment.

Table 38

ESTIMATED MEAN ANNUAL EARNINGS (1992 DOLLARS) AT AGES 16–19
AND AGES 25–27, BY PRESCHOOL EXPERIENCE AND GENDER

Age	Program Females	No-Program Females	Program Males	No-Program Males
16	$ 190	$ 705	$ 95	$ 303
17	1,203	723	1,039	1,116
18	1,944	833	3,410	3,968
19	6,586	2,908	9,480	8,944
25	12,372	8,387	17,669	13,165
26	13,614	9,607	13,621	13,987
27	14,308	8,620	16,397	16,064

It is difficult to know exactly what to conclude from the earnings data for males. On the one hand, earnings and employment reports are likely to be more accurate for the current month than for past years. On the other hand, compared with earnings and employment over a 3-year period, a single month's earnings and employment are more likely to be influenced by transitory fluctuations in the economy and unusual personal circumstances. In addition, the annual comparisons involve same-age persons, while the single-month comparison involves persons of varying ages, because not all "age-27" interviews were conducted precisely at age 27. A final consideration is that estimation of annual earnings for ages 25 to 27 based on educational attainment of the sample and national data on blacks' earnings by educational attainment produces results that are extremely close to the Perry study's self-reported annual earnings by preschool experience and gender for ages 25 to 27.

On balance, the small estimated advantage for program males based on reported annual earnings from age 25 to age 27 seems to be the better indicator of cumulative differences through age 27, especially given the program males' lack of advantage in educational attainment. A small effect on earnings is plausibly explained as due to differences in the quality rather than the quantity of education experienced by the two groups. Qualitative differences might include differences in the acquisition of knowledge, skills, and attitudes, such as motivation to achieve. Whether such qualitative differences could have produced the larger effect on earnings implied by the monthly earnings estimate is unclear. Nevertheless, some concern remains that the preschool program's effect on male earnings could be underestimated by reliance on the annual rather than the monthly estimates.

The annual earnings in Table 38 are only the beginning of a complete estimation of the preschool program's benefits on earnings and employment over the lifetimes of the study participants. It would hardly be reasonable to assume that earnings effects occurred only in those years for which the participants provided adequate data. Thus, additional efforts are required to estimate program effects on annual earnings between age 19 and age 25 and beyond age 27, as well as to extend the analysis of employment-related benefits beyond earnings alone.

The preschool program's effect on earnings for ages 20 through 24 was estimated by assuming a linear trend in real earnings between age 19 and age 26 for each of the four groups defined by preschool experience and gender. To provide a more reliable anchor point at age 26, earnings at age 26 were represented by an average of earnings from ages 25 to 27. This procedure resulted in estimates that the preschool program was associated with earnings being increased by $38,713 per female and by $8,886 per male through age 27. The gender-weighted average program-effect on earnings through age 27 was estimated to be an increase of $23,800 per person.

The preschool program's effect on earnings beyond age 27 can be estimated by a standard procedure for projecting earnings over a lifetime, based on educational attainment (U.S. Bureau of the Census, 1983). The data used to make these projections are (a) national data relating educational attainment to mean annual earnings of blacks by age and gender in 1991 and (b) survival rates (percentage living to each age) for blacks by age and gender (U.S. Bureau of the Census, 1992; National Center for Health Statistics, 1985). Earnings were projected only to age 65, since earnings from employment beyond age 65 are relatively minor, and the data relating earnings to education beyond age 65 are quite limited. Using this procedure to project earnings for females, we estimated that the preschool program increased earnings by $91,000 per female. For males, the effect of the preschool program on earnings beyond age 27 was simply projected to be $0, since educational attainment was virtually the same for program and no-program males. Thus, the average estimated effect of the preschool program on earnings beyond age 27 for both genders was $45,500 per program participant.[43] The total increase in lifetime earnings attributed to the preschool program was $30,331 per program participant. As shown in Table 39, this is the sum of the estimated increase through age 27 and the projected increase beyond age 27. Table 39 also presents the estimated effects on total compensation, which includes fringe benefits *and* earnings.

Fringe benefits   Increased earnings are not the only employment-related benefit that researchers have found to result from improvements in education. Other job-related effects of increased education include higher fringe benefits and greater nonpecuniary benefits, such as improved occupational status, job satisfaction, working conditions, and convenience (Duncan, 1976; Mathios, 1988). However, the only nonearnings

---

[43]Given the apparent earnings advantages of program over no-program males through age 27 in the self-report data, the projection of no preschool program effect on male earnings for subsequent years can be questioned. Moreover, the lack of an earnings advantage beyond age 27 is inconsistent with the estimates of less reliance on welfare and less involvement in crime that are presented in later sections of this chapter. However, there are no data from outside the Perry study that could be used to project the effects of the preschool program *unrelated to educational attainment* on earnings beyond age 27. In this respect, the Perry research is an important part of the larger research program investigating the effects of education on lifetime earnings. Though the estimate of no preschool program effect on male earnings beyond age 27 may be an underestimate, it is the best that we can produce until actual data for such projections are available.

Table 39

ESTIMATED BENEFITS PER PRESCHOOL PROGRAM PARTICIPANT DUE TO THE
PROGRAM'S EFFECTS ON EARNINGS AND TOTAL COMPENSATION

Time Span	1992 Dollars		Present Value (1992 Dollars Discounted at 3%)	
	Earnings	Total Compensation	Earnings	Total Compensation
Through age 27	$23,800	$28,560	$12,082	$14,498
Ages 28–65	45,500	54,600	13,194	15,833
Lifetime total	$69,300	$83,160	$25,276	$30,331

job-related benefit for which it was practical to estimate a monetary
value was the amount of fringe benefits and other job-related costs paid
by the employer. Total compensation (including all employer costs) is
important because it provides a better measure of how society values the
work performed by study participants than do wages alone.

Although there are no direct measures of the fringe benefits earned
by the study participants, fringe benefits and other employer costs can
be estimated from national data relating these to earnings (Woodbury &
Hamermesh, 1992; U.S. Bureau of Labor Statistics, 1992). A reasonable
estimate of the value of fringe benefits to the study participants is that
they equal 10% of earnings. Other employer costs (Social Security,
worker's compensation, and unemployment insurance) add at least
another 10% to the total compensation cost paid by the employer. Thus,
the preschool program's effect on total compensation is estimated to
equal 120% of wages.[44]

Delinquency and Crime

Both self-reports and criminal records indicated that the preschool program reduced crime. Thus, we can expect to find reduced costs of crime
to society. These costs include

- Costs to victims

---

[44]Since 1980, fringe benefits have been equal to 18% or more of salaries across all jobs
(Woodbury & Hamermesh, 1992). The other major costs paid for workers by the employer
(Social Security tax, worker's compensation, and unemployment insurance) are roughly
12%, bringing the cost of total compensation to around 130% of salaries (U.S. Bureau of
Labor Statistics, 1992). Social Security alone accounted for 6.13% (in 1980) to 7.65% (in
1989) of employer-paid compensation costs. Of course, fringe benefits tend to be much
lower for the poorest paying jobs and considerably higher for the best paying jobs. The
Perry study participants had jobs with relatively low pay. Data on the lowest paying
service jobs in 1992 (an average of $6.30 per hour) indicated that their fringe benefits were
equal to only about 9% of wages, while other employer costs brought the total of employer
costs to almost 24% of wages (U.S. Bureau of Labor Statistics, 1992). Since fringe benefits
increase faster than earnings as earnings improve, an effect raising earnings would
increase benefits more than proportionally. Thus, allowing 10% for fringe benefits and an
additional 10% for other employer costs seemed reasonable.

- Costs of the criminal-justice system

- Costs of private-security measures to protect persons, cars, homes, and businesses

In 1985, the estimated annual cost to victims of household and personal crimes (business crimes excluded) in the United States was $92.6 billion dollars, while criminal-justice-system costs were $35 billion and private-security costs were $31 billion (Cohen, 1988; Zedlewsky, 1987). The effects of the Perry study's preschool program were estimated for victim and criminal-justice-system costs, but not for private-security measures. This approach omits a significant portion of the costs of crime, but since it is unclear how private-security costs respond to changes in crime, it did not seem feasible to estimate the preschool program's effect on private-security costs.

The fundamental basis for estimating the preschool program's effects on crime costs is provided by the criminal records collected at ages 19 and 27. These records provided information about arrests, convictions, imprisonment, probation, and parole for the study participants. The effects of the preschool program were estimated separately for the years up through age 27 (using records available to that point) and for the years after age 27.

To estimate victim costs through age 27, the number of crimes actually committed by study participants at each age was estimated by linking participants' arrest histories with national data on the ratio of arrests to crimes actually committed. For example, surveys indicate that for every assault arrest, there are 5 assaults actually committed. Using this ratio yielded estimates, by age, of how many crimes of each type were committed by study participants. These crime estimates were then combined with estimates of victim costs for each type of crime (Table 40) to produce estimates of victim costs from crimes committed by study participants at each age.

Table 40

VICTIM COSTS BY TYPE OF CRIME (1992 DOLLARS)

Type of Crime	Cost
Rape	$65,229
Arson	42,860
Bank robbery	24,031
Other robbery	16,089
Assault	15,596
Auto theft	3,995
Burglary	1,191
Larceny	226

Note. These U.S. victim-cost estimates (Cohen, 1988, 1992), include (a) direct property and monetary losses or out-of-pocket costs; (b) pain, suffering, and fear of injury; and (c) risk of death. The costs of murder are included in the costs of the other crimes and are based on the probability of a murder resulting from the commission of each specific type of crime. For this analysis, Cohen's (1988) estimates of the costs of personal and household larcenies were averaged to produce a single estimate.

Criminal-justice-system costs through age 27 were estimated on the basis of participants' actual arrest and incarceration histories. Police, prosecutorial, and court costs were estimated by combining arrest histories with data on costs per arrest for each type of crime. The costs of corrections (incarceration and supervision of probation) were estimated on the basis of records of study participants' time incarcerated or on probation and on the basis of estimates of the costs of incarceration or probationary supervision.

Obviously, commission of crimes does not cease at age 27, although it does decline with age. Thus, crime and its costs were projected beyond age 27. The *Uniform Crime Reports* (Federal Bureau of Investigation, 1980, 1992) provide data on national arrests by age and gender that were used to estimate the percentages of crimes committed by persons of each age through age 65. These figures were then used to project the cost of crimes committed by study participants at each age beyond age 27. Based on these cost projections, the effects of the Perry preschool program on crime costs were estimated for the years after age 27 (crime committed after age 65 is negligible).

Table 41 presents estimates of the preschool program's effect on crime, by gender. Overall, the estimated effect of the preschool program is to reduce the costs of crime by $148,714 per program participant over a lifetime. The present value of this estimated effect is just over $70,000 per program participant. (If this seems large, consider that crime costs the nation more than $200 billion *each year*.) The estimated effects on costs of crime were larger for program males, who are much more likely than program females to commit violent crimes. When effects on victim costs and criminal-justice-system costs were broken out separately, reductions in victim costs were seen to account for about 80% of the preschool program's total effect on the costs of crime. This percentage seems reasonable, given that estimates for the nation as a whole place victim costs at over 70% of combined victim and criminal-justice-system costs.[45]

---

[45]Arrests rather than convictions were used to estimate the costs of crime, because only arrests can be related to crime as reported by its victims. Data are not available to relate convictions to committed crimes by type of crime. The program and no-program groups differ with respect to both arrests and convictions, but the difference in convictions is somewhat smaller. While this might mean that for some unknown reason, no-program-group members were more likely to be falsely arrested, it is also possible that the effect might run in the opposite direction, with those who are more heavily involved in crime having become better at avoiding conviction. The common use of plea bargaining (which reduces the seriousness and number of crime convictions relative to crime arrests) makes differences between arrest data and conviction data difficult to interpret.

In two respects, it seems clear that the procedures adopted to estimate the costs of crime tend to underestimate the effects of the preschool program. First, lacking a better alternative, we projected that crime committed beyond age 27 would be proportional to crime through age 27 for program and no-program males and program and no-program females. However, it seems more likely that those little-involved in crime would commit their last crime fairly early in life, whereas those more highly involved in crime (career criminals, at the extreme) would commit a disproportionate number of crimes in their later years. This seems to be borne out by data for the no-program females with criminal records, who typically had a single arrest at a young age and no other arrests through age 27. Second, differences in the patterns of arrest by age were sufficiently similar across the various types of crime to allow us to use the pattern for all index crimes to project crime costs beyond age 27. (Since the proportion of violent crimes committed beyond age 27 tends to be somewhat greater than the proportion of all crimes committed beyond age 27, and since violent crimes have higher costs, this procedure tended to underestimate the costs of crime.)

Table 41

ESTIMATED SAVINGS PER PRESCHOOL PROGRAM PARTICIPANT DUE TO
THE PROGRAM'S REDUCTION OF CRIME

	Savings		
Type of Savings	In Victim Costs	In Criminal-Justice-System Costs	In Total Costs
Through age 28			
1992 dollars	$ 72,862	$16,366	$ 89,228
Males	97,964	16,390	114,354
Females	47,760	16,342	64,102
Present value (1992 dollars discounted at 3%)	40,162	8,882	49,044
Beyond age 28			
1992 dollars	43,575	10,911	59,486
Males	65,309	10,927	76,236
Females	31,841	10,895	42,736
Present value (1992 dollars discounted at 3%)	17,423	3,914	21,337
Lifetime			
1992 dollars	121,437	27,277	148,714
Males	163,273	27,317	190,590
Females	79,601	27,237	106,838
Present value (1992 dollars discounted at 3%)	57,585	12,796	70,381

Public Welfare Assistance

Self-report and social-services records at ages 19 and 27 provide evidence that the preschool program reduced participation in welfare programs such as Aid to Families with Dependent Children (AFDC), food stamps, General Assistance (a state program for those without dependents), Supplemental Security Income (SSI), and Medicaid, thus reducing welfare costs. Estimates of the preschool program's effects on welfare payments were calculated for the years up to age 27 on the basis of data on welfare-program participation. Projections of the preschool program's effects on payments over the rest of participants' lifetimes were made on the basis of a few simple assumptions.

To estimate the preschool program's effects on welfare payments, individual welfare-payment histories through age 27 were constructed. The histories were developed by pooling

- Self-report data from the age-27 interview on the number of months welfare assistance was received in the previous 10 years and on the amounts of welfare assistance received

- Social services records on AFDC, food stamps, and General Assistance

- Payment and eligibility rules for these programs

Data on employment, earnings, and incarceration were used to help identify the precise months during which welfare assistance was received, when this could not be verified from records or self-report. Since all SSI, AFDC, and General Assistance recipients automatically qualified for Medicaid or a state-operated ambulatory medical program (confirmed by self-report), the additional costs of these medical programs were estimated for each month on welfare assistance, based on data obtained from the State of Michigan on the average annual cost per person in each type of welfare program.[46]

The problem of projecting welfare payments beyond age 27 was inadvertently simplified somewhat by the State of Michigan, which recently eliminated its General Assistance program, leaving only payments for the federally sponsored AFDC, SSI, food stamp, and Medicaid programs to be projected. Yet, even for AFDC (the most studied welfare program), research provides very little basis for estimating welfare payments over a lifetime. Based on the available research (Ellwood, 1986, 1988), it was projected that persons still on AFDC at age 27 (most of whom had been on AFDC for 8 or more years) had a 15% probability of exiting AFDC each year until age 50, when all AFDC participation was assumed to end. This projection almost certainly underestimates AFDC payments, since it ignores (a) those leaving welfare prior to age 27 and reentering between ages 27 and 50, (b) those leaving after age 27 and reentering at a later time, and (c) those entering for the first time after age 27 (an estimated 24% of all first-time entrants). However, a sound basis for projecting reentry and new entrants beyond age 27 could not be found. In addition, there was no reasonable basis for projecting the state's food stamp costs and medical costs for those who were ineligible for AFDC because they did not have dependents living with them.[47]

Table 42 presents the estimated effects of the preschool program on welfare payments before and after age 27. Because welfare assistance is a transfer payment, the savings given in this table are not benefits to society as a whole. Because welfare payments represent a transfer of resources from one part of society to another (from taxpayers to welfare recipients), they do not by themselves constitute a *cost to society;* there

---

[46]Because Medicaid and similar state program payments are made directly to providers, program beneficiaries have no way of knowing what the costs are for the services they receive. However, state data are available on the average annual cost for each person (with separate averages for adults and children) by type of welfare program (AFDC, SSI, General Assistance, etc.). For 10 study participants, data on type, amount, and timing of welfare assistance were not available (we knew only that they had received welfare assistance). All but 1 were males who would have been eligible only for General Assistance and food stamps. It was assumed that if the 1 female had been on AFDC, this would have been found in the records, as it was for all other cases. Thus, all 10 study participants were assumed to have received state General Assistance and food stamps (these always were found occurring together when the type of welfare assistance was known). The amounts of welfare assistance were estimated for the rest of the sample by preschool experience and gender. Timing was determined from other data on each individual (e.g., unemployment and incarceration) in most cases; where it could not be precisely determined, it was assumed to have occurred at the youngest possible age (because use declines with age).

[47]As an alternative, regression equations relating payment amounts to age were estimated (using a variety of functional forms) on the sample data through age 27. The resulting equations fit the data poorly, severely underestimated payments at ages 25 to 27, and produced estimates for later years that were grossly inconsistent with national data on AFDC participation.

Table 42

ESTIMATED SAVINGS PER PRESCHOOL PROGRAM PARTICIPANT DUE TO
THE PROGRAM'S REDUCTION OF WELFARE USE

Savings	For Males	For Females	Mean
1992 dollars			
Through age 27	$4,719	$3,115	$3,917
Beyond age 27	222	2,096	1,159
Over lifetime	$4,941	$5,211	$5,076
Present value (1992 dollars discounted at 3%)			
Over lifetime	$2,727	$2,580	$2,653

are, however, administrative costs involved in providing welfare payments, and these *are* costs to society as a whole. Over the relevant
period of time, administrative costs of welfare programs have ranged
from 10% to 15% of payment amounts, reaching the higher percentage
in recent years. Thus, the benefits to society as a whole from the Perry
program's effects on welfare-program participation are estimated to
equal 10% of the welfare-payment savings presented in Table 42.

Summation of Costs and Benefits

The primary purpose of this benefit-cost analysis is to assess whether or
not the preschool program was a sound investment—that is, whether its
overall effect (net present value) was positive or negative. The estimates
required to answer that question are summarized in Table 43 and Figure
14 on pages 166 and 167. The last column in Table 43 lists the present
value to society as a whole of each cost and benefit in the table's first
two columns. The bottom line of the last column indicates that the
preschool program was indeed a sound economic investment, one with
an estimated net present value that is positive and quite large, almost
$100,000 per child enrolled. The return on the preschool program
investment compares favorably not only with alternative public uses of
society's resources but also with many private-sector investments.

Distribution

The distribution of costs and benefits between preschool program participants and the public (taxpayers/crime victims) is displayed in the first

and second columns of Table 43.[48] Net present value is found to be positive for both groups.

As shown in Figure 15 on page 168, the estimated returns to the public are quite large, even though the public bears the entire cost of the preschool program. The preschool program's effect on use of welfare assistance takes on special importance when the distribution of benefits is examined, because taxpayers benefit not only from the reductions in welfare payments but also from reduced administrative costs. But the savings in crime costs is the largest benefit by far. Thus, the people most likely to be victimized by crime gain the most from the preschool program. However, even if the reductions in crime were totally excluded from the analysis, the preschool program would still produce a positive net present value for taxpayers.

The estimated benefits that accrue exclusively to preschool program participants seem relatively small, though hardly negligible. One reason that their benefits are not larger is that program participants benefit only from their increase in *after-tax* earnings and fringe benefits. Another reason is that decreased welfare payments are a cost to participants. Perhaps the most important reason is the omission in the analysis of benefits that contribute to a higher quality of life but are difficult to value monetarily. For example, it seems likely that people value being self-supporting and reducing their dependence on welfare per se, but the analysis was unable to take this into account. Nevertheless, the estimated increases in after-tax earnings and fringe benefits alone exceeded the cost of the preschool program. Thus, the preschool program is found to have a positive net effect on participants even when none of the effects on the broader society are considered.

Since there were important differences in the consequences of the preschool program for females and males, the distribution of benefits by gender was examined in some detail. Although there were variations by gender in benefit estimates when benefits were aggregated, both females and males were found to contribute substantially to net present value. Net present value was estimated to be positive for both

---

[48]The division between program participants and taxpayers/crime victims is not dichotomous. Preschool program participants may also be taxpayers or victims of crime (in fact, low-income black Americans like those in the study are at relatively high risk of becoming crime victims). A preschool program participant, as a taxpayer and a potential crime victim, benefits more than most from the preschool program.

It has been assumed that all the costs of crime are real costs to society that are borne by members of the public both as victims of crime and as funders of the criminal-justice system. Although part of the costs of crime might be considered to be forced transfers (e.g., theft), the value of stolen property is a very small portion of the costs to victims, and the value transferred is considerably smaller than the value lost due to loss of legal title. Moreover, no account has been made of the resources devoted to criminal activity. Finally, some part of the costs of incarceration (such as the prisoner's food, clothing, and shelter) might be considered transfer payments. However, the value of these to the recipient would be offset by the conditions under which they are obtained, which impose serious costs on the prisoner.

Table 43

PRESCHOOL PROGRAM'S ESTIMATED EFFECTS PER PROGRAM
PARTICIPANT (PRESENT VALUE, 1992 DOLLARS DISCOUNTED AT 3%)

Effect	For Participant Only	For Taxpayers/ Crime Victims	Total
Measured effect			
Child care	$ 738	$ 0	$ 738
K–12 education	0	6,872	6,872
Adult education	0	283	283
College[a]	0	−868	−868
Total compensation[b]	10,270	4,228	14,498
Crime	0	49,044	49,044
Welfare	−2,193	2,412	219
Total measured	**$ 8,815**	**$61,972**	**$70,786**
Projected effect			
Total compensation	$11,215	$4,618	$15,833
Crime	0	21,337	21,337
Welfare	−460	506	46
Total Projected	**$10,755**	**$26,461**	**$37,216**
Total measured/projected	**$19,511**	**$88,433**	**$108,002**
Cost of preschool program	**0**	**−12,356**	**−12,356**
Net benefit	**$19,570**	**$76,077**	**$95,646**

Note. Present values are in 1992 dollars discounted at 3%; costs appear as negative.

[a]Some small portion of college costs are likely to have been borne by the participants, but these could not be estimated from the available information.

[b]The benefits reported under *total compensation* include all costs paid by the employer to hire a participant; allocations to participants and taxpayers assume a 25% marginal tax rate, 10% fringe benefits, and 10% other costs to the employer.

genders, so the conclusion that the preschool program was a sound investment for society holds for both males and females. There is no suggestion that from a public policy perspective, preschool programs make sense for females but not for males, or vice versa.[49]

Sensitivity Analyses

All the conclusions based on the results presented in Table 43 derive from a single analysis. This analysis has important limitations. The esti-

---

[49]From the perspective of the program participants alone, males appear to benefit much less than females (though net benefits are still positive for males). This result is primarily due to the lack of an effect on male educational attainment, which was assumed to limit the preschool program effect on male earnings up to age 27 and also precluded estimation of earnings benefits beyond age 27.

Figure 14

COSTS AND BENEFITS TO SOCIETY
PER PRESCHOOL PROGRAM PARTICIPANT

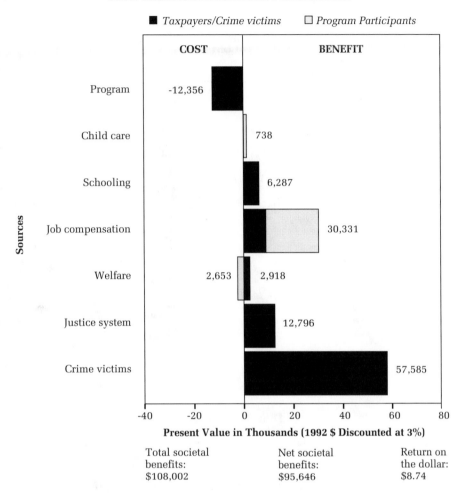

■ *Taxpayers/Crime victims*   □ *Program Participants*

	COST	BENEFIT
Program	-12,356	
Child care		738
Schooling		6,287
Job compensation		30,331
Welfare	2,653	2,918
Justice system		12,796
Crime victims		57,585

Present Value in Thousands (1992 $ Discounted at 3%)

Total societal benefits: $108,002	Net societal benefits: $95,646	Return on the dollar: $8.74

mates are inexact and based on assumptions that may be debated or are uncertain. Also, the monetary estimates provide only a partial picture of the preschool program and its effects. Variations in the assumptions and attempts to take into account what has been omitted from the analysis might alter the conclusions. Sensitivity analyses examined the implications of these matters for the resilience of the conclusions.

With regard to the uncertainty of the estimates, it is reassuring that the estimated net benefits are so large and that most of the benefits accrue by age 27. As Table 43 shows, even if we projected no benefits at all beyond age 27, the estimated net present value would still be $58,430. In addition, the conclusion that the preschool program was a good investment does not depend exclusively on any one benefit estimate. Any one of the specific measured benefit estimates could be set to $0, and there would still be a net benefit *by age 27.*

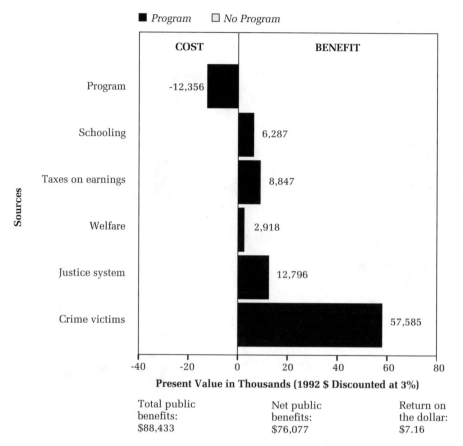

Figure 15

TAXPAYER /CRIME VICTIM COSTS AND BENEFITS
PER PRESCHOOL PROGRAM PARTICIPANT

■ *Program*   □ *No Program*

	COST	BENEFIT
Program	-12,356	
Schooling		6,287
Taxes on earnings		8,847
Welfare		2,918
Justice system		12,796
Crime victims		57,585

Present Value in Thousands (1992 $ Discounted at 3%)

| Total public benefits: $88,433 | Net public benefits: $76,077 | Return on the dollar: $7.16 |

It is also reassuring that many of the assumptions made for projections beyond age 27 were quite conservative with respect to their effects
on estimated benefits. For example, the earnings projections assumed
(over the next four decades) zero growth in productivity, no increase in
women's labor-force participation, and no change in the earnings of
blacks due to reduced discrimination. Reasonable alternatives would
have increased estimated earnings benefits.

Similarly conservative assumptions were made to project the effects
on welfare assistance and crime costs. The welfare projections assumed
no new entry or reentry to welfare programs after age 27. The crime projections assumed that even those with no known arrests for serious
crime after adolescence would contribute a proportionate amount to
crime costs after age 27.

The discount rate chosen may be the most commonly contested
assumption in benefit-cost analysis, partly because of differences of
opinion about the appropriate rate and partly because of the assumption's important effect on the conclusions. In this case, the choice
among reasonable alternatives has little impact. The present values of

costs and benefits were calculated at real discount rates of 3% to 11%. Net present value remained positive even at 11%. Therefore, the conclusion that the preschool program was a sound investment is not highly sensitive to the choice of a real discount rate and is sustained over the range of rates deemed appropriate by various economists.

Finally, it must be acknowledged that the difficulty of measuring and valuing many benefits tends to result in the underestimation of both benefits to the public and benefits to participants. Improvements in education have been found to be related to many social and economic outcomes for adolescents and adults that this analysis did not consider (Haveman & Wolfe, 1984). These outcomes include benefits such as improvements in

- Quality of leisure
- Productivity in household work and childrearing
- Health and longevity
- The timing and spacing of births

In addition, there were some intrinsic values that could not be quantified in economic terms:

- Increased success and satisfaction with school
- Increased satisfaction with work
- Increased socioeconomic status and economic self-sufficiency

Even these partial listings suggest that the value of the preschool program was substantially greater than the estimates in Table 43 indicate.

Policy Implications

The economic analysis of the Perry preschool program is of interest primarily for what it implies for public policy today rather than for what it says about a particular program begun over 30 years ago. In drawing out policy implications, we must extrapolate the analysis results cautiously. No one should expect to exactly replicate the results of the Perry study in a particular location or across the nation. Instead, the economic returns of any preschool program should be expected to vary with

- The people who are involved in the program as participants and providers
- The nature, extent, and quality of the program provided
- The broader environments in which children live

Bronfenbrenner (1991) has aptly portrayed these in his ecological theory of human development as interactions among *person, process,* and *context.* A complete discussion of these interactions is beyond the scope of this chapter, but the following review indicates the kinds of variables that must be considered when extrapolating the Perry study's economic results.

An Ecological Approach

Person   The High/Scope Perry Preschool Project included persons who had much to gain from a high-quality preschool program. They were African-American children who had low IQ-test scores and were from low-income families—a population known to have relatively high probabilities for school failure, special education placement, school dropout, unemployment, criminal activity, and welfare dependency. Clearly, a preschool program has the potential of producing large benefits for any population that is similarly at risk. Children from middle- and high-income families, though they may not stand to gain the same types of benefits from a good preschool program, may stand to benefit in other ways. The Perry study simply does not directly address this question.[50]

Process   It seems reasonable to conclude that results similar to those found in the High/Scope Perry Preschool study can be expected from preschool programs that are similar to the one involved in the study. Since we do know that the Perry preschool program was highly effective, common sense suggests that the further away from this model we move, the greater the risk of reducing program effectiveness. Describing exactly *how* a program should be like the Perry preschool program to achieve similar results requires the expertise of the fields of human development, developmental psychology, and early childhood education rather than economics (this topic is dealt with in Chapter 10). We can surmise, however, that the intensity and quality of the program are the likely keys to its success. Despite the substantial literature on the effects of intensity and quality, there is much that remains to be learned. For example, we do not even know how much is gained by providing two school years of a program rather than one. Also, given social changes since 1962, some thought must be given to the ways in which a preschool program today *should* differ from the Perry preschool program. For instance, how should a preschool program today accommodate families in which the single parent or both parents are at work or in school?

Context   The results of a study such as the High/Scope Perry Preschool Project depend on the political, economic, and social environments in which the program is implemented, as well as on the people involved

---

[50]Another "person" issue that arises has to do with the persons providing the program. To a large extent, provider characteristics fit better under "process," because they influence process—the interactions between teacher and child. One provider characteristic that may be noteworthy in the Perry study is that all of the preschool program teachers were female, and most if not all of the preschool program children had female elementary-grade teachers as well. This might have something to do with the study's differential outcomes for boys and girls (because of differences in interactions or because of the lack of positive early role models in education for boys).

and the program provided. Concretely, this means that there are likely to be important interactions between preschool programs and the families, schools, and neighborhoods in which children live. For example, one reason that studies have found preschool programs to vary in their apparent effects on special education placements and grade retentions is that school districts vary in their policies and practices with respect to special education and retention in grade (Barnett, 1992). Where very few children are placed in special education or retained in grade, little effect on these outcomes is possible, although there may be effects on similar types of outcomes, such as on tracking or ability grouping. As another example, for a number of contextual reasons, extremely poor inner-city neighborhoods may present greater obstacles to producing persistent improvements in educational and social outcomes than other types of neighborhoods, though they may also present greater opportunities for improvement (Anderson, 1990; Jargowsky & Bane, 1991; Jencks, 1991; Wilson, 1987).

What Should Preschool Programs Cost?

While there is no simple answer to the question of what a highly effective preschool program should cost, it is possible to provide some guidance. The High/Scope program model developed in the course of the Perry study was similar to today's special-education programs for preschoolers in terms of its class size, teacher qualifications, teacher salaries, hours of operation, and public-school sponsorship. Thus, it is hardly surprising that preschool special education programs have an average cost of around $7,100 per year (in 1992 dollars), roughly what the Perry program cost (Moore, Strang, Schwartz, & Braddock, 1988). Two school years of a similar public-school-sponsored preschool program for children from low-income families would cost over $14,000 per child. The cost of a similar year-round, all-day program could easily be $20,000 per child over 2 years. Current public policy does not provide this level of funding for programs serving children from low-income families.[51]

Although often motivated by the results of the Perry study and other related research, most large-scale public programs spend far less than $14,000 to $20,000 per child. Costs are reduced in several ways. The greatest cost savings are produced by providing children with only one school year of programming instead of two. The effects of this modifica-

---

[51]These dollar figures are reasonably close to estimates made by others of the costs of high-quality, year-round, all-day programs. Clifford and Russell (1989) estimated the annual cost of a program meeting NAEYC accreditation criteria to be about $6,100 per child (in 1992 dollars). Willer (1990a) estimated the annual "full cost of quality" to be over $8,800 per child (in 1992 dollars). These cost estimates are for the average cost of serving children from birth to age 5 and take into account that accreditation requirements for child-teacher ratios are considerably different for infants and toddlers (3 to 5 children per adult) than for preschoolers (8 to 10 children per adult). However, accreditation criteria allow more children per adult than the Perry preschool program had. According to the criteria, there may be as many as 10 children per adult (based on a teacher and an aide for a group of up to 20 children). Also, neither of these cost estimates (the $6,100 or the $8,800) includes costs of administrative overhead and infrastructure.

tion are uncertain, although Ramey, Bryant, and Suarez (1985), based on their review of 18 experimental studies of compensatory preschool education, concluded that in a preschool program, the amount and breadth of contact with children and families probably bears a direct, positive relationship to the degree of intellectual benefit. The other sources of cost savings are modifications in program structure: larger class sizes, lower teacher qualifications, and lower salaries. These structural modifications are a cause for concern because of their potential effects on the process, particularly on the nature of children's interactions with teachers, peers, and the physical environment (Howes, Phillips, & Whitebook, 1992; Bruner, 1980; Ruopp et al., 1979).

While it is difficult to say how close to the High/Scope program model other programs must stay in terms of cost and structural characteristics, some public programs have strayed so far from this model that the risk of severely reduced benefits is obvious. Public-school preschool programs for children from low-income families tend to have more children per adult than the Perry preschool program, although they do maintain similar formal qualifications and salary levels (Willer, 1990a). Groups of 18 or 20 children with 1 or 2 adults are common. Sometimes these classes have a teacher and an aide, but sometimes they have only one teacher.

Head Start is the program that most people think of when they think about public policy based on the results of the High/Scope Perry Preschool Project. Many more low-income children are served in Head Start than in public-school-sponsored preschool programs. Head Start keeps costs down by having larger class sizes and lower formal qualifications and salaries (less than $10 an hour) for teachers (Willer, 1990a). The federal expenditure for Head Start was only about $3,720 per child in 1993 (U.S. Administration for Children and Families, 1992). Adding the local in-kind match required by Head Start and the contributions from the federal child care food program brings the cost to just about $5,000 per child. Data on enrollment by age suggest that perhaps half of those enrolled attend Head Start for two school years, at both age 3 and age 4 (U.S. Administration for Children and Families, 1992).

There are also many young children from low-income families who attend preschool programs in the private sector. Compared with Head Start programs, these programs—which are both for-profit and non-profit—tend to have even lower requirements for staff qualifications, lower staff salaries, and more children per adult (Willer, 1990a). Thus, the cost per hour of service in these programs tends to be less than it is in Head Start. Although it is recognized that these programs are not explicitly intended to produce the kinds of benefits that the Perry study's preschool program produced, they still absorb significant amounts of public and private funds.

No doubt $14,000 to $20,000 seems like a great deal of money to spend on a poor child's preschool care and education. We are accustomed to spending considerably less than half of that amount. However, by funding programs at such a low level, we risk not producing the desired benefits. The loss of $108,000 per preschooler in benefits is a much greater cost to the nation than the added cost of a preschool program in which we can have confidence. **A conservative, financially prudent policy would be to increase funding levels to the amounts necessary to replicate the quality of the Perry preschool program until research can provide better evidence on how funding level and program structure affect outcomes.**

There is no reason to believe that the Perry study sets an upper limit on the benefits to be gained from producing comprehensive early childhood programs. The preschool program used in the Perry study produced its results by providing only a few hours of programming per day during the school year. Certainly, much greater improvements in the life outcomes of disadvantaged children are conceivable. Year-round, all-day programs that address care, health, and nutrition needs, as well as education, might be found to yield even higher rates of return than the program developed in the High/Scope Perry Preschool Project.

VIII A Causal Model

A causal model of the Perry study data identifies the following paths:

- *From preschool experience to intellectual performance in early childhood*

- *From early childhood intellectual performance to school motivation in elementary school*

- *From elementary school motivation to years spent in programs for educable mental impairment (EMI)*

- *From years spent in EMI programs to literacy at the end of the teen years*

- *From school motivation in elementary school to highest year of schooling completed*

- *From highest year of schooling completed to adult earnings and fewer lifetime arrests*

This chapter develops a rationale for the causal model. To do so, we first present the significant[52] predictors of 1 or more of 3 major variables. These significant predictors were identified from a large correlation matrix between the 3 major variables and all of the plausible predictor variables in the data set.[53] The causal model we present is based on 9 of the significant predictors. Similar analyses were conducted by Schweinhart and Weikart (1980), Berrueta-Clement and others (1984), and Barnes (1991).

Predictors of Adult Success

This report has presented evidence supporting the hypothesis that the Perry preschool program had effects on numerous variables. These effects occurred at various time-intervals after the preschool program—from immediately afterward to 22 years or more afterward. It is reasonable to assume that the immediate effects were directly caused by the preschool program. But since a direct effect usually occurs immediately after its cause, the significant differences in certain variables that were measured years later cannot be considered direct effects. These effects measured years later could be construed, however, as manifestations of some stable, underlying trait that might itself have been a direct effect of the preschool program. (The propensity to avoid misconduct is an example of such a trait.) With such variables, it is necessary to establish the stability and endurance of the trait over several decades.

This chapter focuses on only 3 of the numerous variables involved in the Perry study—*highest year of schooling, monthly earnings at age 27,*

---

[52]**Significance** indicates a two-tailed probability of less than .05.

[53]Parental employment at study entry, a variable on which the program group and the no-program group differed significantly at study entry, was not a significant predictor of any of the 3 major variables considered in this chapter.

and *lifetime arrests.* While other variables might have been used as well, these 3—because of their relevance to participants' adult success—are certainly of central importance.[54] The study has presented evidence that all 3 variables were significantly influenced by the preschool program experience. Highest year of schooling represents the degree of study participants' **school success;** monthly earnings at age 27 represents the degree of study participants' **marketplace success;** and avoidance of lifetime arrests represents the degree to which study participants developed **social responsibility.** As might be expected, these "adult success variables" were significantly correlated with one another. As shown in Tables 44, 45 and 46, *highest year of schooling* was significantly correlated at .516 with *monthly earnings at age 27* and at −.422 with *lifetime arrests,* and *monthly earnings at age 27* was significantly correlated at −.302 with *lifetime arrests.*

The three tables list the significant predictors of highest year of schooling ($n = 123$), monthly earnings at age 27 ($n = 115$), and lifetime arrests ($n = 117$). Table 44 lists scholastic predictors; Table 45 lists economic, family, and general attitudinal predictors; Table 46 lists misconduct-related predictors. The numbers of cases for predictor variables ranged from 88 to 123.

Whereas the three tables divide predictor variables by type, the following discussion reviews the predictors in all three tables for one success variable at a time. A **positive predictor** is a predictor that has a significant positive correlation with the success variable; that is, the larger the value of the predictor variable, the larger the value of the success variable. A **negative predictor** is a predictor that has a significant negative correlation with the success variable; that is, the larger the value of the predictor variable, the smaller the value of the success variable.

Predictors of Highest Year of Schooling

As shown in Table 44 and reported in earlier chapters, preschool experience—that is, participation in the preschool program—was a positive predictor of highest year of schooling.

Various ratings of children's scholastic traits by kindergarten through third-grade teachers were positive predictors of highest year of schooling. Listed from strongest to weakest, these predictors are as follows: school motivation, school potential, social development, socioemotional state, mother's participation, emotional adjustment, and verbal skills. The simplest explanation of these correlations is that the teachers were rather accurately identifying personal traits that endured over the years and played a major role in determining the young people's school success. It is also possible that the teachers' identification of

---

[54]Other study variables are receiving attention in related research: In soon-to-be-completed secondary studies using the Perry data set, Harriette Pipes McAdoo and Thomas Luster of Michigan State University are examining the development of Perry study participants as African-Americans. Sylvia Johnson, an educational psychologist at Howard University, is examining the educational experience of study participants. David Farrington, a criminologist at Cambridge University in England, is examining the predictors of criminal behavior among the study participants.

Table 44

SCHOLASTIC PREDICTORS OF MAJOR OUTCOMES AT AGE 27

Predictor[a]	Age	Highest Year of Schooling	Monthly Earnings at Age 27	Lifetime Arrests
Preschool experience[b]	3–4	.218	.245	−.200
Teacher ratings				
School potential (YRS)	6–9	.452	.291	−.332
Mothers' participation (YRS)	6–9	.328	.306	−.304
Social development (YRS)	6–9	.378	.350	−.297
Verbal skills (YRS)	6–9	.236	.280	−
Emotional adjustment (YRS)	6–9	.274	.352	−.327
School motivation (PBI)	6–9	.457	.369	−.327
Socioemotional state (PBI)	6–9	.367	.421	−.216
Intellectual tests				
Binet IQ after one preschool year	4–5	.390	.242	−.270
Binet IQ after two preschool years	5	.361	−	−.249
Binet IQ	6	.406	.194	−.288
Binet IQ	7	.393	−	−
Binet IQ	8	.382	.232	−
Binet IQ	9	.382	.205	−
Binet IQ	10	.419	−	−
WISC IQ	14	.313	−	−
Achievement and literacy tests				
School achievement (CAT)	7	.241	−	−.247
School achievement (CAT)	8	.358	.273	−.291
School achievement (CAT)	9	.447	.251	−.304
School achievement (CAT)	10	.511	.310	−.357
School achievement (CAT)	11	.445	.214	−.389
School achievement (CAT)	14	.454	.233	−.285
Literacy (APL Survey)	19	.309	.281	−
Literacy (APL Survey)	27	.421	.383	−.213
Special school services				
Years in disciplinary programs	6–18	−.351	−.259	.462
Years in EMI programs	6–18	−.304	−	−
Years retained in grade	6–18	−.491	−.332	.239
Years in EI programs	6–18	−.267	−	.271
Self-reported school suspensions	19	−.214	−.254	.392
Scholastic attitudes				
Thought of college	15	.365	−	−.213
Parent hopes for schooling	15	.277	−	−.303
Self-rated school abilities	19	.276	−	−
Attitude towards school	19	.340	.233	−.182

Continued on next page

Table 44 (continued)

SCHOLASTIC PREDICTORS OF MAJOR OUTCOMES AT AGE 27

Predictor[a]	Age	Highest Year of Schooling	Monthly Earnings at Age 27	Lifetime Arrests
Schooling completed				
Regular high school graduation	18–19	.752	.446	−.306
High school graduation or equivalent	18–27	.830	.429	−.319
Highest year of schooling	14–27	1.000	.516	−.422

Note. Pearson product-moment correlations are presented if $p < .05$, two-tailed. Number of cases = 88 to 123; $n = 123$ for highest year of schooling, $n = 115$ for monthly earnings at age 27, and $n = 117$ for lifetime arrests.

[a]See Chapter 3, Tables 12–15 for names of specific instruments used to measure variables.

[b]1 = no-program group, 2 = program group.

these traits involved some degree of labeling that itself helped shape the children's school experience and success.

Intellectual and school achievement test scores were positive predictors of highest year of schooling—the Stanford-Binet (Terman & Merrill, 1960) from after the first preschool year up to age 10, the WISC at age 14 (Wechsler, 1974), and the California Achievement Tests (Tiegs & Clark, 1963, 1971) from ages 7 to 11 and at age 14.[55] The strongest correlations with highest year of schooling for both intellectual and school achievement tests were at age 10.

Children's placement and time spent receiving various special school services were *negative* predictors of highest year of schooling, that is, the more time spent in special school services, the lower the highest year of schooling attained. Listed from strongest to weakest, these negative predictors are years retained in grade, years in disciplinary programs, years in EMI programs (for educable mental impairment), years in EI programs (for emotional impairment), and suspensions from school. As with teacher ratings, these variables represent both the *identification* of children's problems and the *remedial treatment* of these problems. If this remedial treatment had been a complete solution to children's problems, the correlations would not have been negative. However, the negative correlations do not indicate that remedial treatment was completely unhelpful; it is possible that the negative correlations would have been even greater in magnitude had remedial treatment not been implemented. For example, school dropout rates for these children might have been even higher in a school district that did not offer these special school services. But that is the most positive assessment of these special school services that can be made.

Several scholastic attitudes were positive predictors of highest year of schooling. Listed from strongest to weakest, they are these: thoughts

---

[55]To avoid a sort of redundancy, correlations of the other intellectual and language tests with success variables are not presented.

Table 45

ECONOMIC, FAMILY, AND ATTITUDE PREDICTORS OF
MAJOR OUTCOMES AT AGE 27

Predictor	Age	Highest Year of Schooling	Monthly Earnings at Age 27	Lifetime Arrests
Economic status				
Original socioeconomic status	3–4	.230	–	–
Currently employed	19	.383	.431	−.244
Currently employed	27	.500	.639	−.192
Months unemployed in previous 2 years	27	−.366	−.602	.308
Employed in previous 5 years	27	.458	.395	–
Age–19 earnings (logarithm)	19	.360	.274	–
Monthly earnings	27	.516	1.000	−.302
Annual earnings	27	.545	.848	−.342
Spouse's annual earnings	27	.252	.231	–
Social services in previous 10 years	27	−.406	−.442	–
AFDC in previous 5 years	27	−.273	−.256	–
Food stamps in previous 5 years	27	−.294	−.322	–
General Assistance in previous 5 years	27	–	−.212	–
Months on welfare in previous 5 years	27	−.430	−.408	–
Own home	27	−.214	–	–
Own car	19	.325	.400	–
Own car	27	.426	.483	−.363
Own second car	27	.175	.178	–
Family				
Gender[a]	–	–	–	−.330
Marital status[b] at age 27	27	.272	.342	–
Births	27	−.343	−.205	–
Out-of-wedlock births	27	−.406	−.292	–
Attitudes				
Parent view of own parenting	15	.202	–	–
Youth view of parents' parenting	15	.209	.223	−.207
Meeting others' expectations	15	–	.303	–
Self-confidence	15	–	.254	–
Self-esteem (Rosenberg, 1965)	19	.293	.356	–

Note. Pearson product-moment correlations are presented if $p < .05$, two-tailed, for all variables that had correlations of this magnitude. Number of cases = 105 to 123 for predictors; $n = 123$ for highest year of schooling, $n = 115$ for monthly earnings at age 27, and $n = 117$ for lifetime arrests.

[a]1 = male, 2 = female.

[b]1 = single, 2 = unmarried but cohabiting, 3 = married.

Table 46

MISCONDUCT-RELATED PREDICTORS OF MAJOR OUTCOMES AT AGE 27

Predictor	Age[a]	Highest Year of Schooling	Monthly Earnings at Age 27	Lifetime Arrests
Ratings by others				
Teacher-rated school misconduct (PBI)	6–9	−.237	−	.459
Teacher-rated personal misconduct (PBI)	6–9	−.489	−.420	.399
Parent-rated trouble gotten into	15	−.420	−.283	−
Self-ratings				
Important to avoid trouble	19	.231	−	−.420
Self-reported pickups by police	19	−.483	−.292	−
Self-reported total misconduct	15	−.247	−	−
Self-reported school misconduct	15	−.298	−	−
Self-reported total misconduct	19	−.278	−.262	.584
Self-reported serious misconduct	19	−.280	−.231	.585
Self-reported total misconduct	27	−.255	−.332	.305
Self-reported serious misconduct	27	−.255	−.274	.287
Arrests				
Lifetime arrests	27	−.422	−.302	1.000
Adult arrests	27	−.388	−.313	.970
Juvenile arrests	27	−.342	−	.690
Adult felony arrests	27	−.379	−.278	.833
Adult misdemeanors	27	−.294	−.262	.828
Personal violence crimes	27	−.270	−.205	.669
Drug-dealing crimes	27	−.191	−	.598
Property crimes	27	−.334	−.250	.785
Criminal sentences				
Sentenced to probation or parole	27	−.209	−	.487
Served time on probation or parole	27	−.331	−.314	.629
Sentenced to prison	27	−.235	−.269	.551
Served time in prison	27	−.293	−.307	.599

Note. Pearson product-moment correlations are presented if $p < .05$, two-tailed. Number of cases = 93 to 123; n = 123 for highest year of schooling, n = 115 for monthly earnings at age 27, and n = 117 for lifetime arrests.

[a]A single age indicates events occurring up to that age.

of attending college by 15-year-olds, attitude towards high school at age 19, how much schooling parents *hoped* their 15-year-olds would get (but not how much they *expected* the children to get), and school abilities as assessed by the study participants themselves at age 19.

Highest year of schooling was correlated at .752 with regular high school graduation and at .830 with high school graduation or the equivalent; these are high correlations partly because these variables were incorporated within the total count of highest year of schooling.

Except for the socioeconomic status of the family of origin, the study's economic and family variables generally followed and thus were predicted by highest year of schooling, rather than vice versa. As shown in Table 45, highest year of schooling was a positive predictor of the employment and earnings variables and a negative predictor of months unemployed in the previous 2 years and of social services usage. The one exception to the pattern of highest year of schooling correlating positively with economic well-being is home ownership at age 27 negatively correlating with highest year of schooling, even though ownership of a first car and ownership of a second car were positively correlated with highest year of schooling. This negative correlation of home ownership possibly reflects the delay of financial gratification that frequently accompanies the pursuit of higher education. It seems likely that if the home ownership of study participants were to be assessed again in a decade or so, its correlation with highest year of schooling would be positive.

Highest year of schooling was a positive predictor of marital status at age 27,[56] that is to say, those with more schooling were (a) more likely to be *married* than to be *unmarried but cohabiting* and (b) more likely to be *married* or *unmarried but cohabiting* than to be *single and not cohabiting*. Highest year of schooling was negatively correlated with the number of births to male and female study participants and even more strongly negatively correlated with the number of out-of-wedlock births. Since births may either precede or follow one's completion of schooling, these correlations probably indicate cause and effect in both directions: Births sometimes lead to the ending of schooling and sometimes follow the ending of schooling. The analysis of teen motherhood in Table 17 (Chapter 3) and the accompanying text also address this question.

The 15-year-old study participants' estimates of their parents' parenting ability and the parents' simultaneous estimates of their own parenting ability were both positive predictors of study participants' highest year of schooling.

Highest year of schooling was a positive predictor of self-esteem at age 19 (Rosenberg, 1965). People who said they felt good about themselves completed a higher level of schooling.

As shown in Table 46, all the misconduct-related variables were negative predictors of highest year of schooling—ratings by teachers or parents, self-ratings, arrest rates, or criminal sentences. These correlations of many measures of misconduct with highest year of schooling indicate (a) that young people's conduct plays an important role in

---

[56]Treated as an ordinal variable with 1 = single and not cohabiting, 2 = unmarried-cohabiting, 3 = married.

determining how much schooling they complete and (b) that the amount of schooling completed plays an important role in determining subsequent misconduct and arrests. This relationship is central to the bonding theory described in Chapter 1 (Elliott et al., 1979).

Two misconduct-related measures are of special interest. The strongest correlation of any misconduct-related variable with highest year of schooling, also stronger than almost any scholastic predictor, was personal misconduct as rated by early-elementary teachers.[57] While the earlier-mentioned conjecture about a possible labeling effect regarding teacher ratings of children's scholastic traits applies to this variable as well, it is remarkable that traits visible in children's first years of school could so strongly predict scholastic tenure. Another strong predictor of highest year of schooling was parents' assessment of how much trouble their teenaged children got into.[58] Teenagers whom their parents perceived as getting into trouble did not go as far in school.

Predictors of Monthly Earnings at Age 27

Among the scholastic variables in Table 44 that were positive predictors of monthly earnings at age 27 were all 7 early-elementary teacher-rating scales, Stanford-Binet intellectual performance at some (but not other) ages, school achievement test performance after age 7, literacy test performance at ages 19 and 27, regular high school graduation, high school graduation or the equivalent, and highest year of schooling. Negative predictors were years retained in grade or spent in disciplinary programs and self-reported school suspensions.

The construct validity of monthly earnings at age 27 is supported by its strong correlations with almost all the economic-status variables listed in Table 45, especially by its strong positive correlations with annual earnings and employment status at age 27, and its strong negative correlations with months unemployed in the previous 2 years. It is interesting to note that socioeconomic status at study entry was *not* a predictor of monthly earnings at age 27, which suggests that there was no intergenerational continuation of economic status, at least within the restricted range represented by these study participants. Most of the economic variables that positively or negatively predicted highest year of schooling were *even stronger* positive or negative predictors of monthly earnings at age 27.

Surprisingly, gender was not a predictor of monthly earnings at age 27—perhaps because the program females earned more, on average, than the no-program males (Table 23). Marital status at age 27 was a positive

[57]This scale consisted of 6 teacher ratings from the Pupil Behavior Inventory (Vinter et al., 1966) of absences or truancies, inappropriate personal appearance, lying or cheating, stealing, swearing or using obscene words, and poor personal hygiene; these were scored 1 = very infrequently, 2 = infrequently, 3 = sometimes, 4 = frequently, 5 = very frequently; $r_\alpha = .754$.

[58]The question asked was this: How much trouble would you say your child gets into compared with other teenagers you know—much less, somewhat less, somewhat more, or much more?

predictor of monthly earnings at age 27: Married study participants earned the most, followed by unmarried but cohabiting study participants, and then single participants not cohabiting. Numbers of births and out-of-wedlock births to study participants were both negative predictors of monthly earnings at age 27.

Most of the misconduct-related variables listed in Table 46 negatively predicted monthly earnings at age 27—personal misconduct in early elementary school, parent-rated trouble gotten into by 15-year-olds, self-reported pickups by the police through age 19, self-reported total and serious misconduct at ages 19 and 27 (but not at age 15), lifetime arrests and most categories of arrests, criminal sentences to prison, and time served in prison or on probation or parole. Just as it was for highest year of schooling, the strongest misconduct-related predictor of monthly earnings at age 27 was personal misconduct as rated by early-elementary teachers.

As shown in Tables 44 to 46, most of the noneconomic variables that were positive predictors of highest year of schooling were weaker positive predictors of monthly earnings at age 27, and most of the noneconomic variables that were negative predictors of highest year of schooling were weaker negative predictors of monthly earnings at age 27. The exceptions to this rule are interesting, because they identify variables that were more strongly related to marketplace success than to school success. Slightly better at positively predicting monthly earnings at age 27 than at positively predicting highest year of schooling were

- Preschool program experience
- Verbal skills, emotional adjustment, and socioemotional state in early elementary school
- Marital status at age 27
- Study participants' views at age 15 of their parents' parenting ability
- Study participants' assessment at age 15 of how well they met others' expectations
- Self-confidence at age 15 and self-esteem at age 19

Slightly better at negatively predicting monthly earnings at age 27 than at negatively predicting highest year of schooling were

- Self-reported school suspensions
- Self-reported total and serious misconduct at age 27 (but not at age 15 or 19)
- Prison sentences and time served in prison

Predictors of Lifetime Arrests

The reader of this section should keep in mind that since arrests are undesirable, positive prediction of lifetime arrests is undesirable and negative prediction of lifetime arrests is desirable. As shown in Table 44, many scholastic variables were negative predictors of lifetime arrests.

- Preschool experience
- Early-elementary teacher ratings of school potential, mothers' participation, social development, emotional adjustment, school motivation, and socioemotional state
- Intellectual performance after one preschool year and at ages 5 and 6 (but not at age 3 or after age 6)
- School achievement from age 7 to age 14 (with correlations rising from age 7 to age 11, then dropping slightly at age 14)
- Literacy at age 27 (but not at age 19)
- 15-year-olds' thinking of college
- Parents' hopes for 15-year-olds' schooling
- 19-year-olds' attitudes towards school
- Regular high school graduation
- High school graduation or the equivalent
- Highest year of schooling

Placements in special school services were positive predictors of lifetime arrests.

- Years in disciplinary programs
- Years retained in grade
- Years in programs for emotional impairment
- Self-reported school suspensions

It is interesting that years in programs for educable mental impairment (EMI) did not predict lifetime arrests. As noted earlier, these placements represent both the identification of children's problems and the remedial treatment of these problems. The positive correlations between years in most special school services and lifetime arrests indicate that with respect to preventing crimes, these services were not totally successful, although they might have been successful in reducing crime rates below what they would have been without the services. Perhaps EMI programs were successful in preventing crime.

As shown in Table 45, gender was a negative predictor of lifetime arrests—males were arrested more than females. Among economic status variables, the few negative predictors of lifetime arrests were current employment at ages 19 and 27, monthly and annual earnings at age 27, and car ownership at age 27; the only positive predictor was months unemployed in the previous 2 years. The 15-year-old study participants' estimate of their parents' parenting ability was a negative predictor of lifetime arrests. Several family and economic variables were noticeably

> At the age of 21, **ALICE*** was found murdered in a burned
> building, probably the victim of a drug-related crime. She had
> been one of 10 children and was raised in a small house,
> where 19 people lived. On one home visit, her second-grade
> teacher couldn't walk across the floor because of the litter,
> discarded food, children, and puppies. Alice's mother lay on
> the couch, not raising her head to talk to the teacher. Alice
> missed school about half of the time, was classified as
> mentally impaired, and dropped out of school after repeating
> ninth grade four times.
>
> ---
> *These stories describe real study participants but do not use their real names.

not predictors of lifetime arrests—marital status, socioeconomic status at
study entry, and receipt of various social services.

As shown in Table 46, the consistency of misconduct from childhood to adulthood was demonstrated by strong correlations between
lifetime arrests and ratings by early-elementary teachers of school misconduct and personal misconduct, the importance that the 19-year-old
study participants attached to staying out of trouble with the police, and
self-reported misconduct at ages 19 and 27 (but, curiously, not at age
15). Lifetime arrests had high positive correlations of .598 to .970 with
other arrest and crime categories (adult arrests, juvenile arrests, adult
felony arrests, adult misdemeanors, personal-violence crimes, drug-
dealing crimes, and property crimes), partly because these categories
were in the total count of lifetime arrests. Criminal sentences and time
served also had high positive correlations with lifetime arrests.

A Causal Model

From the significant predictors of the three success variables listed in
Tables 44 through 46, 14 variables that either had significant correlations
with preschool experience or were important for other reasons were
selected as preliminary candidates for a causal model.[59] Table 47 presents
an intercorrelation matrix of the 14 variables, which were measured by the
instruments described in Chapter 2 (with IQ after one preschool year measured by the Stanford-Binet Intelligence Scale [Terman & Merrill, 1960];[60]
school motivation and personal misconduct measured by kindergarten

---

[59]The approach presented in this report was to use variables already presented earlier in the
report rather than to combine these variables into multivariate constructs, as was done for a
causal model presented for the Perry study through age 19 (Berrueta-Clement et al., 1984).

[60]Using IQ after the first preschool year was better than using IQ after the second
preschool year, because *after the first preschool year* included all 5 waves, while *after the
second preschool year* would have included only 4 of the 5 waves.

Table 47

CORRELATION MATRIX OF CENTRAL VARIABLES IN THE STUDY

Variable	Variable						
	A	B	C	D	E	F	G
A. Gender[a]	1.000	−.026	.031	.708*	.056	.089	−.170
B. Entry SES	−.026	1.000	.032	.022	.223*	.237*	−.399*
C. Preschool experience[b]	.031	.032	1.000	.689*	.497*	.184	−.181
D. Preschool by gender	.708*	.022	.689*	1.000	.375*	.207*	.250*
E. IQ after one preschool year	.056	.223*	.497*	.375*	1.000	.423*	−.375*
F. School motivation, K–3	.089	.237*	.184	.207*	.423*	1.000	−.655*
G. Personal misconduct, K–3	−.170	−.399*	−.181	−.250*	−.375*	−.655*	1.000
H. Years in EMI programs	.013	−.168	.237*	−.167*	−.440*	−.507*	.353*
I. Years retained in grade	−.019	−.190*	−.097	−.125	−.278*	−.393*	.349*
J. School achievement at 14	.118	.326*	.339*	.313*	.443*	.696*	−.462*
K. Highest year of schooling	−.042	.230*	.218*	.164*	.390*	.457*	−.489*
L. Literacy at 19	−.062	.257*	.215*	.117	.435*	.450*	−.268*
M. Lifetime arrests	−.330*	−.125	−.200*	−.355*	−.270*	−.327*	.399*
N. Monthly earnings at 27	−.105	.116	.245*	.079	.242*	.369*	−.420*

Variable	Variable						
	H	I	J	K	L	M	N
A. Gender[a]	.013	−.019	.118	−.042	−.062	−.330*	−.105
B. Entry SES	−.168	−.190*	.326*	.230*	.257*	−.125	.116
C. Preschool experience[b]	.237*	−.097	.339*	.218*	.215*	−.200*	.245*
D. Preschool by gender	−.167*	−.125	.313*	.164*	.117	−.355*	.079
E. IQ after one preschool year	−.440*	−.278*	.443*	.390*	.435*	−.270*	.242*
F. School motivation, K–3	−.507*	−.393*	.696*	.457*	.450*	−.327*	.369*
G. Personal misconduct, K–3	.353*	.349*	−.462*	−.489*	−.268*	.399*	−.420*
H. Years in EMI programs	1.000	.366*	−.481*	−.372	−.523*	.052	−.235*
I. Years retained in grade	.366*	1.000	−.387*	−.491*	−.430*	.239*	−.332*
J. School achievement at 14	−.481*	−.387*	1.000	.454*	.564*	−.285*	.233*
K. Highest year of schooling	−.372*	−.491*	.454*	1.000	.399*	−.422*	.516*
L. Literacy at 19	−.523*	−.430*	.564*	.399*	1.000	−.220*	.318*
M. Lifetime arrests	.052	.239*	−.285*	−.422*	−.220*	1.000	−.302*
N. Monthly earnings at 27	−.235*	−.332*	.233*	.516*	.318*	−.302*	1.000

Note. n = 77 to 123.

[a]1 = male, 2 = female.

[b]1 = no-program group, 2 = program group.

*p < .05, two-tailed.

CALVIN's early behavior presaged his future criminal career. Asked as a young child what he would do when he entered school, Calvin replied, "Look for something to do wrong." Teacher reports confirm his self-assessment. His first-grade teacher rated Calvin as most likely to get into fights or quarrels with other students and described him as having to be coaxed or forced to work or play with others, having difficulty learning, making unusual or inappropriate responses during normal school activities, and becoming upset when faced with a difficult problem or situation. His second-grade teacher reported that Calvin had motivational problems affecting his academic performance. At third grade, Calvin was referred for psychological evaluation. His teacher wrote: "Slow in arithmetic and reading (below first-grade level). Becomes frustrated and refuses to do schoolwork that is new to him. He has attempted to skip from school. Needs more help than I can give." At that point Calvin was recommended for special education, but he repeated third grade instead. He dropped out of school after grade 10. His extensive criminal record includes robbery, breaking and entering, assault, attempted murder, and drug dealing; he has served time in prison.

through third-grade teachers' ratings of children on the PBI [Vinter, Sarri, Vorwaller, & Schafer, 1966]; school achievement at age 14 measured by the CAT [Tiegs & Clark, 1971]; and literacy at age 19 measured by the APL Survey [American College Testing Program, 1976]).

For preliminary causal models, the 14 variables from Table 47 were divided into the time periods of early childhood (ages 3–5), early-elementary years (ages 6–9), school years (ages 6–18), post-high-school (ages 17–27), and success at age 27 (the variables did not permit mutually exclusive age delineations). Eventually, 5 variables used in preliminary causal models were excluded from the model we present here, because the sample size for all the variables combined (which ranges from 82 to 123 in the model presented) would not permit statistical confidence in a model of more than 9 variables.

The decisions about which variables to exclude from the 14 were as follows: (1) The variable gender and (2) another variable representing the interaction of preschool experience and gender were excluded because each of them predicted only 1 variable—lifetime arrests—that came at the last stage of the model. (3) The variable school achievement at age 14 was excluded because its relatively large amount of missing data (28 cases missing) reduced sample size to less than 70 in the models that included it and because it was reasonably well represented, conceptually and empirically, by literacy at age 19. (4) The variable retention in grade was first combined with the variable years in programs for educable mental impairment (EMI), but then excluded instead because years in EMI programs correlated extremely well with the combination variable. (5) Personal misconduct was excluded because, like school motivation, it was based on ratings by kindergarten through third-grade teachers but was not linked to as many other variables in the models examined (serving only as a link between IQ after one preschool year and highest year of schooling).

The remaining 9 variables are used in the causal model we present here. Divided into time periods, they are as follows:

- **Early childhood, ages 3–5**
  Socioeconomic status at study entry
  Preschool experience (1 = no program, 2 = program)
  Intellectual performance after one preschool year (Stanford-
  Binet IQ)

- **Early elementary years, ages 6–9**
  School motivation (PBI)

- **School years, ages 6–18**
  Years in EMI programs

- **Post-high-school, ages 17–27**
  Literacy at age 19 (APL Survey)
  Highest year of schooling

- **Success at age 27**
  Lifetime arrests
  Monthly earnings at age 27

Table 48 presents the findings of a series of stepwise regression analyses of the 9 variables. The variables in each time period were treated as dependent variables, with the variables from the earlier time periods treated as independent variables. Thus, the variables from ages 3–27 were treated as independent variables for the analysis of lifetime arrests and monthly earnings at age 27; then, excluding lifetime arrests and monthly earnings at age 27, the variables from ages 3–18 were treated as independent variables for the analysis of highest year of schooling and literacy at age 19; and so on.

The first step in the stepwise procedure analyzed the prediction of the dependent variable by the strongest predictor among all the independent variables. The second step analyzed the prediction of the dependent variable by the two strongest predictors among all the independent variables, and so on, until the final step, in which all the significant predictors (at $p < .05$) were included. However, as can be seen in Table 48, none of the dependent variables in the analyses required more than two steps. Table 48 presents four statistics of the stepwise regression analyses of each variable—the beta weight, representing the strength of the association; the degrees of freedom associated with the analysis; the p-value associated with the T-value of the beta weight; and the r^2, representing the variance in the dependent variable accounted for by the independent variable or variables in the equation at the step at which that independent variable was first included.

Table 48

REGRESSION ANALYSES OF CAUSAL MODEL VARIABLES

Time Period				
Dependent Variable Independent Variable	Beta Weight	*df*	*p*	r^2
Success at age 27				
Lifetime arrests Highest year of schooling	−.449	1, 80	.000	.201
Monthly earnings at 27 Highest year of schooling	.500	1, 80	.000	.250
Post-high-school, ages 17–27				
Highest year of schooling School motivation	.445	1, 84	.000	.198
Literacy at 19 Years in EMI programs IQ after one preschool year	−.441 .252	1, 84 2, 83	.000 .012	.307 .358
School years, ages 6–18				
Years in EMI programs School motivation, ages 6–9 IQ after one preschool year	−.392 −.275	1, 88 2, 87	.001 .006	.257 .320
Early elementary years, ages 6–9				
School motivation, K–3 IQ after one preschool year	.423	1, 93	.000	.179
Early childhood years, ages 3–5				
IQ after one preschool year Preschool experience Socioeconomic status at study entry	.491 .208	1, 121 2, 120	.000 .008	.247 .291

Note. Stepwise regression analyses selecting only the independent variables that are significant at $p < .05$, two-tailed.

Figure 16 represents the information presented in Table 48 in the form of a causal model that takes into account the temporal ordering of the variables. Because of the small sample-size for such complex analyses, this model must be viewed as suggestive rather than definitive. It traces the significant relationships between pairs of variables and does not account for the variance in preschool program effects other than the direct effect of preschool experience on IQ after one preschool year. It *suggests,* for example, that the effect of preschool experience on years in EMI programs is accounted for by the mediation of IQ after one preschool year and early elementary school motivation, but *it does not account for the variance* in years in EMI programs that is indirectly attributable to the preschool experience. Keeping these caveats in mind, we can nevertheless make some interesting observations about this causal model.

The model suggests that the following causal path might be the route through which preschool program effects are transmitted. Since

Figure 16

A CAUSAL MODEL OF THE HIGH/SCOPE PERRY PRESCHOOL PROJECT DATA

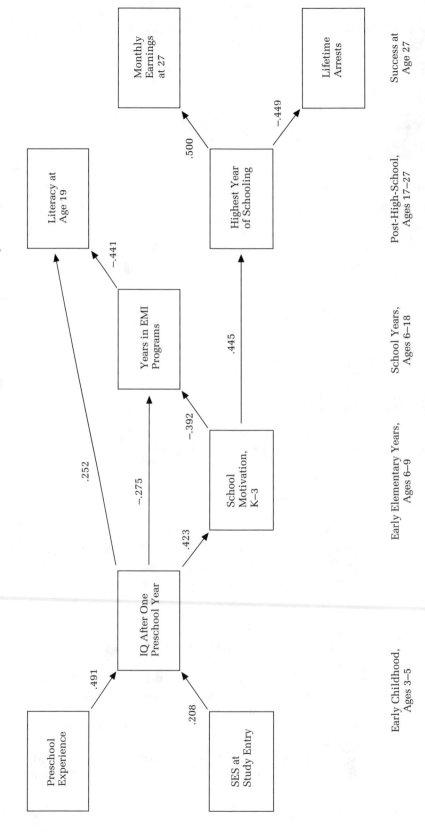

Note. Table 48 presents supporting statistics. Each line presents a path of likely causality, with the strength of the association between the two variable represented by the beta weight.

many of the variables represent individual traits rather than discrete events, the following statements slightly broaden the time periods beyond the times of measurement:

1. Preschool experience directly improves preschool participants' early childhood intellectual performance, which is also positively predicted by family socioeconomic status.

2. Preschool participants' early childhood intellectual performance improves their school motivation in elementary school.

3. Preschool participants' early childhood intellectual performance and school motivation in elementary school reduce the number of years they spend in EMI programs.

4. Because of preschool participants' early childhood intellectual performance and reduced time in EMI programs, they have higher literacy scores as they leave high school.

5. Preschool participants' school motivation leads them to complete a higher level of schooling.

6. Because they have completed a higher level of schooling, preschool participants have higher monthly earnings at age 27 and fewer lifetime arrests.

One of the intriguing aspects of this model is what it suggests about the way preschool experience, intellectual performance, and school motivation are related. Years ago, disappointed by the failure of high-quality preschool programs to permanently improve the intellectual performance of poor children, Zigler and Butterfield (1968) proposed that such programs improved children's motivation instead. The explanation suggested here adds a twist by proposing that high-quality preschool programs do lead to an improvement in children's motivation, but *because of*, not *instead of*, improvement in children's intellectual performance. Further, the reduction in children's personal misconduct because of their improved intellectual and scholastic performance constitutes a sort of early childhood version of social bonding theory (Elliott et al., 1979): Children are better at early elementary school tasks, so they engage in more socially acceptable behavior in school.

School motivation then serves as the foundation of school success, reducing placements in EMI programs and leading study participants to attain a higher level of schooling. It should be noted, however, that it takes some years for high-quality preschool programs to exert their indirect effect on school achievement and literacy. The preschool program used in the High/Scope Perry Preschool Project did not exert a significant effect on school achievement until age 14, probably because of the cumulative effect of children's better school motivation and resultant treatment by school staff.

Literacy at age 19 and highest year of schooling are the two faces of school success, achieved as the culmination of the school processes described in the last two paragraphs. The better children are at avoiding placements in EMI programs, the better their literacy as they conclude their high school experience. The higher children's school motivation, the higher the level of schooling they complete.

The highest year of schooling is a sort of gateway to adult success, a significant positive determinant of adult earnings and a significant negative determinant of lifetime arrests. Despite important concerns about the economy and the availability of good jobs, especially in impoverished communities, the school success of young people born into poverty remains a principal determinant of how much money they make as adults, as this study demonstrates. Moreover, the higher the level of schooling these young people complete, the less likely they are to be arrested—again, a relationship predicted by social bonding theory and examined in depth by Elliott and Voss (1974).

The High/Scope Perry Preschool Project data present a coherent and plausible model of how short-term program effects lead to long-term program effects. The next chapter slices the data another way, taking an in-depth look at the individual lives of 8 of the study participants.

IX A Look at Some Individuals

Ann S. Epstein

Throughout this report, numerous personal vignettes of study participants have illustrated the respective themes of the chapters. Now we explore how these separate themes coalesce to give form and color to entire lives. This chapter presents up-to-date case histories of several study participants whose lives were previously detailed through their early 20s, based on open-ended interviews conducted shortly after the age-19 interviews (Berrueta-Clement et al., 1984).[61] The individuals profiled in their early 20s, and now again at age 27, represent both the program group and the no-program group, males and females, favorable and unfavorable outcomes. As before, this age-27 examination of individual case histories was undertaken to attach personal meaning to the statistical findings of the High/Scope Perry Preschool study.

At the conclusion of the earlier presentation of case studies, the individual narratives were integrated using certain themes that emerged in the lives of the young persons as they were ending their childhood and adolescence. These themes were (a) parental roles, (b) attitudes towards money, (c) role models, (d) church and religion, (e) sense of responsibility, and (f) personality and goal orientation. In the lives studied, success was more likely for those whose parents supported schooling, who found positive role models for achievement within their family or school settings, and who evidenced a sense of responsibility for other people or causes beyond themselves and their own personal gain. We hypothesized that although exemplary role models and experiences exist everywhere, high-quality preschool programs for young children and their parents maximize the odds that children will take advantage of these opportunities.

In the age-27 case studies, the organizing themes that emerged were relevant to the lives of the young persons as they ventured into their first decade of adulthood. Whereas the end of childhood had merited a look backwards at the primary effects of family and school, the entry into adulthood is a time for present and future assessment of one's own family formation and entry into the worlds of work and community. Thus the earlier case study themes pertained to *determinants* of success, but case study issues at age 27 instead involve the present, and perhaps future, *manifestations* of success. The four themes that emerged as these young men and women talked about their lives at age 27 were

- Schooling

- Employment and earnings

- Criminal records

- Relationship to the next generation

In keeping with the statistical analyses reported throughout this book, review of the case study themes explored the relevance of gender as well as age to the path each person's life had taken.

---

[61]All names have been changed to protect the identities of the study participants.

Case Study Methodology

For the case studies, 8 study participants were chosen to represent a range of backgrounds, experiences, and developmental paths. The 8 cases did not constitute a random sample. When initially selected in their early 20s, participants were balanced across three dichotomies: program versus no-program, male versus female, and successful versus unsuccessful in terms of mainstream educational, economic, and social-outcome variables. The reason for including successful members of the no-program group was to investigate the benefits that could be obtained from experience apart from the preschool program. The inclusion of unsuccessful members of the program group allowed the exploration of those barriers that even a high-quality preschool program had little chance of overcoming. Because the same 8 cases chosen at age 19 were followed at age 27, we could not know before the present undertaking whether their lives would continue in productive or problematic directions. Thus, in pursuing these follow-up studies, there was a certain suspense about what would be discovered as well as how sense would be made of the findings.

A solid 30-year data base with only 4.9% sample attrition was as essential to the richness of the case study analysis as it was to the validity and reliability of the quantitative longitudinal research. As detailed in the last comprehensive report (Berrueta-Clement et al., 1984), the sources of case study data for study participants in their early 20s were these: (a) family background information and home-visiting records from the preschool years, (b) teacher ratings and comments from the preschool program and the elementary grades, (c) standardized test scores, (d) school records and psychological evaluations, (e) interviews with study participants at age 15 and with their parents, (f) interviews with study participants at age 19, and (g) open-ended follow-up interviews (shortly after the age-19 assessment) with those selected for the case studies and with their parents. Additional data sources for the case study updates reported here were (h) interviews with study participants at age 27, (i) school records, (j) crime records, and (k) social services records. Interviews conducted when study participants were in their early 20s, as well as portions of the age-27 interviews, were audiotaped; this process allowed us to intersperse participants' own words with the data reported in the following case studies.

Case study analysis and report preparation were carried out by the same researcher who had done the profiles of the 8 study participants in their early 20s. In both instances, the researcher was not involved in the data collection and had no personal contact with the study participants. As before, however, the interviewer familiar with the participants contributed to the development of the measures and verified the accuracy of the case study material.

One caveat: Statistically valid conclusions *cannot* be drawn from the lives portrayed in the following pages. The case studies presented here are meant to complement and illustrate the statistical analyses in the previous chapters. The case histories compiled 8 years ago not only grounded those earlier statistics in everyday lives but were also a rich source of hypotheses and exploration for the age-27 research. Similarly, the updated profiles of these young adults not only make the current numbers come to life; they also help us speculate about the future roads that these study participants and their children may follow.

The Case Studies

Each of the case studies begins with a summary of the profile presented when the study participant was in her or his early 20s (Berrueta-Clement et al., 1984). Following this summary is an update on the person's status at age 27. In the final section of this chapter, the eight narratives are examined from the perspective of the four unifying themes derived from them: schooling, employment and earnings, criminal records, and relationship to the next generation. The lessons learned from these case studies are interpreted in light of the conclusions drawn from the quantitative analyses of the age-27 longitudinal data.

JERRY ANDREWS (Program Group, Male)

Jerry at age 20
The environment . . . the parents and the neighbors and the friends, to me, if they are right, if they want you to do right, then you should do all right. And I would say, really it's the person that makes the difference. When you get to a point where you're out of high school, you got to wonder what you want to do. If you want to do it, you can set your mind to do it, you can do it.

Jerry Andrews, at age 20, was enrolled in a pre-engineering program at a community college. Working half-time as a packer at a large thrift store to finance his schooling, Jerry planned to eventually enter the University of Michigan to obtain an engineering degree with a specialty in drafting. He came from a family in which the importance of education had been stressed for several generations. Jerry's mother was pleased with the opportunity that the preschool program had provided her son, and she herself became quite involved in the program. Not only was Mrs. Andrews an active participant during home visits, she also served as a classroom aide. Living up to the family's educational values, Jerry himself received an academic award for earning all A's in his senior year of high school.

Although his parents divorced when he was quite young, Jerry's uncles provided him with strong role models while he was growing up and encouraged him to attend college. Jerry's mother attributed much of her son's success to the help and support her own mother and brothers gave her while she was raising Jerry and his sisters. She also acknowledged that Jerry's father, even after the divorce, motivated their son to excel academically. Jerry agreed but also saw important influences in his life from outside his family, notably from the friends who shared his academic interests and the teachers and school counselors who encouraged him in his studies. In turn, Jerry was proud to serve as a role model for others. He hoped that his doing well would "rub off" on others in his close-knit circle of family and friends.

Jerry at age 27

I would really like to go back to school to get my degree. I have a choice between engineering and architecture, I'm not sure. Right now, I have around 3 years of college behind me. I know it's going to take a lot of money to finish up, so I'm working every day and trying to save up.

At age 27, although Jerry Andrews has not completely fulfilled his educational goals, they are still a central part of his life. Records show that he earned 87 credits at a community college, 35 of which were transferable to a 4-year degree. He hopes to complete his bachelor's degree in engineering or architecture within the next 2 or 3 years. As he did at age 20, Jerry is working hard to finance his schooling. He currently works 68 hours a week—full-time as a postal mail carrier and part-time as a produce clerk at a supermarket. Jerry's monthly income is $2,600. He is very satisfied with his employment situation and is banking his savings. Although his heavy work-schedule does not allow him much time for relaxation, Jerry enjoys his independence and his chosen leisure pursuits: "I take care of business and I like to treat people nice. I don't have any enemies. I like to play golf, that's my main thing. And I just started trying to travel. I don't drink or smoke, so I don't have any bad habits. I'm my own person."

Jerry lives alone in a rented four-room apartment. He has never been married and does not have any children. As before, however, he continues to have close ties with his family and friends. In his estimation, they think he is "doing great." Looking back at those who influenced him in

Profile of Jerry Andrews at Age 27
Program Group, Male

Variable	Status
Schooling	3 years college completed; plans to complete B.A. in engineering or architecture by age 30
Employment	Full-time mail carrier; part-time produce clerk
Earnings	$2,600 per month
Welfare	None
Marriage	Single, never married, not cohabiting
Children	None
Home ownership	No
Community involvement	None
Criminal record	None
Role model for others	Yes, for younger siblings, cousin, friends

his formative years, Jerry cites his mother, grandmother, teachers, and friends, and the overall school environment. He says, "Everyone just seemed to help me out as I was growing up." Jerry also continues to be conscious of himself as a role model for others. He believes he is an important and positive influence on those who know him: "I have a lot of friends that see the way I do things, and they're influenced by that, and I have some people who say they want to be like me. I have a cousin who says that. There's lots who wish they were in my shoes. I think I influence friends and family members—-all positive."

YVONNE BARNES (No-Program Group, Female)

Yvonne at age 20

If I could, I would change back the hands of time. I'd become a better person 'cause there are a lot of things I want in life, and I came at it the wrong way. For one thing, when I was coming up in school, I should have knew what I wanted to do because now I kind of regret being bad in school and hanging out. I still ain't accomplished what I want in life. I wanted to be somebody and I haven't become that yet.

Yvonne Barnes, aged 20 and the youngest of eight children, lived with her parents in the same house she grew up in. Although she graduated from high school, her school records were dotted with academic problems and disciplinary incidents from the time she entered kindergarten. A first-grade psychological examination noted that Yvonne was highly anxious and withdrawn, gave bizarre responses to questions, and had poor psychomotor coordination. Records also show that Yvonne had several stays in detention centers as a juvenile. Above all, Yvonne herself said she hated to take orders from anyone. The one exception was a fourth-grade teacher whom Yvonne liked because she made Yvonne sit down and do her work and "quit being so bad."

Yvonne described her school days as a time of "hanging out." She did just enough work to get by, but her greatest pleasure was when she skipped classes or hid out in the school building. She liked sports, especially basketball, but her poor academic record prevented her from playing on the high school team. Looking back on her schooling, Yvonne regretted that she did not do better. But she was not yet ready to give up on herself and reported vague plans to get a job or enter college or enlist in the Army. Yvonne was determined to leave home and see more of the world. But she admitted that unless she changed her behavior patterns, she would find herself "hanging out" for a long time to come.

Yvonne at age 27

I grew up a lot and when I look back on the things I used to do, now it's all about the future. I'm very happy being a certified cook. I'd like to have my own restaurant someday soon. That's my goal. I work every day, and I come home after work to help my mother; she's in a wheelchair. I don't run in the streets anymore. I go to work, and I look towards the future.

At age 27, Yvonne Barnes presents a mixed picture of a hard worker and someone with a continuing history of social misconduct and run-ins with the law. She states that she has a culinary arts certificate from the local community college and has worked in restaurants for the past 7 years. Yvonne describes her current job, which she has held for 4 years, as "a certified cook and assistant to the main chef." She is proud of her credential and official title. Yvonne would like to open her own restaurant within the next 5 years. It is clear that she enjoys cooking: "It's my hobby and it's like sports to me. I go in there every day with a smile on my face. Cooking—-that's what I enjoy best." In addition to her full-time job, Yvonne also works part-time as a housekeeper at a hotel. Her combined earnings from these two jobs are $1,500 per month. Yvonne still lives with her mother and grandparents in a six-room house; she contributes to the monthly rent and pays her share of the other bills. Despite living with her family, however, Yvonne says she does not get along with them. She sees them as giving her a hard time and as being disappointed in her accomplishments to date.

Yvonne's troubles with authority have continued into adulthood. Court records show 15 misdemeanor incidents between the ages of 20 and 27, including several assault and battery charges, petty larceny, and drug possession. Yvonne was fined and sentenced to 310 days in jail; she herself reports serving 3 weeks, followed by 6 months probation. Yvonne also acknowledges getting into a serious fight with a member of her family, thefts of cars and other items, and smoking marijuana. She was under psychiatric care as recently as her mid-20s, but there is no specific diagnosis on record. Yvonne insists she has turned her life around, and she is quick to pass judgment on those who persist in the "bad habits" of her younger days: "The world has changed a lot since I

Profile of Yvonne Barnes at Age 27
No-Program Group, Female

Variable	Status
Schooling	Associate's degree in culinary arts
Employment	Full-time cook at restaurant; part-time housekeeper at hotel
Earnings	$1,500 per month
Welfare	None
Marriage	Single, never married, not cohabiting, living with mother and grandparents
Children	None
Home ownership	No
Community involvement	Church; coaches girls' basketball
Criminal record	Juvenile detention center; 15 misdemeanor incidents; assault and battery; petty larceny; drug possession; car theft
Role model for others	No, but skills admired by members of softball team

was in high school. A lot of things disappoint me, seeing people go down. They're cracked out, whatever you want to call it. I hate to see people like that. It looks bad. It makes them look bad."

The inconsistencies in Yvonne's life make it difficult to assess her accomplishments and her prospects. Her recollections of school, for example, obviously conflict with the documented evidence. School records show a pattern of academic failure and disciplinary action; yet 10 years later Yvonne recalls making the honor roll and receiving basketball awards. She says teachers were an important influence on her, but the direction of influence is not clear from her words: "A couple of my teachers always thought I was going to be terrible. And I was terrible a little bit. But then I started changing. I started being more like a lady instead of a bully, because my teachers always thought positive about me. They didn't think I was going to make it. But I pulled the wool over them. I made it."

Yvonne's belief in herself, her conviction that she can and will do better, has not changed in the last 8 years. She says that she is involved in church activities and that she has coached girls' basketball. Yvonne also says that while she is not a role model for others, the members of her former softball team look up to her and wish she had time to play with them again. But her days, says Yvonne, are taken up solely by work. "My mother always thought I was going to be somebody if I wanted to. Growing up, I was already determined that if I wanted to do something, I was going to do it. That's what I'm trying to do now. I am somebody."

CALVIN CHARLES (Program Group, Male)

Calvin at age 23
About third [grade] I got to know where the money was, and I was always trying to think of something to do to get some money. That's the way it's been ever since. I always wanted more than I could get. So you find out that you can steal something and somebody will give you a reasonable amount for it. You do it two or three times and say, "Well, this is it." One thing leads to another. I always liked to be the guy that called the shots. That's the way it was then, and it's the same way now—you get a little money, you can do that.

As age 23, Calvin Charles was interviewed in the state penitentiary, where he was serving 18 months to 5 years for breaking and entering. A high school dropout after grade 10, Calvin had a history of resistance to authority and poor intellectual performance. His preschool teacher noted that Calvin "reacts negatively to a limit or disappointment." Calvin's first-grade teacher rated him as tending to get into fights with other children, having difficulty with learning, and becoming easily frustrated. His second-grade teacher said he was poorly motivated, and his third-grade teacher recommended that Calvin be placed in special education. Calvin's academic and behavioral problems persisted throughout his school years. He entered an alternative education program in seventh grade and was suspended in eighth grade on an assault and battery charge involving another student.

By Calvin's own account, he dropped out of school so he could make money in one illegal activity or another—-larceny, drug dealing, stolen weapons. He even joined a federal job training program at age 18, not for the job training, but because he thought it would lead to useful contacts for his other criminal dealings. Calvin and his parents agreed that they encouraged him to stay in school, but by his early teens Calvin was making his own decisions. Mr. and Mrs. Charles both expressed a sense of helplessness when it came to disciplining their son: "Once they leave here, out on the street, what can you say?" The only enduring role model that Calvin saw in his life was that of Alexander Mundy, the fictional character on the television show *To Catch a Thief*. Calvin aspired to carry out his own crimes with the same cleverness as Mundy. Despite his having been caught and convicted, however, Calvin had no plans to change his means of support after his release from prison: "When my term is up, I'm going to do what I want to do."

Calvin at age 27

As I was coming up, before I got in and out of jail, I was an influence on a lot of people—-friends, people that knew me. I was a friendly type of guy. I'd been out doing wrong all week, so I got spotted for the money. I dressed nice. If I had it, I would try to help out others.

At age 27, Calvin Charles has not changed his self-image or his goals since he was last interviewed. As always, he wishes he had more money, so he could travel to places where the action is, "like the Bahamas, Las Vegas." Currently out of jail, he reports no legitimate source of income in the past 5 years. Although he says he's considering applying for a job at a fast-food restaurant, Calvin admits that his main money supply is from "hustling." He calculates his previous month's earnings at $1,500. Calvin says he completed a Chrysler training program in welding prior to his imprisonment and says he plans to get his GED within the next 3 years. He also talks about getting a job in construction within the next 5 years. Yet he seems content to "take care of business" out on the streets and says he prefers to travel where he wants, rather than to be tied down by work and family commitments.

Calvin was married at age 21 and is recently divorced. He is also the father of two children, born when he was aged 18 and 27, and he pays $50 a month in child support to his ex-spouse. Calvin appears to have no permanent address and "likes to move around a lot." He has had minimal involvement in the upbringing of his children and has no specific expectations for them. Realistically, although Calvin says he is admired by friends and associates, he does not see himself as having any influence on his children. With a history of stealing, breaking and entering, criminal sexual conduct, assault, attempted murder, arson, and drug possession, Calvin obviously does not hope to be a positive role model for the next generation. Yet he adopts a swaggering stance about his life. Asked how someone else would describe him, he replies: "Pretty cool most of the time. He don't socialize much. He don't hang out too much. Pretty much takes care of business. He can pretty much hold his own."

Profile of Calvin Charles at Age 27
Program Group, Male

Variable	Status
Schooling	Dropped out of high school after 10th grade; 3 years of special education
Employment	None within last 5 years; "hustling"
Earnings	$1,500 per month obtained illegally
Welfare	None
Marriage	Divorced after 7 years of marriage
Children	2 children born when he was aged 18 and 27
Home ownership	No
Community involvement	None
Criminal record	1-year jail term and 2 years probation for breaking and entering; arrest for attempted murder; assault; drug possession; theft
Role model for others	No, but envied by others when he has money

GERALD DANIELS (No-Program Group, Male)

Gerald at age 24

The economics and education—-you can't separate them. It's going to be hard, but there are sacrifices one has to make. It has to start when you are a child, it's a long process. But tough it out, because the game is set, this is how it's being played, education is a way. You can frustrate yourself, or you can get in there and play the game.

Gerald Daniels at age 24 said that he was proud to have attended a Big Ten university on a full athletic scholarship and to have majored in criminal justice. He attributed his success to a supportive family, positive role models throughout his school years, and his own sense of importance and determination. The oldest of five siblings, Gerald was raised by his mother, stepfather, and maternal grandmother in a close-knit family unit. Despite some early teacher-comments about his impulsiveness and distractibility, Gerald was nevertheless a good student. Elementary school teachers reported that his mother was highly supportive of her son's schooling and maintained an active involvement in Gerald's school activities.

Although he was a good student, sports were always more important to Gerald than academics. Looking back, he regretted not spending more time on his studies: "I went out for sports. It was the one thing I really knew I could do. I did well in school, but I never took books home in order to study. I just did enough to get by; I didn't really try to do the best or better myself." Fortunately, Gerald's sports activities also provided an opening for him to receive encouragement from other adults in the school system. Gerald was particularly grateful to his athletic coaches and high school counselor for taking a personal interest in him, his study habits, and his future. Gerald said of his high school football coach, for example, "He instilled in me the desire to work hard. He put that ethic in me." Gerald's counselor enrolled him in the Upward Bound program and helped him receive tutoring in college preparatory courses.

In addition to acknowledging the importance of role models, however, Gerald also attributed his success to his own sense of importance and determination: "I have to say that I was a positive influence on myself and that I'm glad I listened to me a lot of times on important decisions." Gerald admitted, for example, that he had to overcome his lax study habits when he entered college. He claimed that his own resolve led him to "take the necessary steps" and that this process of self-improvement made him value education even more as a way to advance in life. Unable to find an attractive enough job after college, Gerald enlisted in the Army. He planned to pursue a master's degree in criminal justice while in the service and then take advantage of military benefits to enter law school. Gerald's long-range plans were to be a corporate lawyer or enter private practice: "Like anything in life, you get out of it what you put into it. Right now, I'm not satisfied, but by the same token I'm not down on myself. I'm still reaching."

Gerald at age 27

Mama never told me life would be easy and, being on my own and away from her, I realize that even more. But if anything goes wrong, I'll be about the business of getting it right. Guess you could call it responsibility. My job is not really what I want to do, but I can see the fruits of that labor will be going back to school to pursue my degree and do something I really want. Not in 5 years, but maybe in 10 years. In the meantime, I have to maintain what I'm doing and just go for what I believe.

A surprising thing about Gerald Daniels' story at age 27 is that a check of his college records reveals that he never graduated. One semester short of completing his degree, Gerald was, his transcript says, "dismissed for academic reasons." This phrase means that his grades were low and he was required to leave school for a period. According to standard procedures, he could then have reapplied for admission. Gerald never took that step. Four years later, he states that he is submitting paperwork to complete his degree at another 4-year institution within the next 2 years. A subsequent check of enrollment records, however, again failed to verify his claim, although his application may have still been in process.

Whether or not his educational plans are currently active, Gerald is working hard and saving money. For the past 3 years, he has been employed full-time in a semiskilled position, as a lathe operator on an assembly line at an automotive supply factory. His monthly earnings are $2,200. Gerald is not satisfied with his current position, however. He has applied for a skilled-trades job as a machine operator and hopes to advance with his present employer or another automotive company.

For his former life as a college student and his plans for a career in criminal justice, Gerald expresses both regret and longing: "I'm happy for the little things most folks take for granted, but it could be better. It just so happens I was blessed, not only with athletics, but also with the insight at that age to distinguish between someone who's just giving you a line and someone who speaks from his own hard work and actions. I listened and I enjoyed a lot of success, the university scholarship." Today, Gerald tries to pass along that help to others—volunteering as a Big Brother and in the Fellowship of Christian Athletes.

Clearly, the influence of his mother and his coaches has remained with Gerald into adulthood. "I've always been more of a listener than a talker, and Mama always had a lot to say. It happened to have been the right advice. In terms of group [influences], it would be my high school football team and my coach. From 15 to 17 was a turbulent time, my life could have gone good or bad. The coach was a heck of a motivator, and I believed what he said and followed him. It just so happens I found a lot of success in that. Sports was my outlet." That determination to hang in and to overcome setbacks continues to operate in Gerald's life. He sees life as an athletic contest that is not over as long as the game is still being played. "I'm just trying to play the game, and when it's right, I'll go for it. I'm just starting out now. I'm not discouraged. It's slower than I anticipated, but I think it's the best route. I was fortunate that significant others came into my life at a point where I could truly listen to what someone had to offer. I believe that with hard work and sacrifice, it's possible to achieve the things that you believe in." With this attitude, Gerald Daniels may yet reach his goal.

Profile of Gerald Daniels at Age 27
No-Program Group, Male

Variable	Status
Schooling	Completed 3.5 years college in criminal justice on athletic scholarship; plans to complete a bachelor's degree and a master's degree by age 30
Employment	Full-time lathe operator (semiskilled)
Earnings	$2,200 per month
Welfare	None
Marriage	Single, never married, not cohabiting
Children	None
Home ownership	Yes
Community involvement	Big Brothers; Fellowship of Christian Athletes
Criminal record	None
Role model for others	Yes, for younger siblings, youth in his community

BONITA EMERSON (Program Group, Female)

Bonita at age 21

I have an aunt who's teaching. She'd been teaching about 10 years when she lived with us for a while. I think she had a big influence. And my parents were always pushing me, too, to get a good education. They always pushed. They pushed us all.

Bonita Emerson at age 21 had completed her bachelor's degree in special education at a local 4-year state university and was planning to obtain her master's degree in learning disabilities. Teaching had been a lifelong calling for Bonita, who began tutoring younger children as early as elementary school. Bonita credits her family and the church with emphasizing education and encouraging her academic achievements. Mr. Emerson, Bonita's father, felt that his daughter's preschool program involvement "gave her a jump" on learning before she entered kindergarten. Both of her parents also emphasized the positive atmosphere they created at home. Mr. Emerson was a minister, and all the members of the family were active churchgoers and community volunteers. Her father summed up Bonita's childhood: "We were involved in school from the beginning of Day One until she completed it. Bonita had the desire to be a teacher, and we encouraged her in every effort, brought her up in a Christian atmosphere, said to keep her goal in mind. She had ambitions from the beginning, and as the parents, we always stood behind her."

In addition to her parents, Bonita cited her aunt as a powerful role model. This aunt, who was also a special education teacher, lived with the Emersons for 3 years beginning when Bonita was 9 years old. Bonita was inspired by her aunt's dedication to helping the African-American community. Junior high school was also a formative period for Bonita. She marked it as the time when her "black consciousness" was raised, when she became active in many school and community organizations. The only discouragement came from a high school counselor who said Bonita would never make it through a 4-year college and advised her to settle for a 2-year community college program. "The other students never challenged him," she said, "but now, every time something positive happens to me, I make sure he hears about it!"

Bonita saw the education system as an ideal organizing force for blacks to help themselves. She believed that parents' involvement in their children's schooling was the primary mechanism for bringing about lasting improvements. After teaching black children locally for a while, Bonita planned to open her own school either within the community or in Nigeria. She envisioned a school in which parents assumed major responsibility for the educational process. Of her plans to raise her own children someday, Bonita had this to say: "I want them to know who they are. I want them to have self-respect. I don't want them to take whatever the teacher says for granted, but to research things and know for themselves whether or not it's right or wrong." Learning from her own experiences, Bonita was determined that others would no longer set limits on the achievements of African-American students.

Bonita at age 27

I'm in a leadership role. I set an example for other people to follow, and I think that's important. And I think I'm a positive role model that the students can look up to. I'm teaching at second-, third-grade level. They have a lot of questions and self-image problems, so we're working on that—just giving them positive strokes and hoping they'll come around.

Bonita Emerson at age 27 is a young woman who has reached her early goals and is now setting new ones. Bonita went on to obtain her master's degree in special education and also received her endorsement in K–12 learning disabled. She plans to continue taking graduate-level courses. Bonita taught middle school for 1 year at the age of 23 but has since been a second- and third-grade teacher in a local school district. As before, Bonita stands up for the youngsters in her community and wants them to have better opportunities in life. She is dissatisfied with the school system, which serves a predominantly low-income population, because of the inequalities she perceives in funding: "I'm thinking of the tax base for the schools. I see certain kids having a lot because of where they live and how expensive the houses are, and other kids just don't have as much, and I don't think that's fair."

Bonita has been married since the age of 25. Her husband is also a college graduate and works as a water treatment specialist. Together, their monthly earnings are $5,000. Currently renting an apartment and without children, they are saving to buy their own home and start a family within the next 5 years. Bonita maintains a close relationship with her parents and siblings and reports that they are proud of her accomplishments. She also remains close to the aunt who inspired her to

Profile of Bonita Emerson at Age 27
Program Group, Female

Variable	Status
Schooling	Bachelor's and master's degrees in special education; endorsement in K–12 learning disabled
Employment	Full-time teacher of second-third grade
Earnings	$2,200 per month; spouse—$2,800 per month
Welfare	None
Marriage	Married since age 25
Children	None
Home ownership	No
Community involvement	Church; teaches Sunday school; member of national and local African-American organizations
Criminal record	None
Role model for others	Yes, for students and other adults

become a special education teacher. Bonita still talks about the years her aunt lived with them and recalls accompanying her aunt to class, so she could observe her work with the youngsters. Together with her family and the influence of the church, Bonita feels she has been fortunate in her role models and early experiences. But she also remembers school counselors who tried to discourage the ambitions of young black students: "The negative influence was counselors who said if you want to work with kids, why don't you just open up a day care center in your back yard, because you can't ever make it through college. I went back and showed them after I made it, and luckily, they're no longer there."

Today Bonita sees herself as an important role model for her students as well as for the other adults around her: "I'm an influence on everyone that I'm around, especially the youth. I try to help motivate them." Bonita also remains active in the church and other African-American organizations. She teaches Sunday school and is a member of the National Black Child Development Institute and the local chapter of the National Association for the Advancement of Colored People. Bonita continues to work for the people and causes she believes in: "If there's something I want to accomplish, I'll do it. I'm churchgoing, friendly. I like being around other people at times, and other times I like to be by myself. But mostly I like to be involved in community groups."

MARLENE FRANKLIN (Program Group, Female)

Marlene at age 22

I hope that I will be sitting back with a lot of money in my pocket and raising my kids to the best of my abilities, and with a new mate that is going to better my life. I am not going to look for no one that's going to make me look bad financial-wise. I am going to look for a much better man than I had, and I am quite sure that I can get one. I am going to go out there and try my best.

Marlene Franklin at age 22 had two children, aged 1 and 2, and was in the middle of divorce proceedings after 3 years of marriage. She was receiving AFDC and food stamps. Marlene attributed the breakup of her marriage to her husband's dissatisfaction with her use of marijuana, although she claimed he exaggerated the problem. It was clear that she had not yet given up on her marriage, although her plans to hold it together through the church or some other counseling were vague. Marlene was adamant about wanting to do a good job of raising her children, whether alone or with their father or a new mate. Being attached was important to Marlene's self-image; if her marriage did break up, she was determined to find someone who could provide for her financially and make her look good in the community.

The youngest of five children, Marlene was the only one of her siblings to graduate from high school. She was a well-behaved but academically marginal student. Marlene said she enjoyed school, particularly because it provided an escape from her mother's strict supervision: "I liked going a lot. I enjoyed that I was getting away from home for a couple of hours." Although her high school grades were typically D's, Marlene loved participating in school sports: "I was on the basketball and volleyball teams and practiced every day after school, so I didn't have to come home. I'm not going to say I was an A student, but I liked it, just being in school." After graduation, Marlene enrolled in a 2-year secretarial program at the local community college. She dropped out after a year. According to Marlene, she left because she did not like her teachers. According to Marlene's mother, her daughter left because she began dating and running around and rushed into starting a family.

Faced with the prospect of raising two children on her own at the age of 22, Marlene was ambivalent about the direction she wanted her life to take. She talked about taking things into her own hands, possibly going back to school or applying for a job—-but usually found some excuse (fees, child care) to explain why she had not yet taken the first step. She planned to rear her children less restrictively than she had been raised—-and in the next breath said that she thought strictness was necessary: "I think I am going to raise them different. I was raised the old-fashioned way. My mother didn't trust me. After I grew up and saw how things were on the street, I really appreciate the way she kept me in the house. I'm not going to be as strict on my kids. She was pretty well strict with me, but I loved it." The confusion evident in this statement was characteristic of the confusion in Marlene's life. She wanted something better, but what—-or how to get it—-still eluded her.

Marlene at age 27

Being in this apartment. This is the main frustration. I don't want to be in these apartments. Bad atmosphere. The way people live around here is terrible, as far as they're rowdy, they want to fight all the time. I've seen people shot right down the street. I want to get out of here.

The first unexpected fact one learns about Marlene Franklin at age 27 is that she is still married. She is living with her husband and their two daughters, now aged 7 and 8, in a rented apartment in subsidized housing. Also living with them is Marlene's 14-year-old niece (whom Marlene is trying to get custody of). Concerned about the drugs and violence pervasive in her apartment complex, Marlene is very unhappy where she is. As before, Marlene wants something better but has no realistic plans for changing her situation.

For the past 5 years, Marlene has been employed as a full-time housekeeper in a convalescent home. She is somewhat dissatisfied with her job, especially the pay, the routine work, and the lack of opportunity for advancement. She would like a job at a nearby university, where the pay and benefits are better. So far, however, all that Marlene has done to seek alternative employment is to look at the want ads in the newspaper. She has not actually submitted any job applications or gone for any interviews. Marlene's husband is employed as a university custodian. She estimates her monthly earnings at $1,000 and her husband's at $1,170. For 6 months, when their marriage split apart, Marlene received AFDC and General Assistance. All told, she has been on welfare for 2 out of the last 10 years. At the present time, by living in subsidized housing and getting occasional help from her husband's mother, Marlene is managing to get by.

Marlene still smokes marijuana but has no record of drug-dealing or other criminal activity. Her life is taken up with work, childrearing, and partying with her friends: "I like to have a good time. I like to party and I like people that's fun to get along with. Partying is my main thing." The lives of her children and niece appear to be similar to Marlene's, except that she is less vigilant as a parent than her mother was. Marlene's involvement in their schooling is minimal; she says she rarely helps them with their homework. According to Marlene, the girls are doing average scholastically and not getting into trouble in school. She expects they will graduate from high school, get jobs, or perhaps attend a community college or technical school.

In her own assessment, Marlene has been "having a good life so far." She is content to "get up and go to work every morning; get in a couple of parties every now and then." Marlene's dissatisfactions are real but not strong enough to motivate her to take concrete steps towards changing her situation. She sees her mother, her stepfather, and one of her brothers, who is a preacher, as having been positive influences in her life. Yet she says that her current relationship with them is "not too good." Marlene states that she is a good influence on her daughters and her niece, yet she cannot specify how she is helping them. Sports were important to Marlene in high school, but she does not belong to any athletic or other community groups now. Although she and her husband live on the edge financially, Marlene is otherwise relatively content with her life of family and friends.

Profile of Marlene Franklin at Age 27
Program Group, Female

Variable	Status
Schooling	High school graduate; enrolled in secretarial program at community college, but dropped out
Employment	Full-time housekeeper in convalescent home
Earnings	$1,000 per month; spouse—$1,170 per month
Welfare	AFDC and General Assistance for 6 months in the last 5 years
Marriage	Married since age 20
Children	2 children born when she was aged 20 and 21; trying to get custody of her 14-year-old niece
Home ownership	No
Community involvement	None
Criminal record	None
Role model for others	Yes, for her daughters and her niece

DWIGHT GAINES (No-Program Group, Male)

Dwight at age 21
It's just money, you know, it's money the main influence. The greens, money, I like to have it. I like to spend it. Get out and have a nice life, 'cause you only live once, so you might as well make the best of it. If you can't do what you want, life wouldn't be worth it.

Dwight Gaines, at age 21, had graduated from high school after receiving a great deal of individualized academic help. His elementary school records painted a picture of a sociable child with academic difficulties, e.g., "poor achievement but may get by on social skills." Dwight's teachers credited him with "trying hard to learn," but by the middle of elementary school his academic difficulties became overwhelming. In fifth grade, Dwight was certified as learning disabled and spent the next 4 years in special education. His school problems were exacerbated by a chaotic home life. Dwight's parents were separated, and he, next-to-the-youngest in a family of six children, was shuffled around among various members of his extended family. His mother was on welfare, and Dwight often had to help care for his grandmother and aunt, both of whom were invalids. Questioned about her son when he was in his early 20s, Dwight's mother admitted to not knowing him very well. Dwight himself, asked about influences and role models when he was growing up, could not think of a single person who had an effect on his development.

From an early age, Dwight's overriding interest in life was making money. Beginning in junior high school, he skipped school regularly to earn money at odd jobs such as cutting grass or washing dishes. He later worked at a fast-food restaurant. During high school, Dwight supplemented his legitimate income by selling marijuana. But after his mother found out and "flushed the joints down the toilet," Dwight went straight and never did anything illegal again. Dwight and his mother were both proud of the fact that he, unlike many other young people in his neighborhood, never took to stealing. His mother said: "I didn't have no trouble on that. Ever since he come out of school, he gonna find him some type of job."

After graduation, Dwight did find a series of unskilled jobs—as a packer, dishwasher, nurse's aide. But none lasted for long, and at age 21 he was unemployed and unhappy with his situation: "I'm not really satisfied, living on social services." Dwight had always been interested in automotive mechanics, and although he did not have a mechanic's license, he was able to pick up odd jobs by word of mouth. He planned to start saving his money to buy the tools he needed to establish himself in the auto repair business. He said: "I need to keep my mind on what I'm doing. Really start banking money instead of just jacking off like I usually do. Otherwise, I'll never get nowhere."

Dwight at age 27
I'll never be at home, I'll be out mainly looking for work. I'm frustrated when I can't get out and do what I want to do, can't take my family out to movies and stuff. Everything goes towards bills right now, so I can't take care of my family as well as I'd like to.

Money is still the central theme in Dwight Gaines's life at age 27. In the past 5 years, he has held a series of unskilled jobs as a stock clerk, maintenance worker, and bus boy. He was unemployed for 6 of the last 24 months. Today, he is a full-time cook at a fast-food restaurant, earning $3.95 an hour, or $700 a month. He brings in an additional $300–$400 each month doing hauling with his truck. His wife, who has an 11th-grade education and whom Dwight married when he was 23, works as a nurse's aide. Dwight estimates his spouse's earnings at $2,000 per month. Their income is supplemented by food stamps and Aid for Families with Dependent Children, which Dwight receives for raising a daughter he had with another woman when he was 16 years old. Dwight and his wife rent a large house, where they live with Dwight's daughter and their own three children, born in quick succession after their marriage.

Dwight is frequently away from his family, looking for work: "My wife gets frustrated with me because I'm not at home." When he is home, he appears to be moderately involved in raising his four children. Although Dwight reports having many educational materials in the house (paper, crayons, books, etc.), he never reads to his children or takes them to such places as the library or local museums. He reports that his oldest daughter attended a preschool program, and he thinks it helped her with her academics. Dwight says she is doing above-average work in school, and he expects her to complete high school and go on to college. Dwight rarely helps her with her homework (less than once a month), but they do enjoy watching television together and talking over dinner. Interestingly, when asked if he has had a positive influence on anyone, Dwight cites his nieces and nephews but does not mention his

Profile of Dwight Gaines at Age 27
No-Program Group, Male

Variable	Status
Schooling	High school graduate; 4 years of special education; hopes to complete associate's degree by age 37; taking home-study program to earn truck driver's license
Employment	Full-time cook at fast-food restaurant; hauling with his own truck
Earnings	$1,000 per month; spouse—$2,000 per month
Welfare	AFDC and food stamps
Marriage	Married since age 23
Children	1 child born out of wedlock when he was 16 (he is raising her); 3 children born in wedlock when he was aged 23 to 27
Home ownership	No
Community involvement	None
Criminal record	None
Role model for others	Yes, for nieces, nephews (but not own children)

own children. Dwight's ties with the family he grew up in continue to be marginal. He characterizes his relationship with them as "fair" and admits that they think he is "not doing anything worth much."

As before, Dwight is dissatisfied with his current work situation. He would like another job, either in trucking or cooking, and says he has submitted several job applications. Dwight is still interested in auto mechanics and has just started a home-study program to become a truck driver. He also says he would like to go back to school and earn his associate's degree within the next 10 years, by the time he is 37. He realizes this plan will take some money, but at the present time all the family income goes towards paying bills, and he is unable to save much at the credit union where he has a savings account. Dwight is unhappy that he doesn't have more discretionary income to treat his family to the better things in life: "It's nice, having my family and a home, but it's not up to par, like it should be."

GLORIA HENDERSON (No-Program Group, Female)

Gloria at age 20
I would give my daughter the same advice my mother gave me, and I would stress that's it's a rough world out there and that it's going to be hard for her. But you can't depend on anybody but yourself; it's your life. If people want to be on AFDC, that's their business, but I'm not. I've worked hard, and all I can do is give my daughter advice and hope it's good. And I would be there for her whenever she needed me.

At the age of 20 Gloria Henderson was in her third year of college at a local 4-year state university. She planned to run her own business when she graduated, most likely in the area of computers or communications. Gloria saw schooling as the most promising means for a young black woman like herself to achieve her goals. It was clear that Gloria's respect for education came from the strong influence of the three prominent women in her life—-her mother and both of her grandmothers. Because her mother worked and was active in the labor union, Gloria and her two younger siblings spent a great deal of time with their grandmothers. She recalls that they always had books for her to read: "They encouraged us to count and learn our ABC's. I always loved to read." When Gloria was in junior high school, her mother returned to college to complete a bachelor's degree in industrial social work. Mrs. Henderson's determination had a profound effect on her daughter. Gloria had become an indifferent student by the start of junior high; by her own admission, she was more interested in boyfriends and cheerleading than in her studies. But after observing the contrast between her mother's values and those of her friends' families, Gloria's attitude changed. She concluded: "I don't want to be like those kids who dropped out. I want to get out of the slums, so I can raise my own kids right."

A potential impediment to Gloria's plans occurred during her senior year in high school, when she became pregnant and gave birth to a daughter. But realizing that her own mother, though married and divorced twice, was able to successfully raise three children convinced Gloria that becoming a mother need not stop her. On the contrary, having a child became a key motivation in Gloria's renewed dedication to make something of herself: "Kids can hold you back if you let them, or they can give you incentive to go on, and that's what mine has done." With the help and support of her mother and grandmothers, Gloria returned to school immediately and managed to graduate from high school with her class.

Perhaps because of her own resolve and good fortune, Gloria was sometimes quick to criticize others. "They should be trying to better themselves. They should be trying to do something with their lives instead of on AFDC. They can go to school, they can get a grant." Gloria stressed that she herself would never settle for anything less than achieving her full potential: "Even if it takes me 20 years to get out of school, you can bet I'll have what I want." But although she could be judgmental, Gloria was also committed to helping the members of her community. She wanted to start her own business, so she could offer employment to other blacks, particularly women struggling to provide their children with a brighter future. Mrs. Henderson was proud that Gloria had inherited her mother's social conscience: "I see my daughter being a very community-minded person. She'll see that once she reaches her goal, she can never go back to the ghetto, but she can help and encourage people. I see her doing that, following right in her mama's footsteps."

Gloria at age 27

I've heard people say they're envious of me because I don't let anything stop me. I'm not an overachiever, but I'm never satisfied. At the job where I am now, I started at the lowest level, and I've been promoted every year since, and now I'm a supervisor. They know how I am, and if they can't offer me more money or put me in a higher position, I won't stay there.

Gloria Henderson at age 27 is in many ways the same determined and independent young woman she was at the age of 20. Family and financial obligations meant that Gloria was unable to continue with college as planned. She earned an associate's degree in criminal justice and enrolled in a 4-year college but dropped out before completing her third year. Gloria expects to resume her schooling and complete a bachelor's degree in sociology within the next 3 years. In the meantime, Gloria is working full-time as a supervisor of computer operations at a large state university, earning $19,000 annually. She is dissatisfied with her job, citing racism and lack of opportunity for advancement as her main grievances. Once she gets her degree, Gloria hopes to get a job in the probation department or some other division of the state criminal-justice system. She maintains a savings account and investments, but admits that she sometimes struggles financially. Fortunately, her family or her boyfriend can help her out when she gets in a tight spot.

Not surprisingly, Gloria continues to be extremely close to her mother and grandmother: "The only reason I'm where I am today is because of them. I had powerful influences and role models standing behind me and telling me everything's going to be okay. Everybody makes mistakes. It's easy to stray in the wrong direction, especially when you have kids at an early age. My mom and my grandmother were there when nobody else was." Gloria also talks glowingly about the boyfriend she has been seeing for the last 3 years and with whom she had her second daughter, a year ago. "My boyfriend is already where I'm trying to go. He's established, he's a positive force and a good role model. He has a house and he's a steady climber, and that's very important to me. I can't be married to anybody that's not trying to better himself." Gloria hopes to marry this man within the next 5 years and own a house. She is still motivated by a strong desire to provide for her children's future. "I look at my daughters and it makes me want to make a better life for them. I don't want my kids to turn to a negative atmosphere, to want things that come easy to people who aren't doing the right things. I didn't do it the way society planned, to get married and then to have a family. But as far as I'm concerned, I'm doing very well."

In addition to her own family, Gloria continues to be concerned about the well-being of African-Americans as a group. She is active in her church and other community organizations; she volunteers as a cheerleader coach for Little League football. Gloria believes that once she gets her degree in criminal justice, she can make a greater contribution to the community. And she is willing to be patient and steadfast in pursuit of her goals. "Right now I'm working on various projects where I'm meeting people, and I'm learning how to communicate and deal with upper management. I think that's going to be a very important role when I do graduate and start on my role within the criminal-justice field. I hope to be very happy with whatever I'm doing. It's not a dream, because it's *going* to happen."

Profile of Gloria Henderson at Age 27
No-Program Group, Female

Variable	Status
Schooling	Associate's degree in criminal justice; dropped out of 4-year college but plans to get bachelor's degree in sociology by age 31
Employment	Full-time supervisor of computer facilities at university
Earnings	$1,580 per month
Welfare	6 months within past 10 years
Marriage	Single, never married, not cohabiting; steady 3-year relationship with man she plans to marry
Children	2 children born out of wedlock when she was aged 18 and 27
Home ownership	No
Community involvement	Church; community organizations; cheerleader coach for Junior Little League
Criminal record	None
Role model for others	Yes, for children, sister, friends, and co-workers

Case Study Themes and Conclusions

Table 49 cuts across the diverse lives of the 8 case studies and summarizes them in terms of the four organizing themes:

- **Schooling**—special education, high school completion, and post-secondary attainment

- **Employment and earnings**—work, income, use of public assistance, and home ownership

- **Criminal records**—misdemeanors and felonies

- **Relationship to the next generation**—children born out of wedlock and being a role model to others

Our intent in drawing up the table is to examine the individual cases with respect to the same variables that accounted for successful adulthood in the full-sample study. It is also interesting to look at the life patterns with regard to some of the gender differences uncovered in the quantitative analyses. The reader is again cautioned, however, that this comparison of 8 cases does not involve statistically valid tests of the variables examined. Our deliberate selection of both successful and unsuccessful cases from the program group and the no-program group alike means the cases cannot be used to compare program outcomes. Nevertheless, by combining case study and full-sample findings, we can better understand the interplay of factors in diverse lives over a 30-year period. The insights gained from these individual narratives allow us to interpret, with even greater certainty, how a high-quality preschool program can contribute to greater accomplishment and fulfillment in human lives.

Schooling

Comparing those with the four highest to those with the four lowest total scores points up that the successful young adults clearly had an educational advantage over the unsuccessful ones (75% vs. 25% of possible positive indicators on the 6 schooling variables). Unsuccessful cases usually ended their schooling with high school, either dropping out or just barely making the grades for graduation. Successful young adults continued their education beyond secondary school. The 4 most successful cases completed 1–2 years of college. Only 1 had thus far earned a bachelor's degree (and a master's), but the 3 others were all actively working towards the completion of college and, in 1 case, graduate training. Their stories illustrate the financial constraints that low-income youths without family resources face in completing postsecondary education according to mainstream timetables. But their persistence also reflects a determination instilled at home, and usually nurtured by supportive school staff, to succeed through educational attainment.

Table 49

CASE STUDY INDICATORS OF SUCCESS

Indicators of Success	Case Study[a]							
	B.E. (P, F)	G.D (NP, M)	J.A. (P, M)	G.H. (NP, F)	M.F. (P, F)	Y.B .(NP, F)	D.G. (NP, M)	C.C. (P, M)
Schooling								
No special education	1	1	1	1	1	1	0	0
High school diploma	1	1	1	1	1	1	1	0
1–2 years of college	1	1	1	1	0	1	0	0
3–4 years of college	1	1	1	1	0	0	0	0
Bachelor's degree	1	0	0	0	0	0	0	0
Master's degree	1	0	0	0	0	0	0	0
Employment and earnings								
Full-time employment	1	1	1	1	1	1	1	0
Earning $2,000+ per month	1	1	1	0	0	0	0	0
No public assistance	1	1	1	1	0	1	0	1
Home ownership	0	1	0	0	0	0	0	0
Criminal records								
No misdemeanors	1	1	1	1	1	0	1	0
No felonies	1	1	1	1	1	0	1	0
The next generation								
No out-of-wedlock children	1	1	1	0	1	1	0	0
Role model for others	1	1	1	1	1	0	1	0
Success score (0–14)	13	12	11	9	7	6	5	1

Note. Each indicator of success is scored 1 for present or 0 for absent.

[a]Initials of persons studied, with information in parentheses as follows: P = program group; NP = no-program group; M = male; F = female.

The 8-member case study sample echoed the full-sample observation that schooling was a more likely success-route for females than for
males (63% vs. 38% of possible positive indicators). Overall, women in
the case study sample had higher educational achievement than men
had. Whether females had been identified as successful or as unsuccessful, they held an edge over males in the number of positive educational
indicators. Moreover, in the unsuccessful group, the males but not the
females required special education services in elementary and junior
high school. Turning to their stories, we can observe that females indicated that school was the place to be as they were growing up. They
could "hang out" and socialize even if they were not paying attention to
academic matters. For males, the action was elsewhere—on the street
earning money through legal or illegal means. Perhaps females felt that
school offered more freedom and opportunity than home; males found

that if they had no interest in learning, then school constrained them from exercising their other options.

Employment and Earnings

Employment history and earnings also clearly differentiated the successful and unsuccessful examples examined. Although only 1 case study participant was not fully employed, the successful young adults earned higher monthly incomes than the unsuccessful ones (75% vs. 0% with monthly incomes above $2,000). Because of these discrepancies in income, successful cases were not dependent on various forms of public assistance, including AFDC, food stamps, and subsidized housing. Job positions and attitudes, as well as earnings, differentiated these two groups. The positions filled by successful individuals were longer term, held more opportunities for advancement, and required the employees to assume more responsibility for themselves and others. Even if study participants saw the jobs as way-stations on the path towards college degrees and work in their chosen field, they nevertheless derived satisfaction from seeing their work as the means towards a valued end. By contrast, the unskilled jobs held by less successful individuals were viewed by them as dead ends. These participants expressed frustration with the lack of promise in their roles, and their comments portrayed workdays that were devoid of satisfaction.

Criminal Records

Criminal behavior was absent from the lives of the successful individuals studied here; juvenile and adult crimes colored the lives of half of the unsuccessful cases. Patterns of problem behavior appeared to become established early. The male and female cases with adult criminal records also had school records citing repeated instances of assaults on peers, destruction of school property, and defiance of teachers. In these lives, unruly behavior in childhood was notably linked with academic difficulties. But children who struggle with learning do not automatically turn to delinquent acts. What distinguished these two was a sense that their parents felt helpless to influence their children's behavior. Carrying out the parental roles of teacher and disciplinarian seemed beyond the personal control of the adults responsible for these youngsters.

Looking at the cases in adulthood, we can see how members of the successful group versus the unsuccessful group handled frustration. The groups appeared equally eager to achieve material success, but their tolerance for delayed gratification differed. One set of young adults resorted to criminal behavior to take what they wanted. The other set worked steadily, persisting as long as necessary, to build up their resources and gradually add to their list of accomplishments. Perhaps their earlier experiences convinced them that legitimate success was not only possible but also likely. A positive personal history not only makes it easier to defer gratification but also allows one to derive pleasure from the very process of pursuing meaningful goals. By contrast, if the future looks bleak and static, persistence foretells repetition but no rewards.

Relationship to the Next Generation

Successful and unsuccessful individuals differed not only in how they conducted their own lives but also in how they affected the lives of others (i.e., 88% vs. 50% of positive indicators). As painful as the self-realization may have been, those who were not doing well were also more apt to admit that they were not influential in the lives of those around them. Those who were successful found that being a role model to others added a further dimension and impetus to their goal seeking. Even potential setbacks, such as becoming a teenage parent, could be turned from adversity to advantage by motivating the adult to secure a solid upbringing for the child.

Looking at the intergenerational relationships of this study population raises the question of what it means to break the cycle of poverty and despair. For the most part, what these cases show are not monumental leaps forward. But from the perspective of where these young people have started, the success of those who made it has been substantial. Breaking the cycle may well be a multigenerational and incremental process. Step by step, those who are making it detour from the roads of a previous generation and from the dead ends of their peers. Instead, they move down the paths of schooling and steady work and invest their intellectual and financial capital in their own futures and the futures of their family members, friends, and communities.

Conclusion

For the case studies, success was manifested by a commitment to learning, an involvement in meaningful and legitimate work roles, and a desire to share with others the influences that shape a positive life. The question remains, How can high-quality preschool programs help youngsters embark on a journey that has success as its destination? From the life stories shared here, we have learned that early encounters establish in children a sense of their own mission and worth. Strands of childhood experience crystallize into patterns that persist into adulthood. Some fortunate children derive a sense of direction, and the skills to pursue it, from family, friends, or community groups—sources outside the school setting. But for children who cannot turn to such sources to translate the dreams of family and community into action, a high-quality preschool program can be the passage to a brighter future. And once the door is opened, new generations may enter.

X The Study in Perspective

When planning for the High/Scope Perry Preschool Project began in 1960, the world seemed simpler than it does today. The problems faced by the Ypsilanti public schools' Special Services staff ranged from the serious—-such as the unusually large number of grade retentions and unacceptably high dropout rate for African-American students from poor families—-to the almost frivolous—-such as students persistently walking up the steps in a high school stairwell marked "down." Newsmakers at the time were the juvenile gangs in the middle school who had an occasional after-school "rumble," and the high school assistant principal who announced that individual student needs would no longer be met by special adjustments in the length of the school day or the content of programs.

But the advent of the civil rights movement in the 1950s had presaged wide-scale social change. First, school desegregation and voter rights dominated the social and political issues of the early 1960s; then the Vietnamese War and its disruptive debates in the late 1960s affected all segments of the nation, shattering forever the orderly social conventions that had governed the immediate post-World War II period.

Employed by a conservative local school board that desired to protect the community from these forces of change and enforce traditional standards, the staff of the Ypsilanti school district's Division of Special Services struggled to find means for effective action. These graduates of colleges and universities of the 1950s responded to the need for change in the way that the young and inexperienced often tackle problems with no obvious solution: They rolled up their sleeves and did something. What they—David Weikart and his colleagues—did was to plan and implement an active learning preschool program to improve the life chances of poor black children. However, because of their academic backgrounds, Weikart and his colleagues also designed a classic scientific experiment to test their idea that early childhood education was a means that schools—and thus society—could use to solve this problem: How could at-risk students be helped to improve school achievement and thereby progress to a fuller measure of real-world success?

From the vantage point of the 1990s, the undertaking could easily be judged hopelessly naive. School districts are not supposed to do research—they serve children. How could a Special Services staff of a public school district select a study group and then deny half of them service? Who would authorize the service, since schools could not legally enroll children under 5 years of age? Who would fund the research even for a year, let alone for three decades? Yet, these issues, one by one, were eventually resolved.

Thus the study now known as the High/Scope Perry Preschool Project was born at a time of great social change in America. The study was created in response to a recognized local situation of low performance in the schools and problems in the community among clearly identifiable poor children. It was executed by trained professionals who solved on a daily basis the theoretical and practical problems that arose, hoping to demonstrate that poor black children can break the cycle of poverty and reach for a decent life in an open society.

With this context of the High/Scope Perry Preschool Project as a backdrop, this chapter summarizes the significant effects[62] of the preschool program and considers what features of the program may have brought them about. The chapter also examines the generalizability of the study's conclusions—to other young children and to other preschool programs. Finally, we discuss the policy implications of the conclusions from this and similar preschool-effectiveness studies.

A Summary of Significant Effects

The principal hypothesis of the High/Scope Perry Preschool study through age 27 was that good preschool programs can help children in poverty make a better start in their transition from home to community and thereby set more of them on paths to becoming economically self-sufficient, socially responsible adults.

To conduct the study, staff (a) identified 123 young African-American children living in poverty and at risk of school failure; (b) randomly assigned them to a program group and a no-program group; (c) operated a high-quality, active learning program for the program group at ages 3 and 4; (d) collected data on both groups annually from ages 3 through 11, at ages 14–15, at age 19, and at age 27; (e) after each phase of data collection, analyzed the data and wrote reports of the study. We report here the significant findings at the age-27 follow-up, along with a summary of the study's previous findings.

Educational Performance

By age 27, the program group on average had completed a significantly higher level of schooling than the no-program group had (11.9 vs. 11.0 years, including postsecondary education).[63]

Findings over time for special school services indicated that compared with the no-program group, the program group averaged significantly fewer years in programs for educable mental impairment (EMI; 1.1 vs. 2.8 years) but significantly more years in compensatory education programs (1.0 vs. 0.4 years)—perhaps because the school problems of the program group were reduced from the EMI-program level to the less intensive, less costly compensatory-program level. The percentages of program females and no-program females ever enrolled in EMI programs were significantly different (8% vs. 37%).

---

[62]This chapter's summary of findings, which presents greater detail than is found in the Executive Summary that opened this report, includes primarily those findings that are statistically significant with a two-tailed probability of less than .05. A more complete picture of the data is found in the opening summaries of Chapters 3–6, where we have also identified findings that are nearly significant ($.05 < p < .10$) and noticeable ($.10 < p < .25$).

[63]Level of schooling was scored as the actual grade of high school dropout: 12 for high school graduation or the equivalent, 12.5 or more for any postsecondary schooling, 14 for an associate's degree, 16 for a bachelor's degree, and 18 for a master's degree.

The group differences in high school graduation rates were due primarily to graduation-rate differences for the females in the two groups (Barnes, 1989). As compared with the no-program females, the program females on average completed a significantly higher level of schooling (12.2 vs. 10.5 years) and had a significantly higher rate of high school graduation or the equivalent (84% vs. 35%). Seeming to account for some of this difference was the fact that nearly significantly fewer program females than no-program females (29% vs. 55%) had been assigned to EMI programs or retained in grade (Barnes, 1989, 1991), and significantly fewer of assigned/retained females graduated from high school or the equivalent (26% of those assigned/retained vs. 85% of those not). Program males and no-program males did not differ significantly in rates of high school graduation or the equivalent (Barnes, 1989).

Over the years, the program group significantly outscored the no-program group on various tests of school achievement and intellectual performance. On the Adult Performance Level Survey (American College Testing Program, 1976), the program group significantly outscored the no-program group at age 27 in problem solving and health information and at age 19 in health information, occupational knowledge, reading, and overall literacy. On the California Achievement Tests at age 14 (Tiegs & Clark, 1971), the program group significantly outscored the no-program group in reading, mathematics, language, and total school achievement. From the end of the first preschool year to age 7, the program group scored significantly higher than the no-program group on the Stanford-Binet Intelligence Scale (Terman & Merrill, 1960) and on several other intellectual and language tests.

Findings during the teen years on the attitudes of study participants and their parents indicated the following: At age 19 the program group had a significantly better attitude than the no-program group towards the last high school they had attended. At age 15 significantly more of the program group than of the no-program group reported spending time on homework. Also when participants were age 15, significantly more program-group parents than no-program-group parents said that their children were willing to talk about school, that their children had done as well in school as they (the parents) would have liked, and that they had college hopes for their children.

Delinquency and Crime

Police and court records showed that the program group had significantly lower lifetime criminal arrest rates than the no-program group (an average of 2.3 vs. an average of 4.6 arrests, with 7% vs. 35% arrested 5 or more times). As compared with the no-program group, the program group had significantly fewer arrests for crimes of drug making or dealing (7% vs. 25% ever arrested). As compared with the no-program group, the program group on average was sentenced to significantly fewer months on probation or parole (3.2 vs. 6.6 months).

Since males were arrested more frequently than females, male group differences involved more arrests than did female group differences. As compared with no-program males, program males averaged significantly fewer lifetime arrests (3.8 vs. 6.1 arrests, with 12% vs. 49% arrested 5 or more times).

Economic Status

As compared with the no-program group at age 27, the program group reported (a) significantly higher monthly earnings (a whole-group mean of $1,219 vs. a whole-group mean of $766, with 29% vs. 7% of the whole group earning $2,000 or more); (b) significantly higher monthly earnings for those group members who were employed (an employed-group mean of $1,556 vs. an employed-group mean of $1,251, with 36% vs. 11% earning $2,000 or more); and (c) significantly higher monthly earnings for study participants and their spouses (a mean of $2,762 vs. a mean of $1,859, with 47% vs. 17% of married couples earning over $3,000).

At age 27, program males reported significantly higher monthly earnings than no-program males (a mean of $1,368 vs. a mean of $830, with 42% vs. 6% earning over $2,000). At age 27, program females reported significantly higher monthly earnings than no-program females (a mean of $1,047 vs. a mean of $651, with 48% vs. 18% earning over $1,000).

According to social services records and interviews at age 27, significantly fewer program-group members than no-program group members reported they were receiving government assistance at age 27 (15% vs. 32%); this was especially the case for females (with 26% vs. 59% on assistance). Also, a significantly smaller percentage of the program group than of the no-program group had received social services sometime during the previous 10 years (59% vs. 80%), owing primarily to a significant difference for males on this variable (52% vs. 77%).

Significantly more program-group members than no-program-group members owned their own homes (36% vs. 13%), and significantly more program-group members than no-program-group members owned a second car (30% vs. 13%).

When interviewed earlier, at age 19, significantly more of the program group than of the no-program group reported being self-supporting (45% vs. 25%) and employed (50% vs. 32%). Compared with the no-program group, the program group averaged significantly fewer months unemployed from the time of leaving school through age 19 (4.9 vs. 10.3 months) and they reported significantly more months employed in their age-19 calendar year (6.1 vs. 3.9 months). Significantly fewer program-group members than no-program-group members, according to the age-19 self-reports, were receiving welfare (18% vs. 32%). Social services records at the time indicated that fewer program-group members were receiving General Assistance (19% vs. 41%) and that the program group, on average, received a significantly lower annual welfare payment than the no-program group ($633 vs. $1,509).

Family Formation, Childrearing, and Health

At age 27, significantly more program females than no-program females were married (40% vs. 8%). As for males, while the same percentages in the program-group and no-program-group were married, program-group husbands were married significantly longer than no-program-group husbands (6.2 vs. 3.3 years).

In a comparison of those in the program and no-program groups who were parenting, the childrearing styles were similar in many ways. However, significantly more program-group parents than no-program-group parents said their children regularly used library cards (85% vs. 53%), and significantly fewer program-group parents than no-program-group parents said their children were turning out better than expected (28% vs. 55%), perhaps because more of the program-group parents had appropriate expectations for their children in the first place.

A Causal Model

A causal model of the Perry study data presented in this report identifies the following significant paths from one variable to the next: (a) from preschool program experience to higher intellectual performance in early childhood; (b) from higher early childhood intellectual performance to higher school motivation in elementary school; (c) from higher elementary school motivation to fewer years spent in EMI programs; (d) from fewer years spent in EMI programs to greater literacy at the end of the teen years; (e) from higher elementary school motivation to completing a higher level of schooling; and (f) from completing a higher level of schooling to higher adult earnings and fewer lifetime arrests.

Why Programs in Early Childhood Can Have Long-Term Effects

What makes a particular program experience at ages 3 and 4 so powerful that it can change the pattern of participants' lives, even when they reach adulthood? Why do the effects of some early childhood experiences last a lifetime?

The transactional understanding of human development views behavior as the result of the continuous interplay between a person's maturation and his or her experiences in settings. As they shape and reshape each other, persons and settings achieve stable patterns of relationship. People grow in the traditional settings of the family of their childhood, the school, the workplace, and the family of their adulthood. Each setting is a context for the formation of habits of interaction between the individual and other persons and events. An *intervention,* such as a preschool program, is an attempt to influence the interactions that characterize these traditional settings.

Because of its timing in the child's physical, social, and mental development, early childhood is an opportune time to provide influential experiences. Physically, preschool-aged children are mature enough to have a fair amount of both fine- and gross-motor coordination and to move about freely and easily; they are no longer toddlers. Socially, preschoolers have largely overcome any earlier fears of strangers or unfamiliar locations, and they usually welcome new settings and new interactions with peers and adults. Mentally, 3- and 4-year-olds have developed extensive ability to speak and understand and can use objects in a purposeful way. Piaget saw preschool-aged children as in the preoperational stage—needing to learn from actual objects—and on the threshold of the concrete-operational stage—being able to learn from symbols and signs (Piaget & Inhelder, 1969). When children are fully concrete-operational in thought processes, at age 6 or 7, schools begin their instruction in the sign/symbol-based skills of reading, writing, and arithmetic.

Thus preschool-aged children are on another kind of threshold—the threshold of participation in the formal school setting. Participating in any new setting entails forming new habits of interaction with persons and objects in the setting, and a person's initial behavior in the setting quite naturally creates expectations by others that affect this formation. Therefore, preparation for a new setting should focus on influencing initial behavior so it leads to the formation of desirable patterns of interaction. If expectations in the new setting were based only on superficialities (knowing colors, knowing letters of the alphabet), desirable initial behavior could be easily achieved (by drilling on color names, memorizing the alphabet). However, because desirable behavior in the new setting also involves positive underlying habits, skills, and dispositions, the initial behavior must be rooted in these habits, skills, and dispositions. Thus, an early childhood program in the year or two prior to school entry is truly the "chance of a lifetime"—the optimal time to develop the child's capacity to respond effectively to the learning opportunities that the school setting will later provide.

The Search for Mediators of Long-Term Effects

In the early 1960s the hypothesis was that early education programs would improve disadvantaged children's intelligence and thereby improve their school performance. Yet, over the years, though effective programs have reported short-term gains, most studies have failed to provide evidence that the programs raise children's IQs significantly for long periods of time. Even the Perry study reports similar average IQs for the program group and the no-program group a decade after intervention. The data from the Consortium for Longitudinal Studies (1983) and Head Start (Westinghouse Learning Corporation, 1969; McKey et al., 1985) indicate similar outcomes. A few studies, such as the High/Scope Preschool Curriculum Comparison study (Schweinhart et al., 1986), do report long-term IQ gains, but such findings are atypical.

Since sustained higher intellectual performance, as measured by IQ tests over time, does not seem to be responsible for the long-term changes in preschool participants' lives, what is? Some might suggest that it is the academic knowledge that early childhood programs provide. Most adults agree that to be successful in later schooling, children need to learn certain skills early in their lives. Yet the High/Scope Preschool Curriculum Comparison study and similarly designed studies (Karnes, Schwedel, &

Williams, 1983; Miller & Bizzell, 1983) found that children who participated in the Direct Instruction curriculum—which has a structured
approach to teaching reading, mathematics, and language—did not do
any better academically a decade after the program than did children
who participated in child-initiated active learning programs. Moreover,
the behavior of young adults who at ages 3 and 4 had participated in the
Direct Instruction preschool program revealed significantly more social
alienation from school, family, and society. Academic content, at least as
a structured objective, is not the link between an early childhood program and successful adult performance.

Personal Dispositions as Mediators of Long-Term Effects

Our best appraisal of the High/Scope Perry Preschool Project results is
this: *It was the development of specific personal and social dispositions
that enabled a high-quality early childhood education program to significantly influence participants' adult performance.* Erikson (1963)
pointed out that the typical psychological thrust of 3- to 5-year-olds is
towards developing a sense of initiative, responsibility, and independence. Katz and Chard (1993), discussing the importance of children
developing the dispositions of curiosity, friendliness, and cooperation,
pointed out that good preschool programs support the development of
such traits. However, personal dispositions are elusive; they cannot be
directly taught as topics or inserted as themes in a program of instruction. They can only gradually emerge, under the right circumstances, as
the by-products of children's engagement in developmentally appropriate, active learning experiences. In particular, chanting "I'm the best, I'm
number one!" cannot substitute for real accomplishment in developing
children's self-confidence. This leads us to the question, What specific
circumstances and program strategies support the development of desirable dispositions?

Attempts to answer this question are important undertakings of early
childhood associations. The National Association for the Education of
Young Children (Bredekamp, 1987) has outlined a set of standards for
developmentally appropriate education that form a basis for educational
quality. In addition, the High/Scope Preschool Curriculum Comparison
study (Schweinhart et al., 1986) has helped to establish the importance of
developmentally appropriate curricula that provide ample opportunities
for child-initiated learning.

The processes described in Table 50 were the essential curriculum
elements that provided the child-initiated active learning experiences
typical of the Perry preschool program. We believe these elements,
which remain central to the High/Scope Curriculum today, led to the
long-term outcomes found in the Perry study. The High/Scope
Curriculum relies heavily on **active learning** and **child-initiated experiences** during which children plan, or express their intentions; carry out,
or generate, their play experiences; and reflect on their accomplishments.

Children express their intentions   A high-quality, active learning curriculum provides numerous opportunities for children to express their

Table 50

HIGH/SCOPE CURRICULUM PROCESSES AND OUTCOMES

Process	Outcome
Children express intentions.	Initiative Responsibility
Children generate experiences.	Curiosity Independence
Children reflect on accomplishments.	Trust Confidence Divergent thinking

own intentions. Initially, children express intentions through both gestures and actions. For example, a very young preschooler may express an intention by picking up or pointing to a specific toy or by taking an adult's hand and walking to the materials she or he wants to play with. As the child matures, intentions are expressed in words: "I want the wagon," "I'm gonna play with sand and water." As the child becomes a writer and reader, intentions are expressed in more detail, through written plans, models, drawings, and detailed discussions with peers and adults. The High/Scope Curriculum calls these expressions of intent *planning;* children in a High/Scope program make plans not only during a designated *planning time* each day but also throughout the day.

Children generate experiences In addition to encouraging children to express their intentions, an active learning curriculum offers opportunities for children to act on their intentions. Effective action comes about when a child is able to interact with people, materials, events, and ideas. There should be enough time for the child to experience trial and error, generate new ideas, make choices, practice, and succeed. The personal independence described here is the key to active learning by self-motivated children. In a classroom using the High/Scope Curriculum, children act on their intentions during *work time.* Throughout other parts of the day, children's choices may be somewhat limited by specific materials, by location, or by decisions made by others, but the children are still free to use materials and respond to situations in ways that make sense to them.

Children reflect on their accomplishments Along with providing opportunities for children to express their intentions and generate their own experiences, an active learning curriculum provides opportunities for children to reflect on their activities and accomplishments. Through this process, they begin to match words to their actions and to construct memories and insights. As children mature, they use increasing verbal ability and logical thinking in their reflections on their experiences. In a High/Scope classroom, the time set aside for the reflection process is *recall time* or *review time.*

These three aspects of an active-learning curriculum—**children's expressions of intent,** their **independently generated experiences,** and their **reflections—define child-initiated learning.** The outcomes are vital to lifelong learning. They include the development of such important dispositions as initiative, responsibility, curiosity, trust, confidence, independence, and divergent thinking. These traits, valued by society, are the foundations of effective, socially responsible adulthood.

Children achieve control   When children participate in an active learning curriculum, they develop self-control and self-discipline. This control is **real power,** not over other people or things, but over themselves. Understanding what is happening in the surrounding environment, realizing that those around them are genuinely interested in what they say and do, and knowing that their efforts have a chance of leading to success give a sense of control that promotes personal satisfaction and motivates children to be productive. While no single factor assures success in life, the **sense of personal control** is certainly a major force. A high-quality, active learning preschool program supports and strengthens this way of thinking.

Research Support for Personal Dispositions as Mediators

The critical outcome of a high-quality, active learning preschool program is the development of dispositions that support the development of school skills and thus lead to better learning and social behavior. This conclusion is supported by the causal model presented in Chapter 8. Preschool experience initially produces improved intellectual performance and ability to respond, as measured by standardized intelligence tests. Better prepared by the preschool program experience to respond appropriately in school, children in the program group, as compared with children in the no-program group, are perceived and rated by early-elementary teaching staff as more motivated learners with greater potential for school success and fewer behavior problems. This performance by the children sets in motion a chain of child behavior and classroom events that helps children avoid assignment to classes for educable mental impairment and leads to higher levels of schooling completed and better out-of-school adjustment, which in turn lead to adult, real-world success. As compared with no-program-group adults, program-group adults obtain better jobs, have more income, commit to home ownership, and engage in family formation within marriage. Crime, with its cycle of drugs, arrests, sentences, and difficult relations with civil authorities, is reduced; and welfare usage, with its accompanying patterns of dependency and single parenthood, is tempered. While other preschool-effectiveness studies have not tracked their participants for as long a time as the Perry study has, they do provide evidence for this pattern of findings extending from the preschool years to adulthood.

Conclusions From the Study

At the end of three decades of research, the **overall conclusion** is that a high-quality, active learning preschool program provided African-American children born in poverty with significant lifetime benefits. It is probable that such a program can do the same for any children whose needs to develop appropriate habits, skills, and dispositions are not met elsewhere. Five **specific conclusions** are warranted.

1. Children's participation in a high-quality, active learning preschool program at ages 3 and 4 created the framework for adult success, significantly alleviating the negative effects of childhood poverty on educational performance, social responsibility, adult economic status, and family formation. Since the program group is now 30 years past the point of the preschool treatment, it is reasonable to assume that the contribution to their lives is *permanent.*

2. The lives of both the program group and the no-program group have followed a predictable pattern of development since their early school years. Any subsequent intervention, such as school remediation, special education, or criminal-justice measures, has not seemed to improve the life course of the participants. In particular, although grade retention and programs for educable mental impairment were intended to help youngsters, girls placed in these situations were nevertheless very likely to drop out of high school (Barnes, 1989, 1991).

3. The effects of the preschool program on females were different from its effects on males during the school years. For females, the preschool program appeared to create the interest and capacity to remain in school and graduate, in spite of difficulties presented by such problems as teen pregnancy. For males, the preschool program appeared to affect not their rate of high school graduation, but their adjustment to society. The preschool program seemed to create for them a chain of events that led to their assuming greater social responsibility; this included a distinct lessening of criminal and other antisocial behavior.

4. The essential process connecting early childhood experience to patterns of improved success in school and the community seemed to be the development of dispositions that allowed the child to interact positively with other people and with tasks. This process was based neither on permanently improved intellectual performance nor on academic knowledge.

5. The lifetime economic benefits to the preschool program participants, their families, and the community far outweigh the economic cost of their high-quality, active learning preschool program. If this program had not been offered, the direct costs to society in lost labor-force participation, increased criminal behavior, and additional welfare support would have far exceeded the program's costs.

Some **qualifications** must be added to the Perry study's conclusions. First of all, we must keep in mind that the findings describe two groups, but not every individual in those groups. While some young people rose above their backgrounds to reach new levels of opportunity and performance, the improvements for most were incremental rather than radical. Although the significant differences between the program group and the no-program group are of extraordinary personal and social importance, not every program participant succeeded, and not every member of the no-program group failed. Even though it can be said that the preschool program, by producing significant benefits, provided participants with a partial "inoculation" against the negative effects of poverty, it cannot be said that the preschool program in any sense offered a "cure" for the problems of poverty.

A second qualification is this. As much as the High/Scope Perry Preschool Project data support the extraordinary value of high-quality early education in breaking the cycle of poverty, preschool programs are only one part of the solution. If the nation is to really confront poverty and its related problems of unemployment, welfare dependence, crime, and drug abuse, much broader social-policy action is needed. Improved educational opportunities at *all* levels, access to medical care, affordable housing, effective job-training programs, elimination of institutional racism—all these must play a part as well. The significance of the role of high-quality, active learning preschool education should be neither overrated nor underrated.

A final qualification concerns the preschool program itself. Special note should be taken that the preschool program responsible for the effects talked about here had these four defining aspects of high quality:

- A developmentally appropriate, active learning curriculum

- An organized system of inservice training and systematic, ongoing curriculum supervision

- An efficient, workable method of parent inclusion and involvement

- Good administration, including a valid and reliable, developmentally appropriate assessment procedure; a monitoring system; and a reasonable adult-child ratio

High quality is essential if the promise of early childhood programs is to be realized. While preservice staff training, adequate staff salary and benefits, appropriate space and materials, and available health and nutrition services all contribute to the quality of a program, full realization of high quality requires an effective curriculum for the participating children and their families. There is probably nothing inherently beneficial about a program in which a child interacts with an extrafamilial adult and a group of peers each day; *a curriculum must be involved, to define the program's organization and delivery.* It is long past time to insist that the delivery and organization of all programs meet standards of quality.

Generalizability of the Findings

We must carefully consider the generalizability of findings from the High/Scope Perry Preschool Project and of findings from similar studies if we are to make good use of the research. Some opponents of preschool programs *undergeneralize* the Perry findings, whereas some proponents of preschool programs *overgeneralize them*. Undergeneralizers say that the preschool program involved unique qualities that cannot be duplicated elsewhere—that it cost too much to be practical, or that the conditions of program operation cannot be duplicated on a widespread basis, or that teachers similarly qualified cannot be found today. Overgeneralizers claim that the Perry study establishes the long-term benefits of Head Start or state-funded preschool programs or child day care programs—without considering the quality of any of these programs. Neither undergeneralizers nor overgeneralizers of the Perry study findings are contributing to the development of sound public policy.

Generalizing the findings of the High/Scope Perry Preschool Project demands attention to two aspects of the project—its *participants* and its *program operation*. Replication of the characteristics of the participants *and* the characteristics of the program should lead to replication of the effects, within the study's intervals of statistical confidence. The question is, How broadly can we define the population and the program and still retain confidence that similar effects will result? Such definition requires careful judgment involving (1) selecting descriptive categories for the participants and the program and (2) estimating what constitutes tolerable variation in these categories if replication of the original study is to be achieved.

Generalization to Children Living in Poverty

For purposes of generalization and replication, we define the Perry study participants as **children living in poverty.** We believe that generalization can be made across all of the following:

- **Specific socioeconomic conditions within poverty:** This includes parents' educational and occupational status, family size and housing, and welfare status.

- **Ethnicity:** Although the study participants were African-American children, specifically ones living in poverty and at special risk of failing in school, we believe that the same kinds of effects would be found for white children, Hispanic children, and children of other ethnic groups living in poverty, even though one or another of these groups might not encounter the same degree of discrimination, crime, or drug abuse as the young blacks in the Perry study.

- **Time:** Although the study began in the 1960s, we believe that the same kinds of effects would be found if the same study began today. The nature of poverty and hopelessness in the United States is substantially the same now as it was then. The most obvious difference is that drug-related crime in poverty areas is much more prevalent today, and such crime does make it more difficult in some places to carry out regular home visits as part of today's preschool programs.

- **Location within developed countries:** The South Side of Ypsilanti was, and is, a typical urban poverty area. Though geographically separated from inner-city Detroit, it faces similar problems of poverty, crime, and drug abuse. Generalization to other urban poverty areas throughout the U.S. and in other developed countries seems quite reasonable.

- **Location within less developed countries:** Generalization to impoverished children in less developed countries requires greater extrapolation and should be done more cautiously—not because poverty itself is so different from country to country, but because opportunity structures vary from country to country. The effects of the preschool program in the High/Scope Perry Preschool Project are clearly related to our nation's opportunity structure, that is, to the prevalence of regular education, special education, high school graduation, home ownership, employment opportunities, and so on. The study cannot tell us whether program effects of similar magnitude would occur in countries where opportunities are more limited. For example, in a country where most children do not complete elementary school, a high-quality preschool program might lead to greater success in the education actually obtained—either higher school achievement or a higher level of schooling completed; or the effect might dissipate because of the lack of opportunities for it to find expression. Woodhead (1988) has argued that the dependence of this type of research on opportunity structure severely limits its generalizability. But generalization to settings of similar opportunity structure seems quite reasonable; and generalization to settings of different opportunity structure should only be made if research in those settings confirms that generalization is reasonable.

Generalization to High-Quality, Active Learning Preschool Programs

For purposes of generalization and replication, we define the program used in the Perry study as a **high-quality, active learning program for 3- and 4-year-olds:** a program designed to contribute to their development, with daily 2¹/₂-hour sessions for children, held Monday through Friday, and weekly 1¹/₂-hour home visits to parents, with 4 adults trained in early childhood education serving 20–25 children. It is reasonable to generalize program effects to other programs with these features, but, again, the question is the degree of tolerance permitted in the variability of the program's features. Three sets of features will be considered here.

The first set of features concerns the sessions held daily for 20–25 children, and the parent outreach:

- **Active learning:** The active-learning approach used in the children's classroom sessions and in the home visits should **encourage children to initiate their own developmentally appropriate activities.** Specifically, the active learning approach used was the High/Scope Curriculum (Weikart et al., 1970; Hohmann et al., 1979; Hohmann & Weikart, in press). This approach has always placed emphasis on providing an open framework in which children initiate their own learning activities. The approach encompasses children's development regarding personal initiative, social relations, creative representation, and music and movement, as well as logic, mathematics, language, and literacy.

- **Parent involvement:** The program should include a **substantial outreach effort to parents,** such as weekly home visits, in which staff acknowledge and support parents as actual partners in the education of their children and model active learning principles for parents. Group meetings for parents are another solution. In communities with a high incidence of drug-related crime, issues of the safety of home visitors call for creative solutions to this challenge.

A second set of features has to do with the program's timing and duration:

- **Age of children:** The program should serve **children at ages 3 and 4,** the years just prior to school entry. The study presents no evidence that the program would have had similar effects if it had served children at an earlier age (0–3) or at a later age (elementary school age).

- **Program duration:** Children should attend the program for **two school years.** This study's evidence for the effectiveness of only one school year is weak, based on a generalization from the 13 program participants in Wave Zero (these attended the program for only one school year and experienced essentially the same effects as did the other 45 program-group members, who attended the program for two school years). Thus, the Perry study alone offers little support for limiting preschool programs to age 4. (Many state-funded preschool programs serve only 4-year-olds and national Head Start and California preschool programs have a "4-year-olds first" policy.) When sufficient funds are available, the implication of the Perry study is that all 3- and 4-year-olds living in poverty should receive preschool programs.

- **Time per week:** The program should have **at least 12½ hours a week of classroom sessions for children**—2½ hours a day, 5 days a week. Variation of an hour or so more or less per week should not matter. Even a full, 9-hour-a-day program, if it meets all the other standards of quality, should produce similar if not greater effects.

A third set of features has to do with the program's staffing, training, and supervision:

- **Staff-child ratio:** The staff-child ratio should be **at least 1 adult for every 10 children and preferably for every 8 children.** While the Perry program had 4 adults for 20 to 25 children, which is a typical ratio for special education classes (Kakalik, Furry, Thomas, & Carney, 1981), the High/Scope Curriculum has since been used with very positive results in classes having 2 adults for 16 young children (Schweinhart et al., 1986), and in classes having 2 adults for 20 young children (Epstein, 1993).

- **Inservice training programs:** Staff need **systematic training in early childhood development and education.** Perry program staff were certified to teach in elementary, early childhood, and special education, but their elementary and special education training had little bearing on the program's active learning approach. Indeed, the Perry program emphasized children's initiative, whereas most special education training focuses on an adult-directed, diagnostic-prescriptive approach.

- **Staff supervision:** The Perry Project's teaching staff worked daily with supervisory staff in training and planning. Staff need **ongoing supervision by trained supervisors or consultants who know the curriculum** and can assist in its implementation by individual teachers and with individual children. Preservice training usually consists of readings, lectures, and discussions that focus on theory and educational philosophy. Too much of the inservice training that is offered deals with disconnected topics and has only a general relationship to the specific needs of practicing teachers. When inservice training has integrated content and is combined with curriculum supervision, the result is high-quality preschool programs with significantly better outcomes for children (Epstein, 1993).

Early childhood programs that do not serve children living in poverty and that are not of high quality, within reasonable degrees of tolerance, cannot lay claim to replicating the program used in the High/Scope Perry Preschool Project and thus are not likely to achieve its long-term effects.

Policy Implications

The issue of insuring program quality (see Willer, 1990b) should be central to the congressional and legislative debate on funding for Head Start and similar publicly sponsored preschool programs. This need for quality was recognized in the last program authorization of Head Start, called the Head Start Expansion and Quality Improvement Act of 1990. Because present funding levels do not allow these programs to serve *all* young children living in poverty, there is a danger that the debate will be framed solely in terms of expanding enrollment. Findings of the High/Scope Perry Preschool Project and similar studies indicate that the congressional debate over increased funding for Head Start ought to be over how much to spend on quality improvement (especially training and assessment) versus program expansion. In light of the documented benefits of high-quality programs, it would be irresponsible to permit current programs to continue or expand without substantial efforts to improve and maintain program quality.

Fundamental to any effort to improve Head Start quality is widespread **formative assessment** of current Head Start program implementation and outcomes for young children. This assessment must focus not only on the performance of teaching staff in implementing high-quality, active learning programs but also on the outcomes regarding children's development. The assessment tools used should embody a vision of what high-quality, active learning programs are about and what they can accomplish. For the assessment of teaching staff, two such tools are the Early Childhood Environment Rating Scale (Harms & Clifford, 1980) and the High/Scope Program Implementation Profile (High/Scope Educational Research Foundation, 1989; Epstein, 1993). One such tool for the assessment of young children's development is the High/Scope Child Observation Record (COR) for Ages $2^{1}/_{2}$–6 (High/Scope Educational Research Foundation, 1992; Schweinhart, McNair, Barnes, & Larner, 1993).

It is essential that the assessment of young children's development be consistent with principles of active learning and the cognitive, social, and physical goals of preschool programs. Many evaluations, even by respected researchers, have used only narrow tests of intellectual and language performance, or worse, brief screening tests noted only for their brevity and inexpensiveness. Such tests are only marginally related to the proper goals of high-quality preschool programs.[64]

Existing research already tells us that Head Start is not achieving its full potential. It follows that program administrators should have access now to the resources necessary for bringing their programs into full conformity with standards of quality. The principal use of such resources should be for sustained inservice training of teaching staff that enables them to provide a high-quality, active learning program for young children and their parents. Until this grand strategy of appropriate assessment and inservice training is fully implemented in national Head Start and other similar preschool programs, it would be unwise to conduct a national evaluation, or a series of national evaluation studies, that would investigate whether these programs are achieving their full potential for influencing young children's development.

Existing research **has defined the full potential of Head Start and similar programs,** establishing that programs—if they are done well— can improve children's success in school, increase their high school graduation rates, reduce their involvement in crime, and increase their adult earnings. But because research findings fail to define the limits of program variation within which these extraordinary societal goals can be realized, it is too easy for policymakers to exceed the limits.

---

[64]Epstein (1993) found that high-quality programs using the High/Scope Curriculum helped participating children score significantly higher than children in other high-quality programs on the High/Scope Child Observation Record in initiative, social relations, creative representation, and music and movement; but these same children did not achieve higher scores on the Developmental Indicators for the Assessment of Learning—Revised (DIAL-R, Mardell-Czudnowski & Goldenberg, 1990).

Some examples, from state-funded preschool programs, show how the process of ignoring limits works. When, in Texas, it seemed politically feasible to establish a staff-child ratio of 1 to 22 in a program for at-risk 4-year-olds, state legislators did not challenge the adequacy of this ratio, fearing that any hesitation in supporting the program might have enabled the program's opponents to eliminate it altogether. When Michigan legislators planning to spend $1,000 per child on a new state preschool program received expert testimony that the minimum cost for high-quality preschool programs was $3,000 per child (a decade ago), they decided to increase spending per child—to $2,000.

Based on existing knowledge, the standards of quality for Head Start and other similar preschool programs should be set high. But, because the nation has finite resources, research on the allowable limits of program variation should begin as soon as possible. One important area for "limits research" would be staff-child ratios. This report recommends a staff-child ratio of 1 adult for no more than 10 children. Because existing research does not answer the question of whether one adult can deliver an effective program for more than this number of children, it would be unnecessarily risky to operate large-scale programming with more than 10 children per adult—unless the programs were operated as part of experimental studies seeking new knowledge about the effectiveness of various staff-child ratios.

Similarly, we need to probe the lower limits of teacher qualifications for delivery of effective preschool programs. Surely, effective programs require training in early childhood development and education, but what level of training is required? Must all members of a teaching team have the same level of training? Many variations are possible. The important question is, What would a well-designed research study be able to determine about minimal qualification?

Any of the other components of preschool program quality presented in this report could, and should, be subjected to like scrutiny. There is widespread acceptance of the importance of an active learning curriculum for young children, but what should it look like? There is widespread acceptance of the importance of a strong outreach to parents, but whereas the parent outreach described in this report has focused on the parent-child relationship, some other forms of outreach have focused on the provision of various social services to parents; what is the proper balance?

The definition of preschool program quality presented in this report is a research-based summary of what is most likely to help young children living in poverty to achieve the striking benefits reported here. But *quality* should have a dynamic definition, constantly under development, constantly being refined by the results of new research studies.

The most important public policy recommendation from this study and similar studies is a call for **full funding** for the national Head Start program and similar preschool programs—enough to not only **serve all 3- and 4-year-olds living in poverty** but also **provide each of them with a high-quality, active learning preschool program.** The national Head Start program is the place to start, because it has a long history as well as experienced teachers and administrators. Congress has already authorized full funding of the program, but sufficient dollars for full funding have yet to be appropriated. Given the quality-of-life benefits as well as the economic return on investment found in this study and in similar preschool-effectiveness studies, the rationale for finding the dollars is compelling. The High/Scope Perry Preschool Project documents a very specific way that we can invest in the future by investing in our children.

References

American College Testing Program. (1976). *User's guide: Adult APL Survey.* Iowa City, IA: Author.

Anderson, E. (1990). *Streetwise: Race, class, and change in an urban community.* Chicago: University of Chicago Press.

Andrews, S. R., Blumenthal, J. B., Johnson, D. L., Kahn, A. J. Ferguson, C. J., Lasater, T. M., Malone, P. E., & Wallace, D. B. (1982). The skills of mothering: A study of parent-child development centers. *Monographs of the Society for Research in Child Development, 47*(6, Serial No. 198).

Arthur, G. (1952). *The Arthur Adaptation of the Leiter International Performance Scale.* Beverly Hills, CA: Psychological Service Center Press.

Auletta, K. (1982). *The underclass.* New York: Random House.

Bachman, J. G., & Johnston, J. (1978). *The Monitoring the Future questionnaire.* Ann Arbor, MI: University of Michigan, Institute for Social Research.

Bachman, J. G., O'Malley, P. M., & Johnston, J. (1978). *Adolescence to adulthood: Change and stability in the lives of young men: Vol. VI. Youth in Transition.* Ann Arbor, MI: University of Michigan, Institute for Social Research.

Bandura, A. (1989). Social cognitive theory. *Annals of Child Development, 6,* 1–60.

Barnes, H. V. (1989). *Gender–related long–term outcome differences in the Perry preschool study.* Unpublished master's thesis, University of Michigan, Ann Arbor, MI.

Barnes, H. V. (1991). *Predicting long-term outcomes from early elementary classroom measures in a sample of high-risk black children.* Unpublished doctoral dissertation, University of Michigan, Ann Arbor, MI.

Barnett, W. S. (1985a). Benefit-cost analysis of the Perry Preschool Program and its policy implications. *Education Evaluation and Policy Analysis, 4,* 333–342.

Barnett, W. S. (1985b). *The Perry Preschool Program and its long-term effects: A benefit-cost analysis.* Ypsilanti, MI: High/Scope Press.

Barnett, W. S. (1992). Benefits of compensatory preschool education. *Journal of Human Resources, 27,* 279–312.

Barnett, W. S. (1993). *New wine in old bottles: Increasing the coherence of early childhood care and education policy.* Unpublished paper, Rutgers University, Graduate School of Education, New Brunswick, NJ.

Becker, G. S. (1964). *Human capital.* New York: Columbia University Press.

Becker, G. S. (1981). *A treatise on the family.* Cambridge, MA: Harvard University Press.

Belle, D. (1982). *Lives in stress: Women and depression.* Beverly Hills, CA: Sage.

Berrueta-Clement, J. R., Schweinhart, L. J., Barnett, W. S., Epstein, A. S., & Weikart, D. P. (1984). *Changed lives: The effects of the Perry Preschool Program on youths through age 19* (Monographs of the High/Scope Educational Research Foundation, 8). Ypsilanti, MI: High/Scope Press.

Berrueta-Clement, J. R., Schweinhart, L. J., & Weikart, D. P. (1983). Lasting effects of preschool education on children from low-income families in the United States. In International Development Research Centre, *Preventing school failure: The relationship between preschool and primary education* (pp. 42–51). Ottawa, Ontario, Canada: International Development Research Centre.

Bloom, B. S. (1964). *Stability and change in human characteristics.* New York: John Wiley.

Brearly, M., & Hitchfield, E. (1966). *A guide to reading Piaget.* New York: Schocken Books.

Bredekamp, S. (Ed.). (1987). *Developmentally appropriate practice in early childhood programs serving children from birth through age 8.* Washington, DC: National Association for the Education of Young Children.

Bronfenbrenner, U. (1991). *An ecological paradigm for research on child care.* Unpublished manuscript, Cornell University, Department of Human Development and Family Studies, Ithaca, NY.

Bruner, J. (1980). *Under five in Britain*. Ypsilanti, MI: High/Scope Press.

Brunswick, A. F. (1988). Young black males and substance use. In J. T. Gibbs (Ed.), *Young, black, and male in America: An endangered species* (pp. 166–187). Dover, MA: Auburn House.

Clifford, R. M., & Russell, S. D. (1989). Financing programs for preschool-aged children. *Theory into Practice, 28,* 19–27.

Cohen, M. A. (1988). Pain, suffering, and jury awards: A study of the cost of crime to victims. *Law and Society Review, 22,* 537–555.

Cohen, M. A. (1992). A note on the cost of crime to victims. *Urban Studies, 27,* 139–146.

Comer, J. P. (1989). Poverty, family, and the black experience. In G. Miller (Ed.), *Giving children a chance: The case for more effective national policies* (pp. 109–130). Washington, DC: Center for National Policy Press.

Consortium for Longitudinal Studies. (1983). *As the twig is bent . . . Lasting effects of preschool programs*. Hillsdale, NJ: Erlbaum.

Danziger, S. (1989, August). *Education, earnings, and poverty* (Discussion Paper No. 881–89). Ann Arbor, MI: Institute for Research on Poverty.

Danziger, S. H., Haveman, R. H., & Plotnick, R. D. (1986). Antipoverty policy: Effects on the poor and the nonpoor. In S. H. Danziger & D. H. Weinberg (Eds.), *Fighting poverty: What works and what doesn't* (pp. 50–77). Cambridge, MA: Harvard University Press.

Deutsch, M. (1962). *The Institute for Developmental Studies annual report and descriptive statement*. New York: New York University.

Dornbusch, S. M., Carlsmith, J. M., Bushwall, P. L., Ritter, P. L., Leiderman, H., Hastorf, A. H., & Gross, R. T. (1985). Single parents, extended households, and the control of adolescents. *Child Development, 56,* 326–341.

Duncan, G. J. (1976). Earnings functions and nonpecuniary benefits. *Journal of Human Resources, 9,* 462–483.

Duncan, G. J. (1992, May 19). E-mail communication.

Duncan, G. J., Hill, M. S., & Hoffman, S. D. (1988). Welfare dependence within and across generations. *American Association for the Advancement of Science*. Reprint Series, *239,* 467–471.

Duncan, G. J., & Rodgers, W. L. (1988). Longitudinal aspects of childhood poverty. *Journal of Marriage and the Family, 50,* 1007–1021.

Dunn, L. M. (1965). *Peabody Picture Vocabulary Test manual*. Minneapolis, MN: American Guidance Service.

Elliott, D. S., Ageton, S. S., & Canter, R. J. (1979). An integrated theoretical perspective on delinquent behavior. *Journal of Research in Crime and Delinquency, 16*(1), 3–27.

Elliott, D. S., & Voss, H. L. (1974). *Delinquency and dropout*. Lexington, MA: Lexington Books.

Ellwood, D. T. (1986). *Targeting the would-be long-term recipient of AFDC: Who should be served?* Princeton, NJ: Mathematica.

Ellwood, D. T. (1988). *Poor support: Poverty in the American family*. New York: Basic Books.

Ellwood, D. T., & Summers, L. H. (1986). Poverty in America: Is welfare the answer or the problem? In S. H. Danziger & D. H. Weinberg (Eds.), *Fighting poverty: What works and what doesn't* (pp. 78–105). Cambridge, MA: Harvard University Press.

Epstein, A. S. (1993). *Training for quality: Improving early childhood programs through systematic inservice training* (Monographs of the High/Scope Educational Research Foundation, 9). Ypsilanti, MI: High/Scope Press.

Erikson, E. H. (1963). *Childhood and society* (2nd ed.). New York: W. W. Norton.

Farnworth, M., Schweinhart, L. J., & Berrueta-Clement, J. R. (1985). Preschool intervention, school success, and delinquency in a high-risk sample of youth. *American Educational Research Journal, 22,* 445–464.

Federal Bureau of Investigation. (1980). *Crime in America* (Uniform Crime Reports). Washington, DC: U.S. Government Printing Office.

Federal Bureau of Investigation. (1992). *Crime in America* (Uniform Crime Reports). Washington, DC: U.S. Government Printing Office.

Fine, M., & Zane, N. (1989). Bein' wrapped too tight: When low-income women drop out of high school. In L. Weis, E. Farrar, & H. G. Petrie (Eds.), *Dropouts from school: Issues, dilemmas, and solutions* (pp. 23–54). Albany, NY: State University of New York Press.

Fitz-Gibbon, C. T., & Morris, L. L. (1987). *How to analyze data.* Newbury Park, CA: Sage.

Flavell, J. (1965). *The developmental psychology of Jean Piaget.* New York: Van Nostrand.

Flax, E. (1990, June 20). Researchers see early signs of adolescent problems. *Education Week,* p. 6.

Frase, M. J. (1989). *Dropout rates in the United States: 1988* (NCES Report No. 89–609). Washington, DC: National Center for Education Statistics.

Freeberg, N. E. (1974). *Development of assessment measure for use with youth-work training program enrollees, Phase 2: Longitudinal validation* (Final Report, U.S. Department of Labor, Document No. ETS PR-74-1). Princeton, NJ: Educational Testing Service.

Freeberg, N. E. (1976). Criterion measures for youth-work training programs: The development of relevant performance dimensions. *Journal of Applied Psychology, 61,* 537–545.

Fuerst, J. S., & Fuerst, D. (1993). *Chicago experience with early childhood programs: The special case of the Child-Parent Center Programs.* Manuscript submitted for publication.

Garber, H. L. (1988). *The Milwaukee Project: Preventing mental retardation in children at risk.* Washington, DC: American Association on Mental Retardation.

Garfinkel, I., & McLanahan, S. S. (1986). *Single mothers and their children: A new American dilemma.* Washington, DC: The Urban Institute Press.

Gottfredson, G. D. (1990, March/April). Resolved: Good preschool programs for young children living in poverty produce important long-term benefits—Con. *Debates on Education Issues,* pp. 1, 3–5, 7–8. (Available from School of Education and Human Development, California State University, Fresno CA 93740–0002).

Gotts, E. E. (1989). *HOPE, preschool to graduation: Contributions to parenting and school-family relations theory and practice.* Charleston, WV: Appalachia Educational Laboratory.

Gray, S. W., & Klaus, R. A. (1970). The Early Training Project: A seventh year report. *Child Development, 41,* 908–924.

Gray, S. W., Ramsey, B. K., & Klaus R. A. (1982). *From 3 to 20: The Early Training Project.* Baltimore, MD: University Park Press.

Gross, J. (1989, April 9). Grandmothers bear a burden sired by drugs. *New York Times,* pp. 1, 16.

Grossman, H. (Ed.). (1973). *Manual on terminology and classification in mental retardation* (3rd ed.). Washington, DC: American Association on Mental Deficiency.

Harms, T., & Clifford, R. M. (1980). *Early Childhood Environment Rating Scale.* New York: Teachers College Press.

Haskins, R. (1989). Beyond metaphor: The efficacy of early childhood education. *American Psychologist, 44,* 274–282.

Haveman, R. H., & Wolfe, B. L. (1984). Schooling and economic well-being: The role of nonmarket effects. *Journal of Human Resources, 19,* 377–407.

High/Scope Educational Research Foundation. (1989). *Program Implementation Profile (PIP) manual.* Ypsilanti, MI: High/Scope Press.

High/Scope Educational Research Foundation. (1992). *High/Scope Child Observation Record (COR) for Ages 2½–6.* Ypsilanti, MI: High/Scope Press.

Hohmann, M., Banet, B., & Weikart, D. P. (1979). *Young children in action. A manual for preschool educators.* Ypsilanti, MI: High/Scope Press.

Hohmann, M., & Weikart, D. P. (in press). *Young children in action* (2nd ed., rev. and exp.). Ypsilanti, MI: High/Scope Press.

Howard, J., Beckwith, L., Rodning, C., & Kropenske, V. (1989). The development of young children of substance–abusing parents: Insights from seven years of intervention and research. *Zero to Three: Bulletin of National Center for Clinical Infant Programs, 9*(5), 8–12.

Howe, M. (1953). *The Negro in Ypsilanti.* Unpublished master's thesis. Eastern Michigan University, Ypsilanti, MI.

Howes, C., Phillips, D. A., & Whitebook, M. (1992). Thresholds of quality: Implications for the social development of children in center-based child care. *Child Development, 63,* 449–460.

Hunt, J. M. (1961). *Intelligence and experience.* New York: Ronald Press.

Irvine, D. J. (1982). *Evaluation of the New York State Experimental Prekindergarten Program.* Paper presented at the annual meeting of the American Educational Research Association, New York, NY.

Jargowsky, P. A., & Bane, M. J. (1991). Ghetto poverty in the United States, 1970–1980. In C. Jencks & P. E. Peterson (Eds.), *The urban underclass* (pp. 274–298). Washington, DC: Brookings Institution.

Jaynes, G. D., & Williams, R. M., Jr. (Eds.). (1989). *A common destiny: Blacks and American society.* Washington, DC: National Academy Press.

Jencks, C. (1991). Is the American underclass growing? In C. Jencks & P. E. Peterson (Eds.), *The urban underclass* (pp. 28–102). Washington, DC: Brookings Institution.

Johnson, D. L. (1988). Primary prevention of behavior problems in young children: The Houston Parent-Child Development Center. In R. H. Price, E. L. Cowen, R. P. Lorion, & J. Ramos-McKay (Eds.), *Fourteen ounces of prevention: A casebook for practitioners* (pp. 44–52). Washington, DC: American Psychological Association.

Kakalik, J. S., Furry, W. S., Thomas, M. A., & Carney, M. F. (1981). *The cost of special education.* Santa Monica, CA: Rand Corporation.

Kantrowity, B. (1991, January 23). A head start does not last. *Newsweek,* pp. 44–45.

Karnes, M. B., Schwedel, A. M., & Williams, M. B. (1983). A comparison of five approaches for educating young children from low-income homes. In Consortium for Longitudinal Studies, *As the twig is bent . . . Lasting effects of preschool programs* (pp. 133–170). Hillsdale, NJ: Erlbaum.

Katz, L. G., & Chard, S. C. (1993). The project approach. In J. L. Roopnarine & J. E. Johnson (Eds.), *Approaches to early childhood education* (2nd ed., pp. 209–222). New York: Macmillan.

Kennedy, W., Van de Riet, V., & White, J. (1963). Normative sample of intelligence. *Monographs of the Society for Research in Child Development, 28*(6, Serial No. 90).

Kopp, C., & Kaler, S. R. (1989a, February 12). The crack children. *Newsweek,* pp. 62–63.

Kopp, C., & Kaler, S. R. (1989b). Risk in infancy: Origins and implications. *American Psychologist, 44,* 224–230.

Krech, D., Rosenzweig, M. R., & Bennett, E. L. (1960). Effects of environmental complexity and training on brain chemistry. *Journal of Comparative Physiological Psychology, 53,* 509–519.

Lally, J. R., Mangione, P. L., & Honig, A. S. (1988). The Syracuse University Family Development Research Program: Long-range impact of an early intervention with low-income children and their families. In D. R. Powell (Ed.), *Parent education as early childhood intervention: Emerging directions in theory, research, and practice* (pp. 79–104). Norwood, NJ: Ablex.

Lazar, I., Darlington, R., Murray, H., Royce, J., & Snipper, A. (1982). Lasting effects of early education: A report from the Consortium for Longitudinal Studies. *Monographs of the Society for Research in Child Development, 47*(2–3, Serial No. 195).

Levenstein, P., O'Hara, J., & Madden, J. (1983). The Mother-Child Program of the Verbal Interaction Project. In Consortium for Longitudinal Studies, *As the twig is bent . . . Lasting effects of preschool programs* (pp. 237–263). Hillsdale, NJ: Lawrence Erlbaum.

Levin, H. M. (1977). A decade of policy development in improving education and training for low-income populations. In R. H. Haveman (Ed.), *A decade of federal antipoverty programs: Achievements, failures, and lessons* (pp. 521–570). New York: Academic Press.

Locurto, C. (1991). Beyond IQ in preschool programs? *Intelligence, 15,* 295–312.

Loeber, R. (1985). Patterns and development of antisocial child behavior. *Annals of Child Development, 2,* 77–116.

Lomotey, K. (Ed.). (1990). *Going to school: The African-American experience.* Albany, NY: State University of New York Press.

Mantel, N., & Haenszel, W. (1959). Statistical aspects of the analysis of data from retrospective studies of disease. *Journal of the National Cancer Institute, 22,* 719–748.

Mardell-Czudnowski, C., & Goldenberg, D. S. (1990). *Developmental Indicators for the Assessment of Learning* (rev. ed.). Circle Pines, MN: American Guidance Service.

Mathios, A. D. (1988). Education, variation in earnings, and nonmonetary compensation. *Journal of Human Resources, 24,* 456–468.

McCarthy, J. J., & Kirk, S. A. (1961). *Examiner's manual: Illinois Test of Psycholinguistic Abilities, experimental version.* Urbana, IL: University of Illinois, Institute for Research on Exceptional Children.

McKey, R. H., Condelli, L., Ganson, H., Barrett, B. J., McConkey, C., & Plantz, M. C. (1985). *The impact of Head Start on children, families, and communities* (Final report of the Head Start Evaluation, Synthesis, and Utilization project). Washington, DC: CSR.

McLanahan, S., & Bumpass, L. (1988). Intergenerational consequences of family disruption. *American Journal of Sociology, 94*(1), 130–152.

Miller, L. B., & Bizzell, R. P. (1983). The Louisville experiment: A comparison of four programs. In Consortium for Longitudinal Studies, *As the twig is bent . . . Lasting effects of preschool programs* (pp. 171–199). Hillsdale, NJ: Erlbaum.

Monroe, E., & McDonald, M.S. (1981). *Follow-up study of the 1966 Head Start program, Rome City Schools, Rome, Georgia.* Unpublished paper.

Moore, M. T., Strang, E. W., Schwartz, M., & Braddock, M. (1988). *Patterns in special education service delivery and cost.* Washington, DC: Decision Resources Corporation.

Murray, C. (1984). *Losing ground: American social policy 1950–1980.* New York: Basic Books.

National Association for the Education of Young Children. (1984). *Accreditation criteria and procedures of the National Academy of Early Childhood Programs.* Washington, DC: Author.

National Center for Clinical Infant Programs. (1986). *Infants can't wait: The numbers.* Washington, DC: Author.

National Center for Health Statistics. (1985). *U.S. Decennial Life Tables for 1979–81* (Vol. 1, No. 1). Hyattsville, MD: Author.

National Commission to Prevent Infant Mortality. (1988, August). *Death before life: The tragedy of infant mortality. Appendix.* Washington, DC: Author.

National Institute of Justice. (1989, July/August). Drug use forecasting update. *NIJ Reports,* pp. 8–9.

Natriello, G., McDill, E. L., & Pallas, A. M. (1990). *Schooling disadvantaged children: Racing against catastrophe.* New York: Teachers College Press.

Ogbu, J. H. (1986). The consequences of the American caste system. In U. Neisser (Ed.), *The school achievement of minority children: New perspectives* (pp. 19–56). Hillsdale, NJ: Lawrence Erlbaum.

Palmer, F. H. (1983). The Harlem study: Effects by type of training, age of training, and social class. In Consortium for Longitudinal Studies, *As the twig is bent . . . Lasting effects of preschool programs* (pp. 201–236). Hillsdale, NJ: Erlbaum.

Phillips, L., & Votey, H. L. (1981). *The economics of crime control* (Sage Library of Social Research, 132). Beverly Hills, CA: Sage.

Piaget, J. (1960). *The psychology of intelligence.* Totowa, NJ: Littlefield, Adams.

Piaget, J. (1968). *Six psychological studies.* New York: Random House.

Piaget, J., & Inhelder, B. (1969). *The psychology of the child.* New York: Basic Books.

Piaget, J., Inhelder, B., & Szeminska, A. (1964). *The child's conception of geometry.* New York: W. W. Norton.

Ramey, C. T., Bryant, D. M., Campbell, F. A., Sparling, J. J., & Wasik, B. H. (1988). In R. H. Price, E. L. Cowen, R. P. Lorion, & J. Ramos-McKay (Eds.). *Fourteen ounces of prevention: A casebook for practitioners* (pp. 32–43). Washington, DC: American Psychological Association.

Ramey, C. T., Bryant, D. M., & Suarez, T. M. (1985). *Preschool compensatory education and modifiability of intelligence: A critical review.* In D. Detterman (Ed.), *Current topics in intelligence* (pp. 247–296). Norwood, NJ: Ablex.

Rescorla, L., Hyson, M. C., & Hirsh-Pasek, K. (1991). *Academic instruction in early childhood: Challenge or pressure?* San Francisco, CA: Jossey-Bass.

Ricketts, E. (1989). The origin of black female-headed families. *Focus: Newsletter of the Institute for Research on Poverty, 12*(1), 32–36.

Rodes, T. W. (1975). *National child care consumer study, 1975: Vol. 2. Current patterns of child care use in the United States.* Washington, DC: U.S. Department of Health, Education and Welfare, Office of Child Development.

Rodes, T. W., & Moore, J. C., (1975). *National child care consumer study: Vol. 1. Basic tabulations.* Washington, DC: U.S. Department of Health, Education and Welfare, Office of Child Development.

Rosenberg, M. (1965). *Society and the adolescent self-image.* Princeton, NJ: Princeton University Press.

Ruopp, R., Travers, J., Glantz, F., & Coelen, C. (1979). *Children at the center: Summary findings and their implications* (Final report of the National Day Care Study, Vol. 1). Cambridge, MA: Abt Associates.

Sameroff, A., & Chandler, M. (1975). Reproductive risk and the continuum of caretaking casualty. In F. Horowitz (Ed.), *Review of child development research* (Vol. 4, pp. 187–244). Chicago: University of Chicago Press.

Scanzoni, J. H. (1971). *The Black family in modern society: Patterns of stability and security.* Chicago: University of Chicago Press.

Schweinhart, L. J. (1985). *The preschool challenge.* Ypsilanti, MI: High/Scope Press.

Schweinhart, L. J. (1987). Can preschool programs help prevent delinquency? In J. Q. Wilson & G. C. Loury (Eds.), *From children to citizens: Families, schools, and delinquency prevention* (pp. 135–153). New York: Springer-Verlag.

Schweinhart, L. J. (1988a). How policymakers can help deliver high-quality early childhood programs. In Council of Chief State School Officers (Ed.), *Early childhood and family education: Analysis and recommendations of the Council of Chief State School Officers* (pp. 163–176). New York: Harcourt Brace Jovanovich.

Schweinhart, L. J. (1988b). *A school administrator's guide to early childhood programs.* Ypsilanti, MI: High/Scope Press.

Schweinhart, L. J. (1990, March/April). Resolved: Good preschool programs for young children living in poverty produce important long-term benefits—Pro. *Debates on Educational Issues,* pp. 1–2, 5–7. (Available from School of Education and Human Development, California State University, Fresno CA 93740–0002).

Schweinhart, L. J. (1992). Early childhood education. In M. C. Alkin (Ed.), *Encyclopedia of educational research* (6th ed., pp. 351–361). New York: Macmillan.

Schweinhart, L. J., Berrueta-Clement, J. R., Barnett, W. S., Epstein, A. S., & Weikart, D. P. (1985a). Effects of the Perry Preschool Program on youths through age 19—A summary. *Topics in Early Childhood Special Education, 5*(2), 26–35.

Schweinhart, L. J., Berrueta-Clement, J. R., Barnett, W. S., Epstein, A. S., & Weikart, D. P. (1985b). The promise of early childhood education. *Phi Delta Kappan, 66,* 548–553.

Schweinhart, L. J., McNair, S., Barnes, H., & Larner, M. B. (1993). Observing young children in action to assess their development: The High/Scope Child Observation Record. *Educational and Psychological Measurement. 53,* 445–455

Schweinhart, L. J., & Weikart, D. P. (1980). *Young children grow up: The effects of the Perry Preschool Program on youths through age 15* (Monographs of the High/Scope Educational Research Foundation, 7). Ypsilanti, MI: High/Scope Press.

Schweinhart, L. J., & Weikart, D. P. (1981a). Effects of the Perry Preschool Program on youths through age 15. *Journal of the Division for Early Childhood, 4,* 29–39.

Schweinhart, L. J., & Weikart, D. P. (1981b). Perry Preschool effects nine years later: What do they mean? In M. J. Begab, H. C. Haywood, & H. L. Garber (Eds.), *Psychosocial influences in retarded performance: Vol. 2. Strategies for improving competence* (pp. 113–126). Baltimore: University Park Press.

Schweinhart, L. J., & Weikart, D. P. (1983). The effects of the Perry Preschool Program on youths through age 15—A summary. In Consortium for Longitudinal Studies, *As the twig is bent . . . Lasting effects of preschool programs* (pp. 71–101). Hillsdale, NJ: Erlbaum.

Schweinhart, L. J., & Weikart, D. P. (1985). Evidence that good early childhood programs work. *Phi Delta Kappan, 66,* 545–551.

Schweinhart, L. J., & Weikart, D. P. (1987). Evidence of problem prevention by early childhood education. In K. Hurrelman, F. -X. Kaufmann, & F. Lösel (Eds.), *Social intervention: Potential and constraints*. Berlin: de Gruyter/Aldine.

Schweinhart, L. J., & Weikart, D. P. (1988a). Education for young children living in poverty: Child-initiated learning or teacher-directed instruction? *Elementary School Journal, 89*, 213–225.

Schweinhart, L. J., & Weikart, D. P. (1988b). The High/Scope Perry Preschool Program. In R. H. Price, E. L. Cowen, R. P. Lorian, & J. Ramos-McKay (Eds.), *Fourteen ounces of prevention: A casebook for practitioners* (pp. 53–65). Washington, DC: American Psychological Association.

Schweinhart, L. J., & Weikart, D. P. (1989). Early childhood experience and its effects. In L. A. Bond & B. E. Compas (Eds.), *Primary prevention and promotion in the schools* (pp. 81–105). Newbury Park, CA: Sage.

Schweinhart, L. J., & Weikart, D. P. (1991). Response to "Beyond IQ in preschool programs?" *Intelligence, 15*, 313–315.

Schweinhart, L. J., & Weikart, D. P. (1992). The High/Scope Perry Preschool study, similar studies, and implications for public policy in the U.S. In D. Stegelin (Ed.), *Early childhood education: Policy issues for the 1990s* (pp. 67–86). Norwood, NJ: Ablex.

Schweinhart, L. J., & Weikart, D. P., & Larner, M. B. (1986). Consequences of three preschool curriculum models through age 15. *Early Childhood Research Quarterly, 1*, 15–45.

Scott, J. P. (1962). Critical periods in behavioral development. *Science, 138*, 949–957.

Shepard, L. A., & Smith, M. L. (Eds.). (1989). *Flunking grades: Research and policies on retention*. New York: Falmer Press.

Smilansky, S. (1968). *The effects of sociodramatic play on disadvantaged preschool children*. New York: John Wiley.

Smolensky, E., Danziger, S., & Gottschalk, P. (1988). The declining significance of age: Trends in the well-being of children and the elderly since 1940. In J. L. Palmer & B. B. Torrey (Eds.), *The vulnerable: America's young and old* (pp. 29–54). Washington, DC: Urban Institute Press.

Spitz, H. H. (1986). *The raising of intelligence: A selected history of attempts to raise retarded intelligence*. Hillsdale, NJ: Erlbaum.

Steinberg, L. (1987). Familial factors in delinquency: A developmental perspective. *Journal of Adolescent Research, 2*, 255–268.

Steinberg, L. D., Catalano, R., & Dooley, D. (1981). Economic antecedents of child abuse and neglect. *Child Development, 52*, 975–985.

Terman, L. M., & Merrill, M. A. (1960). *Stanford-Binet Intelligence Scale Form L–M: Manual for the third revision*. Boston, MA: Houghton-Mifflin.

Thompson, M. S. (1980). *Benefit-cost analysis for program evaluation*. Beverly Hills: Sage.

Tiegs, E. W., & Clark, W. W. (1963). *California Achievement Tests: Complete battery, 1957 ed.* Monterey Park, CA: California Test Bureau (McGraw-Hill).

Tiegs, E. W., & Clark, W. W. (1971). *California Achievement Tests, 1970 ed.* Monterey Park, CA: California Test Bureau (McGraw-Hill).

Tobias, T. N., Baker, M. W., & Fairfield, B. A. (1973). *The history of Ypsilanti—150 years*. Ypsilanti, MI: Ypsilanti Sesquicentennial Committee.

U.S. Administration for Children and Families. (1992). *Head Start statistical fact sheet*. Washington, DC: Author.

U.S. Bureau of the Census. (1983). *Lifetime earnings estimates for men and women in the United States: 1979* (Current Population Reports, Series P-60, No. 139). Washington, DC: U.S. Government Printing Office.

U.S. Bureau of the Census. (1992). *Money income of households, families, and persons in the United States: 1991* (Current Population Reports, Series P-60, No. 180). Washington, DC: U.S. Government Printing Office.

U.S. Bureau of Labor Statistics. (1992, June). *Employer costs for employee compensation— News, March 1992*. Washington, DC: Author.

U.S. General Accounting Office. (1992). *Early intervention: Federal investments like WIC can produce savings* (GAO/HRD-92-18). Gaithersburg, MD: Author.

Varden, S. A. (1982). Public school systems. In R. E. Anderson & E. S. Kasl (Eds.), *The costs and financing of adult education and training* (pp. 33–56). Lexington, MA: Lexington Books.

Vinter, R. D., Sarri, R. S., Vorwaller, D. J., & Schafer, W. E. (1966). *Pupil Behavior Inventory: A manual of administration and scoring*. Ann Arbor, MI: Campus Publishers.

Weber, C. U., Foster, P. W., & Weikart, D. P. (1978). *An economic analysis of the Ypsilanti Perry Preschool Project* (Monographs of the High/Scope Educational Research Foundation, 5). Ypsilanti, MI: High/Scope Press.

Wechsler, D. (1974). *Manual for the Wechsler Intelligence Scale for Children* (rev. ed.). New York: Psychological Corporation.

Weikart, D. P. (Ed.). (1967). *Preschool intervention: Preliminary results of the Perry Preschool Project*. Ann Arbor, MI: Campus Publishers.

Weikart, D. P., Bond, J. T., & McNeil, J. T. (1978). *The Ypsilanti Perry Preschool Project: Preschool years and longitudinal results through fourth grade* (Monographs of the High/Scope Educational Research Foundation, 4). Ypsilanti, MI: High/Scope Press.

Weikart, D. P., Deloria, D., Lawser, S., & Wiegerink, R. (1970). *Longitudinal results of the Ypsilanti Perry Preschool Project* (Monographs of the High/Scope Educational Research Foundation, 1). Ypsilanti, MI: High/Scope Press.

Weikart, D. P., Rogers, L., Adcock, C., & McClelland, D. (1971). *The Cognitively Oriented Curriculum: A framework for preschool teachers*. Urbana, IL: University of Illinois.

Weikart, D. P., & Schweinhart, L. J. (1993). The High/Scope Curriculum in early childhood care and education. In J. L. Roopnarine & J. E. Johnson (Eds.), *Approaches to early childhood education* (2nd. ed., pp. 195–208). New York: Macmillan.

Westinghouse Learning Corporation. (1969). *The impact of Head Start: An evaluation of the effects of Head Start on children's cognitive and affective development* (Vols. 1–2). Washington, DC: Clearinghouse for Federal, Scientific, and Technical Information.

Whitebook, M., Howes, C., & Phillips, D. (1989). *Who cares? Child care teachers and the quality of care in America*. Oakland, CA: Child Care Employee Project.

Willer, B. (1990a). Estimating the full cost of quality. In B. Willer (Ed.), *Reaching the full cost of quality in early childhood programs* (pp. 55–86). Washington, DC: National Association for the Education of Young Children.

Willer, B. (Ed.). (1990b). *Reaching the full cost of quality in early childhood programs*. Washington, DC: National Association for the Education of Young Children.

Willer, B., Hofferth, S. L., Kisker, E. E., Divine-Hawkins, P., Farquhar, E., & Glantz, F. B. (1991). *The demand and supply of child care in 1990*. Washington, DC: National Association for the Education of Young Children.

Wilson, J. Q., & Herrnstein, R. J. (1985). *Crime and human nature*. New York: Simon and Schuster.

Wilson, W. J. (1987). *The truly disadvantaged: The inner city, the underclass, and public policy*. Chicago: University of Chicago Press.

Wilson, W. J., & Neckerman, K. M. (1986). Poverty and family structure: The widening gap between evidence and public policy issues. In S. H. Danziger & D. H. Weinberg (Eds.), *Fighting poverty: What works and what doesn't* (pp. 232–259). Cambridge, MA: Harvard University Press.

Woodbury, S. A., & Hamermesh, D. S. (1992). Taxes, fringe benefits, and faculty. *Review of Economics and Statistics, 74*, 287–296.

Woodhead, M. (1988). When psychology informs public policy: The case of early childhood intervention. *American Psychologist, 43*, 443–454.

Zedlewsky, E. W. (1987). Making confinement decisions. *Research in Brief, July*. Washington, DC: National Institute of Justice.

Zigler, E. (1987). Formal schooling for four-year-olds? No. *American Psychologist, 42*, 254–260.

Zigler, E., & Finn-Stevenson, M. (1992). Applied developmental psychology. In M. H. Bornstein & M. E. Lamb (Eds.), *Developmental psychology and advanced testbook* (3rd ed.), Hillsdale, NJ: Erlbaum.

Zigler, E., & Butterfield, E. C. (1968). Motivational aspects of changes in IQ test performance on culturally deprived nursery school children. *Child Development, 39*(1), 1–14.

Invited Comments on *Significant Benefits: The High/Scope Perry Preschool Study Through Age 27*

Edward Zigler, Sterling Professor of Psychology
Victoria Seitz, Research Scientist
Department of Psychology
Yale University

The High/Scope Perry Preschool Project is of enormous significance for researchers and policymakers seeking ways to improve the lives of our nation's poorest children. The presentation of the results of this preschool program more than 20 years later makes it clear that high-quality preschool programs can lead to benefits in such societally important areas as education, employment, and reduction of criminal behavior.

Scientifically, this study is a major resource because of its excellent design and execution. This is a prospective, controlled-trials, longitudinal study of substantial duration, with astonishingly little attrition. The researchers have chosen to assess real-life outcomes of considerable importance. Instead of relying solely on self-report, they have conducted an impressive search of educational, criminal, and social service records that gives great weight to their findings. Therefore, the results of this study need to be taken very seriously. They show both that it is possible to use early intervention to change poor children's life prospects and that it is cost-effective to do so.

As is true with all research, this study also raises numerous questions. The most important question concerns the causal mechanisms involved: What precisely should we replicate to obtain the long-term benefits found in this study? This program provided a relatively brief (2½-hour-a-day) preschool program for children over a period of two school years. Because the child's teacher visited the home for 1½ hours each week, the program also provided for a considerable amount of intervention with parents. From a program perspective, the teachers spent their mornings teaching children and their afternoons making home visits. From the participants' point of view, the home visit took about two-thirds as long as the average amount of teacher time claimed by each child.[65] Although the study's authors attribute the long-term benefits to changes brought about in children through exposure to the preschool curriculum, what they may have discovered instead is the great value of having preschool teachers work extensively with parents as well as with children.

The major weakness of the present report is that the researchers say very little about the parental component of the program and provide no information on how parents may have changed in response to all this home visitation. The authors do not relate what transpired in the weekly home visits—whether the teacher taught the parent how to provide a more stimulating home environment, or whether the mother and teacher became friendly and began to view themselves as allies in educating the child. If parents learned the benefits of becoming familiar with their child's teacher and trying to provide home activities that complemented what the child was learning in school, this could have led to the better early school motivation and performance these children later showed and to a consistently more supportive parental attitude towards schooling.

For both practical and theoretical reasons, it is important to determine what role home visiting by teachers plays in producing later benefits. On the one hand, if it is possible to generate long-term benefits purely by exposing children to a stimulating preschool curriculum, it would be cheaper and easier to do that than to provide a preschool program including home visits. On the other hand, if the home visitation is a critical factor underlying the long-term benefits obtained, the particular educational curriculum employed may be relatively unimportant. Or it may be that *both* a stimulating curriculum and home visits are needed to produce the kinds of results seen here. From a scientific standpoint, what is greatly needed now is a follow-up study replicating the original study with and without the home visitation component.

Despite early intervention, a high percentage of the females in this study became pregnant as teenagers, and approximately half became teenage mothers. This finding has the policy implication that the effects of preschool programs could be maximized if such programs were combined with other forms of intervention at other times in the person's lifespan. School-based health clinics, for example, have shown promise in reducing the incidence of student pregnancies, and special programs for pregnant students have been shown to be effective in improving birth outcomes and in reducing the likelihood of rapidly repeated childbearing. Had such programs been available for the many teenagers who became adolescent mothers in this study, one might have expected to find even more-dramatic long-term program effects. In general, the principle here is that a preschool intervention of the present kind—even when it is highly effective—is not a panacea for all the child's later life problems. The High/Scope Perry Preschool Project's kind of early childhood program may well be what we should be providing for impoverished 3- and 4-year-olds, but we should not invest all our efforts in the preschool period alone.

---

[65]With the program's 750 minutes of class time per week and overall average of 5.7 children per teacher, the individual child's portion of teacher attention in class was 132 minutes per week (750 minutes divided by 5.7). The 90-minute weekly home visit, during which the child and parent shared the teacher's attention, was 68% as long as the child's portion of teacher time in class.

Taking into account all that we now know about the effectiveness of intervention, one could envision an ideal dovetailed network of programs at various points in the child's life. Such programs could productively target the next generation, before it is conceived, by working with adolescents to prevent school-age pregnancy. When such pregnancies do occur, however, it is societally imperative to provide the special prenatal programs that reduce the otherwise-high likelihood that the babies will be born unhealthy, with lifelong costs to themselves and society. For both teenaged mothers and older, impoverished first-time mothers, postnatal intervention can reduce the risk of child abuse as well as the frequency of childbearing; such intervention can even lead to mothers' long-term educational and socioeconomic improvements. Before poor children enter school, it is clearly to their benefit to attend a high-quality preschool program. Once children are in school, an early-elementary version of the preschool intervention can also improve their school performance.

We know a great deal in principle about what can be done to improve the life prospects of poor children. The results of the High/Scope Perry Preschool Project add a very strong link to the chain of evidence. What we now need is the resolve to put principle into practice. The potential benefits of doing so are enormous in both financial and human terms.

Now Adults! The Perry Preschoolers

Sadie A. Grimmett
Department of Counseling and Educational Psychology,
*   School of Education*
Indiana University—Bloomington

The Significance of *Significant Benefits* in 1993

The year 1993 is very appropriate for a report from the High/Scope Perry Preschool Project because care of young children is again a national topic. Lively discussion of child care was recently fueled by the child care decisions of two candidates for President Clinton's cabinet, and the discussion is being sustained by middle-class parents across the country who are intent on simultaneously fostering their careers and parenthood. Their interest is not in child care per se; instead, they are addressing the *quality* of child care. This interest suggests a tacit belief in a relation between care and child outcomes. Middle-class parents now seem to be seriously considering how early care experiences may influence their children's futures.

The instigators of the Perry preschool program, 30 years ago, had such a concern about the early experiences of poor children, when concern about early experiences—for any kind of children—was not much talked about. The Perry preschool program and similar early education programs (e.g., Gray & Klaus, 1970) were interested in demonstrating that high-quality early educational experiences would make a difference in the immediate and future lives of poor children. Underlying these demonstrations were bold questions, largely unasked at the time, that had implications for (a) the malleability of intelligence, (b) the definition of *early childhood,* (c) the relationship between parent and educator, and (d) the representation of the social category of the child. Support for these researchers' hunches and beliefs came from *Intelligence and Experience* (Hunt, 1961), a synthesis of early-experience findings. This landmark book challenged the notion that intelligence was inherited and fixed, and in doing so, opened the door to the great possibilities of early childhood intervention.

My personal support for these ideas was strengthened at a meeting of the American Psychological Association. I observed Harold Skeels receiving an APA award from a fellow psychologist. The award-giver recalled having been a toddler in an IQ-manipulation experiment directed by Skeels. I am sure there were many other experiences, between toddlerhood and adulthood, that had influenced this person. Nevertheless, it was noteworthy that the former research subject had grown up to be a *psychologist.* I would certainly say that early experience had made a difference in *his* life. Both recipient and researcher were white males. I could not help but think about the implications for poor minority children.

Historical Perspective—Success Against the Odds

The early 1960s was a period of optimism about improving the life chances of the poor, and for poor children early education was a popular approach to providing for such improvement. With the War on Poverty under way, Head Start began in 1965. Head Start, however, was not designed for scientific study; there were no original intervention and control groups, as there were in some other preschool programs designed at the time to test preschool effectiveness for poor children. Nonetheless, it was an evaluation of Head Start itself that led to public disillusionment about the impact of early education on poverty. The evaluation, by the Westinghouse Learning Corporation (1969), revealed that the gains children made during Head Start disappeared soon after they entered elementary school. This finding was a shot to the heart for malleability of IQ and a strong reinforcement for the view of development as static!

The subsequent public pessimism about the potential effects of preschool programs on poverty had a political influence that in turn affected support and funding for high-quality preschool programs. Consequently, these programs' contributions to the knowledge about early experience and its long-term outcomes were curtailed.

Contributing to the decline in interest in preschool education was a debate about the concepts "disadvantaged" and "deprived" and their underlying premise that there was something lacking in the experience of poor children—the premise behind the deficit model. Some American researchers who belonged to non-Caucasian ethnic groups were critical of the philosophical underpinnings of this model, since a negative representation of poor children was obviously involved. There is still sufficient dispute today about the deficit model to prompt Edward Zigler (Zigler & Finn-Stevenson, 1992) to declare that Head Start was *not* founded on this model. I am not sure if the implication of Zigler's statement is that whereas no deficit emphasis existed in Head Start, such an emphasis did characterize other programs of that time. But clearly, such an inference would be in error concerning the Perry preschool program and its guidelines and content. This program emphasized *building* on the child's competencies. Moreover, if the deprivation model's influences could not be seen in the boardroom, they surely could be seen in the Head Start trenches. I was in those trenches in 1965, and deprivation had a strong influence there.

A number of environmental shifts were also occurring during the 1960s. Two of these were school changes and neighborhood changes. A major event was *school desegregation*. As the former Perry preschoolers confronted school desegregation, either directly or indirectly, they could not help but receive messages devaluing African-Americans, messages that ran counter to some of the Perry program's goals. By that point in our history, segregation should have been viewed as an anachronism; desegregation, based on democratic values and principles, should have been supportive of African-American school children and citizens. Instead, lingering attitudes were antagonistic to these values.

In the years after the Perry preschool program, while schools were undergoing the changes of desegregation, urban neighborhoods were changing as well. In general, *urban areas were becoming more dangerous,* with more illegal drugs and associated crime and violence. At the same time, the rich of the 1980s, with their show of affluence, reminded us all about the power of money. A new term came into use—the *underclass*—to describe the powerless.

Some Possible Explanations for the Program's Long-Term Effects

This backdrop to the growing-up years of the High/Scope Perry Preschool Project participants was not positive for African-American children. The negative attitudes were seldom overt, and they were probably not obvious to Caucasian-Americans, but they were very real to the young African-American males and females who were organizing their lives. Given the environmental complexity and the barriers it involved, how could early experiences in the Perry preschool program have contributed to the lives of these young adults? I shall propose two motivational possibilities that are not necessarily independent.

One possibility is that preschool program participants developed a sense of *self-efficacy* (Bandura, 1989), which is a belief in one's competence in achievement contexts and an anticipation of being capable of new tasks. It seems reasonable to me that the preschool program experiences initiated in children a new appraisal of their self-efficacy. Moreover, their preschool learning prepared them for the cognitive demands of the primary grades, allowing them to persist in their confident, positive self-appraisals. Of course, some of their appraisals may have been in error, but Bandura has said, "Development of resilient self-efficacy requires some experience in mastering difficulties through perseverant effort" (p. 47). The program group's rate of regular high school graduation and their employment records are arguments in favor of self-efficacy.

Another possible source of motivation may have been derived from being special children in the neighborhood. The program group went to the preschool program although others in their neighborhood did not. Every year from ages 3 to 11, the children from the High/Scope Perry Preschool Project were sought out by an interviewer/tester, while other children not participating in the study did not have this distinction. Perhaps, in the next phase, Perry study researchers will ask study participants, now adults, about their feelings about being involved in a research project. I propose that the continuing contact was itself motivational and that the low attrition of study participants was indicative of a satisfying relationship with the study.

The Perry preschool program maximized both the academic and the life potential of its participants. Perhaps this experience succeeded because it developed internal motivations strong enough to counteract the powerful and negative societal barriers faced by these young African-Americans during their formative years. This process, repeated many times over with youngsters today, may influence the direction of all our lives tomorrow.